So This Is Normal Too?
Second Edition

Also by Deborah Hewitt, with Sandra Heidemann

Play: The Pathway from Theory to Practice

So This Is Normal Too?

Second Edition

Deborah Hewitt

Redleaf Press®
www.redleafpress.org
800-423-8309

Published by Redleaf Press
10 Yorkton Court
St. Paul, MN 55117
www.redleafpress.org

First edition published 1995. Second edition 2012.
Cover design by Jim Handrigan
Cover photograph © ZenShui Photography/Veer
Interior design by 4 Seasons Book Design/Michelle Cook
Typeset in Gill Sans and Minion Pro
Printed in the United States of America
18 17 16 15 14 13 12 11   1 2 3 4 5 6 7 8

Image on page 25 from *Play: The Pathway from Theory to Practice* by Sandra Heidemann and Deborah Hewitt (St. Paul, MN: Redleaf Press, 2010), 72. Reproduced by permission.

Library of Congress Cataloging-in-Publication Data
Hewitt, Debbie, 1958-
    So this is normal too? / Deborah Hewitt. — 2nd ed.
      p. cm.
    Includes bibliographical references.
    ISBN 978-1-60554-072-6 (alk. paper)
    1. Child development. 2. Child care. 3. Early childhood education—Parent participation.   I. Title.
HQ772.H456 2012
305.231—dc23   2011026538

Printed on acid-free paper

To all the children doing their best to cope and the adults who help them.

The rabbits thought and thought, "If we're normal and Leo is normal, then normal is whatever you are!"

—*Leo the Lop* by Stephen Cosgrove

Contents

Acknowledgments

Thank you to Sandy Heidemann, who developed the chapters on numbers and patterns. She also assisted in revising the chapters on activity level and tantrums. I want to thank Jeff for believing I could write another book. I am especially appreciative of the work of my daughter, Marcia, who researched, edited, and helped format the manuscript. As always, she went above and beyond the call of duty, and I am proud of her in so many ways. Thanks go to my son, Reid. He continues to provide me with reasons to step away from the involvement of a book and brings me great joy. I am grateful to those who read the manuscript and provided valuable feedback, which helped shape the book. I am especially thankful for the thoughtful comments of Sandy Heidemann and Cindy Croft. Finally, I want to thank Kyra Ostendorf and David Heath for their constructive ideas and advice throughout the project.

Introduction

In the children's book _Leo the Lop_, the rabbits strive to be just like one another until they learn that normal is whatever you are. For people, normal encompasses a huge range of behavior and development. "Normal is whatever you are." It's what you are used to. It's what you know.

At times, however, what children currently know doesn't provide them with the skills to further their development or get along with others. They need teachers and parents to teach them skills that adequately prepare them for what is to come. Parents and teachers use research to learn what to expect of children's behavior and what children need to learn. In most states, these expectations have been articulated in a set of guidelines, or standards, that outline what is currently known about the skills children should be able to attain by certain ages. When parents and teachers know what the standards or expectations are, they can arrange environments and interactions that give children opportunities to reach these goals to the best of their abilities.

Children come to early childhood settings with a wide variety of backgrounds, experiences, and skills. Those are their "normal." Teachers need to accept children where they currently are in their development and design activities and instructional strategies that help them grow and develop. Children develop at their own pace and in their own way. Therefore, even as a group of children moves toward a standard, they will vary greatly in skill level. This book helps you recognize that many lags in skill development and challenging behaviors are normal but can still be improved upon and moved toward the standards.

The second edition of _So This Is Normal Too?_ briefly discusses some of the basic elements of a strong classroom environment and the importance of relationships. These are essential to successfully working with all children. The book is based on the assumption that these elements are understood and in place. If not, take classes and find resources for further study.

This book is not meant to be a curriculum with breadth of scope or to offer sequences of development. It is intended to give you basic information on a variety of skills and behaviors that preschool children are working on. _So This Is Normal Too?_ helps identify children who need more specific planning and support to expand their skills. It provides you with observation questions and suggested strategies for working with individual children who are struggling or need extra support. It encourages you to work with families to develop consistency between the home and the early childhood setting. This consistency helps children learn skills more quickly. Family involvement helps children see education as valuable. Practical information and suggestions that can be distributed to families are provided.

A great deal of research has been done since the first edition of *So This Is Normal Too?* was published in 1995, and it has led to the development of state early learning standards. In the new edition of the book, early learning standards are used as a guide to help teachers develop goals for each child. Strategies are provided to reach each goal while adapting what is normal to each individual's needs. New research on brain development has been highlighted and is incorporated throughout the book. Ideas and strategies for working with dual-language learners are included. Information on the impact of stress on children is presented for you to consider as you work with children who are trying to cope. *So This Is Normal Too?* Second Edition is intended to be a practical guide and easy to use.

How to Use This Book

So This Is Normal Too? discusses many of the skills children are developing from three years of age to kindergarten entry. After part 1, Laying a Foundation, the book is divided into five parts based on domains, or areas, of learning. These include social and emotional development, approaches to learning, language and literacy development, cognitive development, and motor development. Each domain is introduced with general information on what the domain is, why it is important, what children need to be successful, and which standards have been included. The domains included in this book were chosen because they are common. Each domain includes chapters based on a standard included in the guidelines of many states. Depending on the state in which you live, there may be more or fewer standards.

Each chapter is divided into two sections. The first section, For Teachers, contains information about how a behavior or developing skill may look in an early childhood setting and provides activity suggestions for you to use. It also contains A Plan for Action, which consists of suggested goal statements as well as a summary of actions teachers and parents can take. The second section is for parents and offers similar information. This section is written with the family in mind and has examples of how a behavior or skill may present itself at home. You will find that these sections are intentionally similar and give the parent and teacher a similar base of information. A planning form is found at the end of the book.

The section for teachers contains five subsections. These include

What Is It? This provides a description of the standard. It identifies what children need to learn and some of the challenges they face as they learn the skill.

Observe and Decide What to Teach In this subsection, you are encouraged to observe a child to gather information about what is taking place and reflect on actions you can take. You'll find observation questions to pose and teaching suggestions based on developmentally appropriate practices. Use the teaching strategies to help you start to think of things you can do in your setting. You are encouraged to be creative and add your own activities to help a child to learn the desired skill. Also included are ideas for working with children who are demonstrating mistaken behaviors, such as tantrums or aggression. Suggestions are made about how to avoid problem situations and how to respond to situations that cannot be avoided.

I hope that those new to the field of early child education or to parenting will find the suggestions insightful as well as filled with common sense. People who have worked or lived with children for a number of years will find the suggestions worth revisiting when a situation becomes momentarily baffling. Your efforts may not succeed on the first day, in the first week, or even in the first month, but when you offer support and guidance, you show children that you believe in them and that they are worth the effort.

Work with the Parents   In this section, you are reminded to work with the child's family. You'll find information to help support parents and understand their point of view. This insight can bring about honest communication about instructional techniques that can be used.

When to Seek Assistance   Here you'll find guidelines to follow when you need additional help, including when to have a child's skills screened for further evaluation. Also included are general suggestions about whom to contact. Get to know the resources in your community so you can make more specific referrals when needed.

Another way to seek assistance is by learning more about the expectations set forth in the standard, the skills that lead up to the standard, and how to teach it. Attend classes or workshops. Look for books and journals in your public library, college or university library, or the library of a nearby parent education program. Conduct Internet searches for information from reliable sources. Talk with a colleague or mentor. Ask a consultant, coach, or parent educator to help develop strategies specific to a situation. (Be sure to obtain written permission from a parent before sharing confidential information with others.) Share any information that would benefit the child with the parent.

A Plan for Action   This section helps teachers work with parents to develop a course of action. The Plan for Action overview contains language that can form the basis for a goal. In addition, it contains a list of ideas *both* teachers and parents can use. This list helps teachers and parents focus on the things they can do to promote consistency between the early childhood setting and the home. When parents and teachers use the same strategies, a child receives more practice in needed skill development as well as clearer messages. Following these ideas are a few suggestions that are appropriate to implement in an early childhood setting. Finally, actions unique to the home setting are listed.

The second section in each chapter is information specific to parents. It provides practical information and ideas for parents to try at home to support skill development. You may reproduce copies as needed to hand to a parent with whom you are working, use as part of a parent newsletter, or post on a parent board. In addition to the parent handout, be sure to communicate regularly with the parents to build a strong relationship and to enhance their understanding of skill development. This same content is available as PDF files online at www.redleafpress.org. From the Redleaf Press home page, search for *So This Is Normal Too?* Second Edition; the PDF files are posted there.

Use the appendix Parent and Teacher Action Form, to organize your thoughts as you plan. It provides spaces for you to write a goal, the actions to be taken by both parents and teachers, and those that will be taken independently. It asks that you set a date when you will come together to look at what progress has been made. Reflection questions are included to prompt you to consider what is working and what is not. The Parent and Teacher Action Form can be used as an informal tool to assist during a planning meeting or as an agreement to which each party commits (see section called Coming to Agreement in chapter 1 for more information).

This book is intended for people who provide care to young children in a variety of settings, including child care centers, family child care homes, preschools, state pre-K programs, early childhood family education programs, special education programs, Head Start, and faith-based programs. No one term best fits all the settings. An effort has been made to use inclusive language by referring to the wide variety of programs as early childhood settings. Similarly, no one term best fits all those who care for and educate young children. Regardless of whether you call yourself teacher, provider, caregiver, educator, or practitioner, if you have regular contact with a child, you are teaching him. You teach through your actions, your words, and the ways in which you interact with him and others. The term *teacher* has been chosen to refer to all those who work with young children.

Parents are a child's first and most important teachers. It is extremely important to develop a partnership with them as you work with their child; work especially closely with those whose child needs extra support. The term *parent* is used throughout the book, but many other family members play significant roles in a child's life. The partnerships you make can include guardians, grandparents, and other family members. The recommendations apply to all.

Because both boys and girls will be working on developing the skills described in the standards, I use "he" or "she" in alternating chapters.

Part I

Laying a Foundation

During the preschool years, young children are learning many of the skills they need in order to be prepared for school and life. They develop social-emotional skills, including expressing their feelings, getting their needs met in appropriate ways, and interacting with others. They also learn cognitive skills, such as observing and asking questions, using language to describe what they see, counting, and quantifying. During this time, children develop physically, learning large-motor skills like sitting, standing, walking, and jumping. At the same time, they learn to use the small muscles in their hands and fingers to manipulate tools and to care for themselves when they dress and use a spoon to eat. Most children develop skills in a predictable pattern. Each individual, however, learns at his own rate.

Most states have developed early learning standards that describe the development and learning that is likely to take place by a certain age. Standards articulate what children should know and be able to do. These standards help teachers of young children know what is expected so they can arrange learning activities and opportunities that give children practice.

Teachers can do much to address the standards and to support learning. One key element is the nurturing relationship they establish with each child. Through interactions based on each child's interests and abilities, a teacher helps a child grow, develop, and learn. In addition, teachers plan environments that encourage all of the children in their class to actively explore; arrange schedules that help meet children's needs; and offer activities that encourage children to practice new skills that build on what they have already learned.

Teachers who look for ways to help each child reach his highest potential observe to discover each child's likes, interests, and current skills and abilities. They know the path of typical development and help move children from where they currently are to the next skill by offering challenging yet achievable activities that expand on each child's interests. They recognize when a child might need additional, focused attention to develop certain skills and plan individualized instruction.

Teachers help children develop when they recognize the roles of parents and other family members as a child's first teachers and work to establish partnerships. These partnerships help children receive consistent messages about what is expected, increase the opportunities for practice of challenging skills, and help children see that their families and their families' involvement are valued.

Parents and other family members help a child develop the skills described in the standards by developing loving relationships, talking about experiences, meeting the child's basic needs, and offering activities that support learning. When a child attends an early childhood setting, family members can work with his teacher to focus on skills and behaviors that might be difficult for him to learn. Parents can help support their child by recognizing the challenges to the child and the teacher during hours spent in a large-group setting.

When both teachers and parents enter into a partnership that focuses on helping the child learn skills needed to be prepared for school, they help him move ahead. When they are committed to working jointly and project a confident attitude, they can work out developmental issues together. The chapter that follows looks at early learning standards, what teachers can do to help children develop these skills, and ways teachers and parents can work together.

1 ◆ What Is Normal?

Grace, a preschool teacher, describes three of the children in her four-year-old classroom. Each uses a different approach to join a group of children who are already playing. "When Joshua comes to school, he puts his coat away and rushes to the block area to join the children who are already playing there. Hayden usually comes in, gets a puzzle, moves the pieces around, but watches the other children out of the corner of his eye. More often than not, another child joins him. When Isabel comes to school, she walks over near the housekeeping area and watches the other children. Eventually she joins the group by offering to help with something they are doing or by locating a toy the others are talking about." Are all three approaches considered normal? Should Grace be concerned about any of these children?

Brian, a parent of two boys, talks about his experience. "My older son started writing his name a few months after he turned four. Thomas, my younger son, is about to turn five, and he still isn't interested in working on it. Every time I try to suggest that we practice, he finds something else he would rather do. When I finally get him to try, he struggles to form the letters." Is Thomas developing skills at a normal rate? Should his father be worried about him?

The term *normal* encompasses wide variations and individual rates of development. It describes the widely held expectations society has for behaviors, skills, and approaches to learning. It includes a broad range of individual differences, such as those used by the children in Grace's preschool class—all are normal ways children become part of group play. *Normal* also describes the time range during which children are expected to develop certain skills. Brian's sons were interested in writing their names at different ages, but each is developing at a normal rate. When children demonstrate behaviors within the typical range and skills within the expected time frame, their development is considered normal. Most children develop skills and behaviors within the range of what is expected.

During the preschool years, children learn to regulate their emotions and develop internal controls. As they learn these important personal skills, they make behavioral mistakes. Certainly behaviors like swearing, hitting, and temper tantrums are upsetting. But most often, these and the other behaviors described in this book are considered normal. While it can be reassuring to know a behavior is normal, it doesn't make it easier to deal with. Teachers can expect young children to make mistakes while they learn appropriate behaviors. It is important that you accept these mistakes while helping children learn new skills that allow them to be more successful.

Preschool children are also learning many academic and cognitive skills, such as emerging reading and writing and mathematical concepts like counting and patterning. Some children show a great deal of interest in these skills and seem to pick them up readily. Others seemingly don't want anything to do with these foundational skills, or they may find them challenging to perform. There are many things adults can do to help children practice skills in ways that are meaningful to them, including practicing while at play. This book provides ideas about how to capture children's interest and ways to help them develop these important skills that prepare them to succeed.

Sometimes parents and teachers worry that a child is not developing skills or behaviors at a normal rate. You might think that he is lagging in development when you compare him to other children. Or you might think his behavior is out of the norm for a child his age. While there are patterns of typical development, each child progresses at his or her own rate. The more familiar you are with typical development patterns, the more likely you are to find that a child's skills and behaviors are considered normal. Children develop at individual rates, and growth isn't always steady. There are times when he will need additional help to develop needed skills.

All children in an early childhood setting need a strong, nurturing relationship with their teachers. They need a well-planned environment, schedule, and activities to help them be successful. They need teachers who plan activities that build on their interests and challenge them to develop new understandings. With these supports in place, most will develop the skills and the behaviors they need to be prepared for kindergarten. A few children need explicit instruction and more structured opportunities to learn important skills. This book will look briefly at some of the foundational pieces that must be in place for all children and then help you consider ways to individualize as you and a child's family members provide additional learning supports for those who need them. In the rare situation when a child is not developing as expected, this book will help you work with his family to recognize when to seek additional assistance and what steps to take to help him reach his full potential.

Early Learning Standards

State-developed early learning standards for young children reflect current research, articulate what is considered normal, and describe expectations about what children who are developing typically should know and be able to do. Standards are established in the belief that the majority of children will be able to reach the standard by a certain age. Understanding the standards allows early childhood teachers to arrange environments and learning opportunities to ensure children reach them.

The early learning standards in this book describe the skills and behaviors that the majority of children are likely to learn before entering kindergarten. This book provides ideas and suggestions for helping children three years of age to kindergarten entry. A standard can be thought of as one step along a path of development. This makes it easy to see that there are many steps that lead up to the development of a certain skill as well as many skills that will build upon it in the future. Early learning standards are often aligned to K–12 standards, so one feeds into the next. Standards provide teachers with clear indicators to use in determining if a child is on track for what is to come. You can set goals, plan activities, and offer learning opportunities that help children reach the age-level standards. Preparing for the future success of a child is one goal of early childhood teachers. Another is to make sure learning is taking place for the sake of learning, for fun, and with a sense of wonder.

Standards are generally grouped into areas of learning, or domains. These domains are a convenient way to organize thoughts and talk about learning, but a standard listed in one domain could easily be listed in another too. They are often interrelated—learning that takes place in one area influences learning in others. For example, a child's fine-motor development is related to and influences his emerging writing skills.

Although individual states may differ, the five domains addressed in this book tend to be included in early learning standards:

- ◆ Social-Emotional Development: includes learning to regulate emotions and behaviors as well as to get along with others

- ◆ Approaches to Learning: includes how children acquire information, their attitudes toward learning, and how they put information together to form new understandings

- ◆ Language and Literacy Development: includes learning to listen to others, learning to express themselves, and developing early reading and writing skills

- ◆ Cognitive Development: includes mathematical and scientific thinking

- ◆ Motor Development: coordinating the movements of large and small muscles

Teaching Early Learning Standards

Children learn best by doing. Teachers help children learn by creating environments they can safely explore and providing toys they are free to use and materials with which they can experiment. When children are given ample time to play, they learn to get along with others, share resources, and express thoughts and ideas. There are many ways you can help ensure that children meet standards:

- ◆ Develop a close relationship with each child

- ◆ Maintain a positive attitude that each child will learn the necessary skills and behaviors when given guidance and an opportunity

- ◆ Help each child succeed by creating an environment that is safe to explore

- ◆ Create a schedule that helps each child pace his activity level and meet his physical needs

- ◆ Arrange activities that are of interest to a child and challenge him to learn new things

Play, as well as everyday routines and activities, provides perfect opportunities for children to learn the skills that are described in standards. For example, if a standard states that a child "shows an interest in numbers, counting, and grouping

Effective Instruction Matters

Using effective instructional practices can make a big difference in how children feel, act, and learn. First, set the emotional tone of your classroom to foster a child's sense of belonging and well-being:

◆ Develop a relationship that is supportive, caring, and respectful

◆ Enter into and maintain a long-term relationship that helps a child discover how to treat others and develop an interest in the world around him.

◆ Offer support when a child feels out of control, and guide behavior in ways that protect his self-esteem

Second, use your time to provide high-quality early childhood programming:

◆ Pay attention to your schedule and organization of the day

◆ Provide a balance of active and quiet activities

◆ Offer both teacher-directed and child-led activities

◆ Plan waiting times and routines so they are efficient and children do not have to wait long

◆ Use transitions as opportunities for learning

Finally, facilitate learning:

◆ Set clear learning goals and engage children in activities that will promote the development of those skills

◆ Include visual, auditory, and movement activities for different types of learners

◆ Gain a child's attention and maintain it so he is fully engaged in learning activities

◆ Expand on a child's current understanding

◆ Ask open-ended questions to extend a child's thinking

◆ Help a child connect new information to past experience

objects," he can practice this by helping set the table and counting as he places one napkin on each placemat. The standards "shows strength, balance, and coordination of large muscles" and "tries out pretend roles in play" are practiced when a child acts as if he is one of the goats from *Three Billy Goats Gruff* who is crossing a bridge on the playground.

Create a Supportive Environment

Children do best when adults provide an emotional and a physical environment that supports healthy development. Help children feel safe in your setting by creating an emotionally safe setting. Develop a supportive, nurturing relationship with each child. Project a confident attitude that each child will learn new things as well as behave in ways that are appropriate when he is taught how to express his feelings and problem solve. Establish a consistent schedule that children can count on to have their needs met. Arrange an environment that allows them to explore and learn through interactions with toys and others while moving about safely. Plan activities that are challenging yet achievable to give children an opportunity to succeed.

Develop a Supportive Relationship

Children who feel safe, valued, and accepted are more likely to be interested in learning and getting along with others. Children who experience a supportive relationship in which they are nurtured learn that the world is a place they can trust that it will meet their needs, and that they are worthy of care and attention. Supportive relationships are made up of interactions built on children's unique interests and capabilities. When children are in a supportive relationship with an adult, the adult's approval, attention, and recognition are motivating. Children want to please the adult and will respond to his or her suggestions more readily. Children share their excitement with adults and seek contact with them (Gallagher and Mayer 2008). Help children learn necessary skills by first developing a strong, supportive relationship with each of them.

Building or strengthening a relationship with a child takes time and effort. It is well worth it when you see him flourish. There are many ways you can develop strong relationships with the children in your program:

- Greet each child and his family warmly
- Include in your setting toys and materials that reflect each child's customs, activities, and routines
- Talk with each child about his family
- Get to know the community in which each child lives
- Spend one-on-one time with each child
- Learn each child's likes and dislikes
- Talk about each child's experiences and ideas
- Cook each child's favorite meals
- Plan each child's favorite activities
- Take an interest in each child's activities
- Play next to each child and follow the child's play suggestions
- Enjoy things you have in common
- Read books together and talk about what you read

It may be difficult to nurture a relationship with a child who is demonstrating challenging behaviors. But each child has endearing qualities and strengths on which to build. Look beneath the surface and find what makes a child special. If a child engages in an upsetting behavior, make sure your own emotions are in check before you work with him. Take a moment to gain your composure, and then help the child learn the skill he needs in the upsetting situation (Croft and Hewitt 2004).

Project a Confident Attitude

Children need adults who believe in them. Children who are resilient can do well in spite of stresses that may enter their lives in part by developing close relationships with adults who believe in their abilities. These caring adults can be family members, teachers, or community members (Hewitt and Heidemann 1998). Projecting confidence that you know children will learn new skills or demonstrate friendly behavior, communicates your belief in them. In addition, the attitude you communicate can become a self-fulfilling prophecy, because children tend to live up or down to the expectations of others.

How you think and feel about skill development and behaviors lays a foundation for your work with a child. You will respond quite differently to situations when you think he is not trying, incapable, out to get you, or purposefully

A Relationship Can Buffer the Effects of Stress

Many believe childhood should be stress-free. The reality is that all children experience stress, but the level and the effect of stress differ. Three levels of childhood stress have been identified (National Scientific Council on the Developing Child 2007). They are positive, tolerable, and toxic. These levels depend on how often a child is exposed to a stressful situation, if it is controllable, and to a large extent the availability and quality of relationships a child has with adults. Adults can act as a buffer for stress and help children learn to cope.

Positive stress occurs when a child is learning something new, dealing with frustration, or learning to separate. A child's autonomic responses to stress temporarily cause an increase in heart rate, blood pressure, and the production of hormones and proteins. When a child has an adult who supports his learning or reduces the frightening situation, he learns to cope. His physical reactions dissipate, and his body returns to normal fairly quickly.

Tolerable stress occurs when a stressful situation is time limited and an adult can help the child manage. Children may experience tolerable stress when there is a divorce, a prolonged illness of a loved one, or a natural disaster. They react strongly to this level of stress. All of their survival mechanisms kick in, and they prepare for "fight or flight." The autonomic responses can be detrimental. But when an adult is there to ease the stress, their bodies return to normal before long-lasting effects take hold.

Toxic levels of stress occur when children experience unpredictable, uncontrollable, and frightening situations. These children experience toxic levels of stress if they are exposed to violence in their families or communities, are victims of abuse or neglect, or have mothers struggling with severe depression. Children in these situations often lack a supportive relationship with someone who can help them cope. Toxic levels of stress activate the body's autonomic response system. When a child's response system is running at high alert for long periods of time, the prolonged presence of high levels of stress-related hormones and proteins released can have a negative impact on his developing brain. This can lead to learning, memory, and behavioral challenges.

You play a critical role in helping children who are experiencing stress at any of these levels. While you can't take the place of a supportive, responsive parent or family member, you can contribute to a child's ability to weather a difficult storm. You can do the following:

◆ Enter into a long-term, positive relationship that promotes growth and development

◆ Provide a consistent, safe, nurturing environment

◆ Learn to effectively work with children who are reacting to prolonged levels of stress or who are communicating the stress they feel through their behavior

- Learn to recognize signs that a child and family need additional support

- Arrange an assessment of a child's skills if you believe he is lagging in development

- Locate resources in your community that support families when they experience stress, such as parent education classes, financial support services, and family counseling programs

- Encourage a parent who needs help to seek it

- Report suspected cases of child abuse and neglect

misbehaving instead of believing he hasn't yet learned a skill or is inexperienced. For example, if a child is playing in a plastic tub filled with sand and spills some, you can assume he is being sloppy and doesn't care about keeping things clean, or you can assume he is having so much fun he doesn't realize the sand is flying. Or you can assume he hasn't yet learned the standard "shares responsibility in taking care of their environment."

Depending on your perspective, you are likely to choose very different ways of handling this situation. Your tone of voice, facial expressions, and body language will reflect your feelings. These subtleties may speak louder than the words you use. If you believe the child is intentionally making a mess, you are more likely to go to him with a stern face and use a demanding voice to tell him, "You need to clean up this mess. Come on get busy. Come! Now!" Statements like these, and the manner in which they are said, suggest you are fed up and perhaps do not have enough strategies to use in coping with this situation.

On the other hand, if you recognize this as an opportunity to work on the standard, you can help the child learn to clean up his messes. If you view this as a teachable moment, you are more likely to use a matter-of-fact manner and encourage him as you speak. You might say, "When you were playing, some of the sand fell out. I need you to clean up your spills. Here is the whisk broom and the dustpan. I'll use the big broom, and we can work together to clean it up." In this scenario, you are assuming the child was not aware of the mess and that he needs more information or a direction to clean up. By responding in this way, you have taught him that he is responsible and that he can do many things for himself.

Arrange the Schedule

A consistent schedule and well-planned routines can offer children comfort and a sense of security. A schedule must meet the physical needs of the children in the group. It needs to be consistent so children know what to expect. Well-planned routines help children know how to move from one activity to the next. When they know the schedule and routines, they can move through the day with greater confidence and ease.

Give careful thought to the schedule you arrange. You can help children pace themselves throughout the day by creating a schedule that alternates strenuous and restful activities. Balance child-choice activities with adult-directed activities to help children learn independent and interactive skills. Plan transitions, teach children what is expected of them, and reduce waiting time by being prepared. Make it clear where children are to go and what they are to do during changes in activity. Reduce confusion by keeping things similar from day to day.

Your schedule should not be so rigid that it cannot be changed if a problem (or unexpected opportunity) occurs. You might find that you need to change your schedule by a few minutes so a hungry child can eat. Perhaps you can avoid problems by making sure that a tired child can rest although it isn't naptime yet. Or you may need to take a break from a hectic schedule to help a frustrated child find a way to calm down or be successful.

Plan the Environment

Arranging the environment is an important element in helping children succeed. They need a pleasant space in which they can move about safely—an environment that allows them to explore and learn through hands-on activities. They need a space that allows them to interact with others and to learn to cooperate while sharing materials. Children also need an environment in which they can make choices in order to learn independence and self-control. As you plan your environment, critically examine your surroundings. A few questions you might ask yourself include the following:

- Are materials and toys arranged so children can make independent play choices?

- Are there too many things, making it difficult for children to choose?

- Are there enough things to occupy each child?

- Is the play space large enough for the activity?

- Are materials challenging without being frustrating?

- Are there things with which each child is familiar?

- Does each child see himself and his culture reflected in these things?

Make adjustments to your space so children are safe and comfortable and are encouraged to try new things and practice existing skills.

Changing the environment can be a simple and effective way to provide opportunities for children to practice new skills. Arrange activities and materials so children can practice a skill in related ways. For example, if you are working on fine-motor cutting skills, set out tongs for them to use to pick up cotton balls, playdough to squeeze, and scissors to cut construction paper. You might also change the environment to encourage practice in the standard "demonstrates good hygiene" by placing a stool and picture directions next to the sink so children can wash their hands by themselves.

When a behavioral problem arises, consider how you might change your environment to avoid the situation or to cut down its frequency. For example, you might use a seating arrangement or put more space between children who are having difficulty sitting next to each other at group time.

Plan Developmentally Appropriate Activities

Children learn best when they are actively involved with materials and engaged in interactions with others. They need activities that match their developmental level. If activities are too hard, they may become frustrated or feel inadequate. Materials that are too easy may be uninteresting and lead to wandering or inactivity. Materials and activities that are well matched encourage children to feel challenged yet successful.

In a group setting, offer the same kind of materials at varying levels of difficulty. For example, if you know that a number of children in your group are working on eye-hand coordination, you might put out pegboards and pegs with large knobs, pegboards and pegs with small knobs, and a Lite Bright set (a pegboard and pegs without knobs). Offer activities and variations of them many times so that children have adequate opportunities to practice.

Be aware of and plan ways that you can change group activities to meet the needs of each individual. How might you adapt an activity so it matches each child's skill level? How can you make it participatory to capture a child's attention? How will you shorten it for a child who is unable to sit for very long? One teacher knew that children in her group had varying levels of comfort in talking in front of the group as well as varying levels of language development. She felt it was important for the children to practice speaking in front of the group and wanted to give each child a chance to answer a question before leaving group time. She thought carefully about how she could phrase a question in a way that matched the skill levels of each child. She asked some children an open-ended question that could be answered with a short phrase, others a question that could be answered with just one word, and others a question that could be answered with "yes," "no," or a nod of the head. She asked the children who were most comfortable with group situations to answer the question first and then dismissed them. Then, when the group became smaller, she asked the children who were less comfortable to answer in front of only a few of their peers.

The Value of an Instructional Approach

Instructional approach to teaching refers to the way in which early childhood teachers plan learning activities for their group and for individual children. An instructional approach is based on an understanding of widely held expectations, early learning standards, and child development. When a teacher uses an instructional approach to teaching, learning is facilitated by setting clear goals and engaging children in activities that develop their skills.

An instructional approach requires that a teacher not only plan for her group of children but learn about each child's skill level, interests, and learning styles. The teacher then uses what she knows about each individual to guide her planning. You can use an instructional approach to teach any of the early learning standards included in this book. The following pages outline the steps to take as you help a child make progress toward meeting standards.

Continuous Cycle of Improvement

An instructional approach to teaching incorporates a continuous cycle of improvement. Informally, many teachers engage in this cycle by watching children, recognizing what they are capable of, and building on it to teach them new skills. When a child learns a new skill, teachers begin again at the first step of the cycle: observing. Formally engaging in these steps can improve your effectiveness and help children reach the goals you set for them. This continuous cycle of improvement includes several steps:

1. Observe

2. Determine where the child is developmentally

3. Write a goal

4. Plan and implement activities

5. Repeat the process

(Heidemann and Hewitt 2010)

Observe the Child

Teachers have so many demands on their attention that they have very little time for thorough observation. However, vital information about a child's skill development or behavior may be missed unless the time is taken to step back and assess a situation. Planning for an individual starts with systematically observing him to learn about his likes and dislikes, his current skill level, how he interacts with others, his approach to new activities, and signs that he may be becoming frustrated.

Look for a child's strengths and the areas in which he is doing just fine. Consider the areas in which he needs to grow or develop new skills. Watch other children too. Observe the other children in your program who are approximately the same age and temperament. This can give you perspective as well as a baseline for comparing how others of approximately the same age are doing. The information you gain from your observations will help you to do the following:

◆ Identify skill strengths and areas that need improvement

◆ Find insights into behaviors

◆ Gain perspective

◆ Talk with others about the child's skills and behaviors

◆ Determine if the child's skills need to be screened for special services

◆ Determine how to proceed

◆ Gauge if you are making progress

If you are working with a child who is demonstrating a challenging behavior, ask yourself the following general questions when you observe:

◆ Under what circumstances is the behavior taking place?

◆ Who else is involved?

◆ Does it take place at certain times of the day or during certain activities?

◆ What happens right before the behavior?

◆ What takes place immediately following?

◆ Does this child have the skills needed for the task?

◆ How much verbal or nonverbal communication is taking place?

The answers will guide your plans for working with this child. Questions specific to each standard are included in the following chapters. In addition, there are a number of general observation questions you can ask to help determine a child's level of skill development. These include the following:

◆ Is this child exploring the material as if it were the first time he saw it?

◆ Does this child seem highly interested in the activity?

◆ Is this child showing signs of frustration?

◆ Is an adult offering support?

◆ How much support is needed?

Document your observations. Keep samples of each child's work to show parents and/or specialists what he is capable of doing. Take photographs of each child at work or play, and label the skill he is demonstrating. Write down what he says to provide a sample of his language. Retain a project in which he used fine-motor skills or a paper that shows how he writes his name. Collect similar samples every couple of months. Be sure to date each one. When you place similar samples in chronological order, you can see the progress over time in much the same way you can see a child grow through a series of photographs.

Authentic Assessment

Many early childhood teachers agree that it is important to assess the skill development of young children in an authentic manner. This means that assessment is part of everyday activities rather than a single test. In this type of assessment, well-known adults observe a child's performance while he engages in everyday activities in a familiar setting. Authentic assessment relies on many sources of information, such as observation, work samples, and parent reports. Assessment is ongoing and provides rich information.

Authentic assessment is especially helpful in working with a group of children who have diverse skills. It allows children who are dual-language learners to show what they know in ways that are not dependent on language. It is also helpful in working with children who have special needs, because it focuses on progress rather than performance at an age-level standard.

Take notes as you observe a child at work and play. Your notes can help you recall a situation or skill you observed so you can analyze it along with work samples. They also help you provide specific examples when you talk with a parent, coworker, or specialist. Use descriptive words and phrases to recreate the situation on paper. Use objective terms that do not assign value to what is taking place. For example, in observing Tyler, record, "Tyler stands at the sandbox. He does not respond to Sue's comments. He looks down. He draws circles with his car." These are facts that are observable to all. Be careful not to include judgments in your description of what is taking place. If you write, "Tyler pouts. He stands at the sandbox and ignores Sue when she talks to him," you are judging what is taking place.

In addition to your written narratives, there may be times when your records are more helpful and factual if you count the number of times a behavior or skill is demonstrated during a specific time period. How many times does a child initiate conversation with others? How many times does he take turns when he is asked to? How many times does a child hit another in one week? One day? One hour? While you log situations you are concerned about, be sure to also record examples of times a child handles a difficult situation well. Recording a child's strengths as well as his need for help provides balance and helps you keep a positive attitude.

Observe three or four times or collect three or four samples before drawing any conclusions. If you use limited information, your conclusions may not be accurate. For example, if you only watch a child one time, his ability to perform a skill or a behavior he demonstrates may be influenced by an oncoming cold, a fight with a sibling, or an upcoming visit from grandparents. These, and many other factors, can cause a child to behave or perform a skill in a way that is not typical or does not show him at his best.

Factors That May Influence Behaviors

Many factors can affect a child's behavior. Sometimes you're fortunate enough to be aware of the influences. However, many times you are not aware of what is affecting behavior. Some factors can be controlled while others cannot. Some possible influences are these:

- Change in routine, teachers, or home
- Frustration
- Boredom
- Toys that are too hard or too easy
- Feeling too crowded
- Lack of language skills
- Fatigue
- Overstimulation
- Hunger or poor nutrition
- Illness or oncoming illness
- Prolonged illness of a family member
- Need for attention
- Adult expectations that are too high
- Adult expectations that are too low
- Taking a medication
- An allergy
- Disagreement with a friend, sibling, or adult
- Visit from a relative
- Anticipation of an upcoming activity
- Loss of a loved one through divorce, deployment, or death
- Experiencing or witnessing violence

Determine Where a Child Is Developmentally

Use your observations and samples of a child's work to determine where he is developmentally. Analyze your records to determine the skills and behaviors the child is capable of performing independently, what he needs help with, and what he isn't yet attempting. This can help you decide what he is currently able to do and what skills to work on next.

Pinpoint what skills a child is capable of performing with some assistance. In general, the skills a child is trying to do but needs a little help to perform are the ones that he will be performing independently in a short time. The skills he isn't yet trying are too advanced and would be frustrating for him if you tried to work on them at this point. When you help a child move from things he can do with assistance to independent performance, you are operating in what Lev Vygotsky, a Russian psychologist of the early twentieth century, calls the zone of proximal development (ZPD). Your efforts to help a child learn a new skill will be most successful when you stay within the ZPD.

Write a SMART Goal

Use your observations, your knowledge of widely held expectations for young children, and early learning standards to write an appropriate goal that is challenging but achievable. Your goal should move a child from where he is to a skill slightly more difficult. Writing a SMART goal can be helpful in focusing on a desired outcome. SMART goals are

- ◆ Specific
- ◆ Measurable
- ◆ Attainable
- ◆ Realistic
- ◆ Timely

SMART goals contain specific information—they answer the questions "Who? Does what? Where? How well or how often? By when?" When you write a goal, state it positively, stating what you want a child to be able to do by a certain time.

Determine how you will make their goal measurable and judge if you have met it. Will you count the number of times you see the skill and watch for an increase? Or will you make a goal slightly more complex by looking at what a child is doing currently and increasing your expectations? For example, if a child is currently following one-part directions 80 percent of the time, it might be realistic to increase your expectations and write a goal asking the child to follow two-part directions 25 percent of the time.

It isn't always necessary or appropriate to expect that a child will reach 100 percent proficiency. For example, if a child is taking turns 50 percent of the time, perhaps he has reached a developmentally and individually appropriate level. In this instance, it isn't necessary or appropriate that he gives up a toy he is using 100 percent of the time.

Any goal you write needs to be attainable and realistic. It must help a child move from his current level of skills to the next level of difficulty. Your goal is more likely to be within a child's reach when it is within his zone of proximal development and based on what he is likely to do within the near future.

Pay timely attention to your goals by setting a target date for completion or to evaluate the progress being made. The target date should be two to three months away to give you time to teach the skill and the child time to practice. (Example goals are listed in the Plan for Action found at the end of each chapter.)

Plan and Implement Activities

Once you have decided what to teach, you must decide how you will teach it. Plan and implement activities that give a child a chance to practice the new skill. Each chapter of this book suggests many strategies. Learn more about the expectations set forth in the standard you are trying to teach, the skills that lead up to it, and effective ways to teach it by attending classes or workshops, reading more about it, or talking with a colleague or mentor. Ask a consultant, coach, or parent educator to help develop strategies specific to a situation. (Be sure to obtain written permission from a parent before sharing confidential information with others.)

Develop a plan for how you will help a child reach his goals, consider what words you will use or questions you will ask, what activities you will offer, how you will avoid problems, and how you will respond to mistaken behavior (unintentional inappropriate behavior). Use scaffolding as you help a child move from skills with which he needs assistance to things he can do more independently. When you scaffold his learning, you provide support for the child to get to the next stage or level of development. For instance, he might need your hand-on-hand assistance as he first learns a new skill. As he becomes more competent, he might be able to perform the task when you verbally remind him of the steps to take. Perhaps as the next step, the child might need only picture cues to stay on task before finally being able to perform the task on his own. In this way, you start with the amount of assistance needed and gradually withdraw your support by matching it to how much the child can do for himself.

Work with Parents

Children who are learning new skills and behaviors do best when those who work with or care for them throughout the day are consistent in their messages and approach. Consistency provides stability and helps a child learn a new skill more easily. Ideally, you would develop a team of people made up of parents, family members, staff, and if needed, specialists. Your team works together to create goals and a plan to reach them. Gathering busy people together can be challenging and may not be realistic in every situation. However, the more serious the behavior or skill lag, the more essential it becomes for everyone to work together. Keep in mind that the documentation you gather may be useful in a formal assessment process at a later time. At a minimum, work with the parents to develop goals and discuss activities to help the child reach the goals. If it is impossible to bring more of the child's planning team together, be certain to communicate the plans you and the parents make to all involved.

It is critical that you and the child's parents work together to help him learn the skills and behaviors he needs. It is well understood that parent involvement positively influences a child's school achievement. Parental involvement begins in early childhood and sets the stage for future involvement.

Ask parents open-ended questions to help you get to know and understand them. Your conversations with parents should allow for all of you to appreciate one another's experiences, knowledge, and values. Most child-rearing practices are embedded in cultural beliefs. People learn these through how they were cared for as they grew up and by watching how those around them talk to, touch, dress, and feed young children. Learn from people who are like you as well as those who hold ideas that may be different from your own. Assume parents want what is best for their child and are capable in helping their child achieve goals. Remember: there are many ways to support the development of young children.

Teachers and parents need to communicate with one another. You can share information about a child in your setting to help bridge the gap between home and school. One teacher made a mental note of something entertaining or interesting that a child did each day to share with his parents. This helped the parents know the teacher was really tuned in to their child. Some parents want to know about the eating, sleeping, and toileting habits of their child. Some are more interested in the social relationships the child is building. Others want to know about the activities in which their child is involved. Find out what types of information a parent is most interested in, and keep them up-to-date. Ask parents to support your efforts by sharing information that may be helpful in caring for their child, such as changing sleep patterns or stressful situations in his life. When you need to share sensitive information, be sure to do so confidentially to protect a child's self-esteem. Explain to a child, "I need to talk with your mom alone." Then walk out of hearing distance. Or set a time to talk either in person or on the phone.

Technology provides opportunities to keep in touch with parents in many

Conversation Starters

Get to know parents and build a team from the very beginning. Ask questions to build your relationship and to learn about a parent's experiences, cultural beliefs, values, and family style. Your purpose in asking questions and getting more information is to understand—not to judge responses that might be different from your own. Strive to learn about others' worldviews and to appreciate their strengths. Remember: there is more than one way to support growth and development. Arrange for an interpreter if one is needed. Avoid using family members as interpreters, because doing so may place them in an uncomfortable position. Here are some questions you might ask to get a conversation started:

- What would you like to see your child do at our program?
- What do you think is important for your child to learn?
- How would you teach your child _____?
- How do you talk with your child about _____?
- How does your child learn best?
- Tell me more about _____.
- What are your thoughts about _____?
- Tell me about a time when _____.
- What have you found works best when _____?
- How do you respond when _____?
- What have you tried when _____?
- How do you help your child to _____?
- How does your family acknowledge your child when he does something well?

ways. Websites, e-newsletters, text messages, and e-mails can be valuable forms of communication. They can be a great way to stay in touch about routine things and upcoming special events. But challenging situations or messages that might be difficult to absorb are better discussed in person. Often text messages and e-mails are misunderstood or misinterpreted. Other methods of communicating, such as social networking sites like Facebook, might be fun, but they should be used with caution. Information about children needs to be highly confidential. Posting pictures of children on the Internet poses additional questions, and safeguards need to be taken. While access to computers is spreading and many families find them convenient for communicating, please remember that not all families have easy access to computers. Be sure to use the appropriate method of communication for each family.

Parents are experts on their child, and because they know him intimately, they are often the first to notice a problem. But sometimes teachers recognize problems that are not obvious to parents. Teachers offer a different perspective, having seen typical patterns of development in the groups of children with which they have worked. Sometimes a problem is noticed because it occurs only in a group setting. Sometimes a behavior or skill lag becomes apparent in the early childhood setting because of the "academic" activities offered.

Both parties have a right to honest communication that fosters teamwork in caring for a child. Usually it is best to talk when you first see a pattern developing or notice a skill with which the child is struggling. If you have already been concerned by what you see, you may have moved ahead in your thinking—don't wait until you are frustrated or convinced of a child's skill delay to begin to talk about it. Tell the parents you want to talk with them about what you are noticing.

Sometimes parents and teachers try to discuss concerns during drop-off or pickup. Things are generally hectic during this time; parents are in a hurry, children are tired, and teachers may be frustrated after dealing with a behavior or group of children all day. It is better to arrange another time to discuss a difficult situation or a skill you are concerned about. Say, "I have noticed that Nathan is swearing a lot lately. I would like to talk with you about it. When are you available to meet in the next two or three days?" It is best if the meeting is not during a time when children need attention. It might be better to meet during naptime or your preparation time. Set aside enough time to talk without interruption.

Keep your expectations about what can be done at home realistic. Parents may be able to do little about a problem like hitting if it seems related to the group experience and is taking place only in the early childhood setting. It is inappropriate and ineffective for parents to punish a child for something that has taken place hours earlier. Make it clear that you are not asking parents to do that. Instead, inform them of what is taking place and tell them that you want to work together to come to an agreement on how best to handle the situation.

Expectations about what teachers can do must be realistic too. Most teachers will do all they can to respond to the individual needs of a child. However, teachers are responsible for a group of children and are unlikely to implement complicated or time-consuming requests. This is not because they are unwilling to help, but because of the numerous demands on their time and attention.

Be sure to recognize the emotional investment parents have in their children. Acknowledge that you may be sensitive about the work you do with children too. The information you share may be received by parents as if it is a personal attack if you are not careful to phrase things sensitively. If you have more than one concern, use good judgment about how many concerns to share during your first discussion. It is better to talk about digestible pieces of information that will not alienate parents from further discussion. Choose the most important skill or behavior to focus on first, and discuss other concerns at another time. After planting a seed about your concern, continue to note how the child is progressing and come back to the concern later if needed. Chances are that once you mention it, parents will begin seeing examples of the same thing.

Keep a positive attitude about working together. Build a cooperative effort by viewing emerging skills and challenging behavior as something you can work on together. Be careful to avoid blaming anyone for skill lags or mistaken behaviors. This is unproductive, builds resentment, and leads to defensiveness. Attend to the situation at hand and determine what can be done to improve it.

Create a Team

Whenever possible, invite the team of people who will work to help a child develop the skills he needs to your planning meeting. Include parents as well as other significant caregivers, such as other family members or coworkers. People who work with or care for a child during specific times of day, such as an assistant teacher, a bus driver, or a grandparent, can be helpful in reaching goals too. Make sure you ask for and consider their observations while you assess a child's development. The team can work together to establish a goal and develop a plan to teach it. Communicate the plan to those who work with a child but are not able to attend a planning meeting.

Some children attending your program may be identified as having special educational needs. By attending school with other children, they learn from their more typically developing peers, and their peers learn from them. A child with special education needs is likely to have an Individualized Education Program (IEP) that outlines a goal, target date for completion or reevaluation, and strategies to help him achieve the goal. Work with this child's early childhood special education teacher to implement the child's IEP in your setting.

If possible, attend this child's early childhood special education team meeting. The special education team may be made up of early childhood special education teachers as well as specialists. At this meeting, you will learn about their goals for the child and what you can do to support the child's growth and development. Using the strategies a special education teacher identifies as well as those you plan for all the children in your program, you can help a child with special needs become more successful.

Putting It All Together

The following puts it all together by providing you with a sequence of steps to take as you use this book to teach a child new skills. It shows you how to embed the continuous cycle of improvement and effective instructional practice within the steps. To help a child develop a skill, do the following:

1. Observe and assess. Gather detailed information.

2. Plan for success by attending to your relationship and attitude as well as adjusting aspects of your environment, schedule, and activities to meet the child's needs.

3. Read all the materials on a skill or behavior as well as others that are closely related.

4. Give the parents the corresponding section(s) in this book written for them.

5. Arrange a meeting with the child's planning team so you can work together. Determine where the child is at present; develop goals and a Plan for Action.

6. Implement your plan.

7. Observe again.

8. Meet to discuss progress.

9. Modify your plan if necessary. Cycle back to step 6.

1. Observe the Child   Begin by observing the child to identify specific skills or behaviors to work on. Use the recommendations for observing presented earlier. Ask yourself the specific questions in the chapter(s) that address what you are focusing on to help you gather more information about what is taking place.

2. Plan for Success   Build or rebuild your relationship. Adjust your attitude. Change aspects of your environment, schedule, or activities to avoid problems.

3. Read Appropriate Chapters   As you plan to teach a skill or behavior, you may find that more than one chapter applies. Read all the chapters that are related to the skill a child needs to learn. Piece the appropriate information together and reflect on what is taking place. For example, expanding a child's vocabulary may help in situations where he needs to use words to solve problems. Information in the chapters "It's My Turn to Talk!" Speaking and "Whack!" Aggression might help you determine an appropriate way to work with a child to develop essential skills. Read the whole chapter even if you don't think an observation question applies 100 percent. Many of the suggestions listed under one question will be useful in or can be modified to fit a number of situations.

4. Give the Parents the Corresponding Sections Written for Them   Give the For Families pages to the parents you are working with so they have developmental information similar to yours when you talk together. If needed, have the materials translated into the language with which the parent is most comfortable. Avoid using web-based translation programs—they are often inaccurate. Allow a few days for the parents to study and digest the information and to look for examples of their own before meeting.

5. Meet to Develop a Plan for Action   Arrange a meeting with the parents and as many members of the team as possible. When you meet, set an expectant tone that says you can help the child develop necessary skills when you work together. Be open and alert to topics the family may want to discuss. (Additional information about parent meetings can be found later in this chapter.)

6. Put Your Plan into Action After you meet, implement the strategies to which you agreed. Use your copy of the Parent and Teacher Action Form as a reminder to use the words you have prepared or do the activities planned. Post your plan in a place where you are sure to see it. Of course, in a setting where people are coming and going, keep the reminder confidential. Perhaps you can put it inside a cupboard door that you open often.

Once you have developed your Plan for Action, limit daily conversation about the skill. It isn't necessary or productive to look for growth each day. Instead, offer plenty of opportunities and time for a child to learn a new skill. If you need to vent frustration or talk further about your concerns, find someone outside of the situation who can keep information confidential and provide a listening ear. A coworker, family member, director, or mentor may be able to provide support.

Continuous Cycle of Improvement

The continuous cycle of improvement is important to use when you are helping a child learn new skills. Begin by observing and assessing a child's skills. Reflect on what you have seen and the examples of work you have collected to determine a child's current developmental level. Create a goal that is challenging but achievable. Plan and implement activities and actions to teach the child new skills.

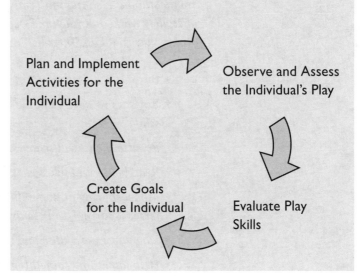

Plan and Implement Activities for the Individual

Observe and Assess the Individual's Play

Create Goals for the Individual

Evaluate Play Skills

7. Observe Again Formally observe the child again a week or two before your next meeting so that you have current, accurate information to share. Look for progress as well as what should come next on the path of skill development.

8. Meet to Discuss Progress The purpose of a second and perhaps subsequent meeting is to decide if the child's skill has improved and if your strategies have been helpful. When you evaluate, you may find that he has made good progress toward the goal you set. If so, pat yourselves on the back and congratulate each other for helping him learn this new skill. Other times, you may find a child has made some progress but more work is needed.

9. Modify Your Plan If your goal was not met, reevaluate your plan. Make sure the goal is appropriate for this child; be sure your expectations are appropriate, and do not ask him to take too big a step. Adapt your goal or change your strategies to make a good match. Eliminate the strategies that were not effective and replace them with ones that you think will be more meaningful to the child. Agree once again with the parents to check in with each other in two to three months. Skill growth is neither quick nor easy. It takes time and patience. If you are working to improve a behavior, you can still expect mistakes to occur even after improvement is evident.

If your goal was met, engage in the continuous cycle of improvement. Each time you reach a goal, determine what can be learned next and how you will continue to support the child in his growth.

Sarah, the early childhood teacher, was excited to meet with James's parents, James's grandma, and an assistant teacher. She had had a couple of quick conversations with his parents about helping him learn to share toys, and she knew that they were willing to do anything they could to help him work on the standard "shares materials when appropriate." When the whole team met, they worked through the steps described here and began to brainstorm things they could do. Their list included the following:

- *Buy duplicates of the most desired toys*
- *Buy toys to have at home that are most difficult for him to share at school*
- *Refer to the toys at school as "school toys"*
- *Read books and tell stories about taking turns*
- *Model sharing at home during everyday experiences, emphasize the terms "sharing" and "taking turns"*
- *Do puppet plays at school that demonstrate waiting for a turn*
- *Help James find something to do when he needs to wait for a turn*
- *Teach James to ask for a turn*
- *Ask James if he will give the toy to another child now or in two minutes*
- *Play board games in which James practices taking turns*
- *Give James clues about when his turn will come by saying, "Your turn is after Mom's"*
- *Teach James to make trades*
- *Teach James to ask for help when he is frustrated*

When they looked at their list, they realized these were all good ideas and that they could add still others. They decided to try to be more specific about what James needed to learn and what the most helpful activities would be. They narrowed their focus to teaching James to wait for a turn. They decided to limit the ideas they would try so that they wouldn't overwhelm themselves or James with too many at one time. Their list became more manageable when they decided to try the following:

- *Do puppet plays at school that demonstrate waiting for a turn*
- *Teach James to ask for a turn*
- *Help James find something to do when he needs to wait for a turn*

- *Play board games in which James practices taking turns*

- *Give James clues about when his turn will come by saying, "Your turn is after Mom's"*

- *Teach James to ask for help when he is frustrated*

Sarah and James's parents planned to try the things they outlined a number of times before meeting again. During this time, they would look for evidence of growth and improvement. They agreed to check on progress made toward the goal in six weeks.

When they came back together, they were happy to report that James had made progress at school and at home. He waited more calmly when he didn't get his turn right away, and he had learned to ask for help when he couldn't wait any longer. However, he wasn't always successful in waiting without becoming upset. He still cried occasionally when he didn't get his turn right away, but he had made significant progress and showed as much emotional control in this situation as others his age.

They knew their work didn't end here. They decided they would continue to work on this standard and started the process again. Now they would focus on teaching James to give up a toy when someone asked him to.

Reasons Some Plans Are Ineffective

Some of the suggestions for helping a child call for changes in routine, activity, environment, or your responses. Change is often met with resistance. Yet when you make the effort and see how successful you can be in helping a child learn or prevent problems, you will find it well worth the effort. For some children, the change may mean the difference between success and continued frustration. So keep an open mind as you consider which of a chapter's suggestions will help a child and which you will implement.

Steps in Problem Solving

You may recognize that the steps in the continuous cycle of improvement are similar to those used in problem solving. The steps in problem solving can be helpful to both children and adults when they approach a challenge, learn something new, or engage in scientific inquiry. Teach children to use the following steps:

1. Identify the problem.

2. Gather information.

3. Generate solutions/strategies.

4. Choose the best one or ones.

5. Decide on a plan.

6. Implement your plan.

7. Evaluate how your plan is working.

8. Revise your plan as needed.

You can help children use these steps when engaged in a conflict with another child by using these helpful phrases:

- "I see _____." (*Describe what you see taking place. For example,* "I see you both want a turn on the swing.")

- "Tell me about your argument."

- "What could you do to work this out?" or "How could you work this out so you're both happy?"

- "What might happen if you tried that idea?" or "Which idea will you try first?"

- "Try it."

- "Is that idea working?"

- "Is there another idea that might work?" or "Is there an idea that will work better?"

There are other reasons plans are ineffective. Sometimes a plan will fail if it is discontinued too soon or if activities are not offered often enough for a child to learn a new skill. It takes time and a great deal of practice to learn a skill. Changing a habit or replacing one behavior with another may take even longer. Be sure to offer ample time and activities for a child to practice. If a goal is not well matched to his skill level, it may be outside of his zone of proximal development and may ask too much of him. He will not be able to reach the goal without learning the skills or behaviors that lead up to it. A plan may also be ineffective if the written goal is not specific enough or does not reflect what he needs to learn. For instance, if a goal states that a child "learns to take turns," but it does not pinpoint one of the skills that make up turn taking, it will not be a practical one. To be more specific, the goal should indicate that a child needs to learn to ask for a toy and wait for a response. Planning strategies that are not meaningful to the child or do not build on his interests will cause a plan to fail. If a goal is to encourage a child to write his name, strategies need to include signing his name as part of activities he enjoys rather than pulling him away from those to practice writing at a table.

When to Seek Assistance

Many children learn skills and behaviors a few months ahead of or behind the average age at which a skill is expected to appear; they are still considered normal. Children who develop at a typical rate will develop the skills they need when they have teachers who create nurturing and supportive relationships with them, provide a high-quality learning environment, and use effective instructional practices. Other children may experience neurological, physical, cognitive, speech, language, or environmental challenges that cause lags in skill development. They may avoid performing certain skills, may not be able to perform an activity independently, or may lack the ability to perform a skill proficiently. If, in spite of your concerted efforts to teach a skill, some children's development seems to be lagging by six months or more, they are likely to benefit from specialized help.

In addition, there are some children who do not learn to control inappropriate behaviors as quickly as others. Their behavior may be severer or more frequent or may persist for a longer period of time than that of others. If challenging behaviors don't significantly decrease even though you have implemented the techniques suggested in this book—these are usually found to be helpful—you may need to seek additional help. Early intervention can help children who are displaying challenging behaviors make great gains in learning to interact successfully with others.

You will find guidelines about when to seek assistance in each chapter. (General information follows.)

If you remain concerned about a child's skill development, you may want to talk to his family about having his skills assessed further. Deciding to take this next step can be difficult for teachers and parents alike. Seeking additional help does not mean that you have been unsuccessful. Instead, it means you have recognized the limits of your setting or your expertise. It is not necessary, nor should you try, to make a diagnosis. There are many different reasons a child may experience challenges. It will take a team of experts to determine potential causes and, if needed, make a diagnosis or determine eligibility for services. Even then, a diagnosis may not fully reflect the complexity of the child's experience.

Usually where there is a concern, a child should have his skills screened. Screening is a quick look at a child's health and developmental progress. It can assist in identifying whether his skills are lagging in development. Encourage his parents to have their child's skills screened through the school district's early childhood screening program, early intervention program, or Child Find activities.

If a child is found to be at risk for learning problems, he is likely to be referred for further testing. Testing involves a comprehensive evaluation of his skills and abilities by a team of experts. From these tests, experts or medical personnel can determine eligibility for services, make a diagnosis, or determine if he has a disability that might interfere with learning. If this is the case, the child is eligible for and will benefit from early intervention services. Early intervention programs serve children with special educational needs in a variety of ways, including working directly with the child, offering support for him and his family, and in many cases, providing consultation with a classroom teacher or child care provider.

In addition to the resources found in your school district, specialists to contact may include a primary health care provider, parent resource center, community or public health service, county/regional or state social service program, or private agency. County or regional services may offer a variety of helpful programs. Their services often include financial assistance, child care resources, and mental health services. Check to see which are available in your area. Gather the names and phone numbers of support services. Make calls to obtain more information on services while you consider options. Suggestions for whom to contact are made in each chapter.

Limited income prevents some people from obtaining needed services. Services available through the public schools are free. However, if you need to look beyond the schools, contact programs that have a sliding fee scale based on family income. Service organizations, such as Shriners, Kiwanis, and Salvation Army, are groups that may be able to provide financial help. There may be additional groups in your community.

Talk with the parents about the need for additional services for the child. Discuss the resources within your community. Set a date to talk after a screening or an evaluation. After meeting with a specialist, encourage the parents to discuss anything they learned that would be helpful when you work with their child.

Your observation records of a child's skills and behaviors can be helpful to specialists. This information, if written objectively, can be a critical piece of collected data. You might offer to send your notes or to talk directly with a specialist about the concerns you have. Written permission from parents must be obtained before releasing any information. Parents can also request that you share your records as background data and give them to a specialist.

If a child is found to have a disability, your work with him does not end. Children with special educational needs, behavior needs, or disabilities have the right to be included in all early childhood settings. When children with disabilities are included in general education settings, they benefit from learning alongside their more typically developing peers. Children with typically developing skills learn to appreciate, accept, and respect children whose development differs from their own. They also increase their own skill by teaching and supporting others.

Conducting Meetings with Parents

Begin your conversation by describing the standard or the skill that is expected. Use conversation starters (on page 21) to learn more about the parent's expectations and point of view. Describe the skill level you see the child demonstrate in your setting. Provide specific, factual examples of your observations. Include skills that concern you as well as things this child does well. Ask if the parents see similar examples. Chances are they do. Sometimes, however, children act differently in different settings. Even if the parents don't see what you are concerned about, most will do all they can to help their child learn what is needed.

Including Children with Special Needs

The children in your program possess a wide range of skill levels and include some children with special education needs, behavior needs, and disabilities. Including a child with special needs adds value to your program. It gives a child with a disability an opportunity to play and learn with his peers, and it gives typically developing children an opportunity to respect people with differing abilities. To include a child with disabilities in your setting, do the following:

* Learn about his strengths and the areas in which he needs additional support

* Create a caring, supportive environment for all children

* See this child as a child first and his disability second

* Model supportive behavior that allows him to do as much as possible for himself

* Be flexible in your schedule and routines

* Find ways to modify your environment to make room for adaptive equipment

* Include materials showing positive images of people with disabilities

* Use observations to plan and to individualize instruction

* Learn how to use assistive technology that supports a child with disabilities in the classroom

* Work with specialists to determine the best course of action in working with the child

Set a Goal

Develop one or two SMART goals for the child by using the information from your observations, what you know of your setting, the goals of the program, the parents' goals, and your state's early learning standards. Concentrating on what the child needs to learn helps you stay focused on an instructional approach and frames the goal in positive language. Remember that different cultures may value different goals. For example, some cultures value and want to teach their children to be independent at early ages. Other cultures value and want to teach their children to be interdependent; in such cultures, parents encourage their children to give up personal goals for the good of the group (Maschinot 2008).

You will find sample language for the root of a goal in each chapter's Plan for Action. Modify or write other goals to more closely reflect the needs of the child with whom you are working. If he needs to work on more than one standard, you may need to prioritize and decide which to address first. How well he needs to perform a goal may be suggested in the examples, but this must be decided on an individual basis. Stay within a child's zone of proximal development by developing goals that he can soon accomplish without assistance. Your goals should be challenging yet achievable. Keep your expectations realistic. Look for improvement, not perfection.

Brainstorm Strategies

After setting a goal, brainstorm a number of strategies for achieving the goal. List as many ideas to teach the goal as you can. Begin with the suggestions given in each chapter and summarized in the Plan for Action. These suggestions are based on sound child development practices and usually are effective in helping children learn skills. Add your own ideas.

Decide on a Plan

The focus of the conversation should be to strive for an understanding between parties and to decide on a plan. Determine which of the activity ideas are most appropriate to your situation. Write three or four actions you will take in the early childhood setting and at home on the reproducible Parent and Teacher Action Form (in the appendix). Write additional strategies to be used at home or in the early childhood setting. Be careful not to overwhelm yourself, the parents, or the child with too many changes/activities at once. The techniques can be difficult to implement if you try to do too many at once. Multiple techniques also make it hard to know which of the strategies were helpful and are most important to continue.

Complete the planning form by setting a date two to three months (depending on the urgency of the situation) later to meet again. Be sure to communicate positive expectations that together you will be able to teach the child the expected skills and behaviors. Signatures on the Parent and Teacher Action Form are optional unless you are using the form as an agreement.

Coming to Agreement

Opinions about a child's skill development may differ for many reasons. Parents may not view a skill lag as a problem. What they see their child do seems normal to them. They may not have opportunities to see what other children are capable of. They may not see a behavior at home, or it may not be a problem when only one or two children are present. Parents may hold different expectations or value different behaviors as part of their cultural beliefs. Or they may deny the existence of a problem they are unprepared to confront.

Sometimes a child presents very different challenges at home than at school. You may not see the child as loud or argumentative as his parents report. Or you may not view the skill the parents are concerned about as a problem, because you feel, for example, that their child will learn to write his name in time. Or you may view a normal skill or behavior as a problem because of the demands of caring for a group of children—for example, you may wish a child would play independently for longer periods of time so that you have time to care for other children. Sometimes a behavior that is acceptable at home is difficult to allow in the group setting because of the increased noise level, activity level, or number of disputes it seems to cause. You may inadvertently have difficulties or create frustrations for a child because you ask too much of him. You can cause a child to become upset by sticking to a rigid schedule or being unaccepting of his individual differences.

Sometimes parents may experience challenges that require your help. Ask them what they are trying to help their child learn. Find a standard that addresses the goal behavior and develop teaching strategies that you can use to help their child move toward the standard.

Obviously, when there is a disagreement, you and the parents will want to reach some sort of agreement that benefits the child. At the heart of any conversation should be "What is best for the child?" Focusing on him will also help both parties reduce defensiveness. When situations arise in which you and the parents hold differing points of view, avoid either/or thinking. Instead, use both-and thinking and look for new solutions and creative ideas.

You may also hold differing opinions on how to approach a situation. Be flexible in your planning and be open to different approaches that may be effective. Respect the parents' thoughts and ideas. Perhaps you can agree to try something they suggest until your next meeting. If you do, take note if it is helpful and continue it, or explain why it didn't work and decide on something more effective. Teachers must keep best practices and their state regulations in mind when a Plan for Action is determined. Your state may require you to do something different from what is recommended in this book or what parents recommend. If parents recommend something that you consider unkind, unethical, or impractical, indicate that you are unable to use the idea; then provide an alternative. You might say, "I'm not able to do that with seventeen other children in the class; I could do this instead" or "Rules of our center don't allow me to do that. What would you think of encouraging more . . . ?" Your licensing takes priority over parents' suggestions.

If parents you are working with choose not to work cooperatively, this book can still serve as a valuable tool. Use the strategies presented and continue to work toward your goal. If you continue to have concerns in a few months, bring them up again. If the parents are still unwilling to work with you or they disagree with you, you may want to use the Parent and Teacher Action Form as a formal agreement. In these difficult cases, the success of your relationship may become contingent on taking a certain action, such as working with a specialist before your next meeting. If this is the case, hold your meeting, describe the action that must be taken before your next meeting, and make it clear that you will no longer be able to work together if this action is not completed. Sign and then ask the parents to sign the Parent and Teacher Action Form. If the action is not taken by your next meeting, you may have to make a difficult decision.

On rare occasions, it may become necessary for you to decide if a child's enrollment in a program continues to be in his best interest. You will have to weigh the importance of a stable relationship against the challenges you are facing in coming to agreement. You will need to consider if you are continuing to treat this child with respect and if you are offering high-quality services. Develop skills that enable you to work effectively with children who demonstrate a broad range of skills and behaviors. Parents need to evaluate if the child is receiving the best possible care in your setting. Having him leave the program is a rare solution that should only be used as a last resort, but it may occasionally be what is best for the child. Sometimes a move to another program can alleviate problems. But more often, when a child doesn't learn the skills and behaviors needed in one program, the problems follow. In fact, the feelings resulting from a change may complicate matters and make it more difficult for a child to cope.

More often than not, you and a child's parents can work together to help him learn the skills and behaviors he needs. Develop a strong, respectful relationship with the parents. Communicate confidence that you can help the child learn the skills he needs when you work together, and his parents will be more likely to work with you.

Teaching young children can be challenging. You will find it easier if you take the time to observe, reflect on what you see, develop the skills you need to work with children effectively, and develop and implement Plans for Action. When you do this, you help children learn the skills and behaviors that form the foundation for future learning and success.

Part 2

Social-Emotional Development

The social-emotional domain involves a complex set of skills in which a child learns to separate from her family and take part in an early childhood program, express a range of emotions in a way that is appropriate to the situation, join groups of children and interact for extended periods, and take increasing responsibility for solving problems.

These important skills begin to develop when children are very young and continue to develop over their lifetimes. Children learn their first social-emotional skills from interaction with their parents, families, and the adults who care for them. Through these early relationships, they learn skills they need to successfully interact with their peers. For example, simple games in which babies and adults coo back and forth to one another form the underpinnings of turn taking.

During early childhood, children begin to understand their feelings and the feelings of others. They develop ways to regulate the intense feelings they have and to express them in ways that do not hurt others. They learn to have their needs met in ways that do not infringe on the rights of others. They learn that at times, they need to wait, take turns, and coordinate their behaviors with others so that play can continue. When children learn these self-regulation skills, they are learning how to function effectively in groups and be successful in a variety of settings.

Children need early childhood settings that support them while they learn social-emotional skills. They need settings that accept them as individuals, include them as a part of the classroom community, and help them learn to maneuver group settings. They need to feel safe and emotionally secure in order to experiment with different responses while they gain self-control. They need teachers who model appropriate responses. They need adults around them who accept mistakes and teach them what is appropriate.

They also need parents who set realistic boundaries that allow them to explore but also keep them safe. They need to be able to trust that their parents will provide for their physical needs. They need their parents to show them acceptable ways of behaving and interacting within their culture and their community.

Eight standards have been included in part 2, Social-Emotional Development. As in all the domains, states may have more standards than those included in this book. The standards presented here, or similar standards, are common in a number of states. Many focus on expressing feelings and developing self-regulation. It is important to help children learn to reach each standard while they learn to control their emotions, express themselves appropriately, get their needs met in acceptable ways, and interact successfully with others. The following standards are included:

- Separates from family to participate in early childhood setting, chapter 2

- Demonstrates confidence in own abilities, interacts and plays with others, and regulates own emotions and behaviors most of the time, chapter 3

- Enters group and plays with others, chapter 4

- Shares materials when appropriate, chapter 5

- Seeks assistance from an adult when needed, chapter 6

- Uses words to express feelings that are appropriate to the situation, chapter 7

- Demonstrates increasing use of words instead of actions to express emotions, chapter 8

- Uses problem solving to resolve conflicts, chapter 9

Not Getting Enough Sleep?

In her book *Sleepless in America*, Mary Sheedy Kurcinka describes a number of challenging childhood behaviors that may be due, in part, to overtiredness. She suggests that when children are overtired, they find it more difficult to focus, pay attention, control their emotions, problem solve, and get along with others. Children who have not had enough sleep may be whiny, argumentative, or clumsy. Children who are overtired may look as if they aren't tired at all. In truth, they are fighting to stay awake. Overtired children are more likely to be irritable, find it hard to fall asleep, and have difficulty staying asleep. Without enough sleep, a child's brain activates the arousal system, which causes her to keep going. Turning off the arousal system can be difficult for many children.

Children need plenty of sleep to deal with everyday challenges. Getting a good night's sleep can be a key to good behavior. Infants from birth to twelve months need an average of fourteen to eighteen hours of sleep including naps. Toddlers need an average of thirteen hours. Preschoolers three to five years need an average of twelve hours to feel well rested.

Children are unlikely to tell you they are tired. Instead, their behaviors give you reason to wonder if they have had enough sleep. If you have reason to believe a child is exhausted, there are a number of things you can do to help her get more sleep and feel better prepared to cope with the challenges of the day.

What parents and teachers can do:

- Keep the child on a regular schedule for waking, eating, and sleeping to help set the internal body clock

- Make sure the child has plenty of exercise early in the day

- Avoid caffeinated treats (chocolate) and sodas

- Be mindful of things that overly excite or distress the child and limit them

- Decrease the stimulation to which the child is exposed

- Limit screen time; the light can signal to a child's body that it is time to be awake

- Connect with this child throughout each day

- Offer comfort when this child is tense or anxious

What teachers can do:

- Help this child feel safe and accepted

- Set the stage for nap with room-darkening shades, quiet activities leading up to nap, and calming music in the background

- Give this child a back rub, rub her forehead, or rock her for a few minutes while she falls asleep

- Give this child a private space, away from toys and other children, in which to nap

What parents can do:

- Stay on schedule, even during the weekend

- Help your child meet her sleep needs by making sleep a priority

- Make choices about activities so your child gets the sleep she needs

- Avoid exciting or active play for at least one hour before bed

- Help your child unwind from exciting activities

- Create a safe, comfortable place for your child to sleep

- Establish a bedtime routine

- Watch for cues that indicate your child is ready for sleep; get her to bed when these become evident

- Assist your child as she learns to fall asleep

"Don't Go!" Separating

2

FOR TEACHERS

Anna has been coming here for weeks. Now, all of a sudden she cries every time her mom drops her off. I don't understand what is going on.

❖ **Standard**
Separates from family to participate in early childhood setting.

What Is It?

One of a child's first experiences separating from her parents comes when someone else cares for her. Fear of being separated can be stressful for the child, whether the separation is for a short or a long period. A child periodically experiences developmental peaks in separation anxiety. A number of these peaks take place during the infant and toddler years. Preschool age children experience them too.

All preschool children experience some feelings of separation anxiety. Being upset when parents leave is a normal, expected response. The intensity, however, varies from child to child. The degree to which they show their feelings depends on their personality, culture, and previous experiences with separation. Some children approach a new setting enthusiastically, seemingly unaffected by the separation. Others become upset, cry, or cling to their parents when it is time for the parents to leave. Others are taught not to cry but still miss their parents. A few children withdraw and refuse to talk or engage in activities. Helping an anxious child separate from her parents is an important step in helping her participate in an early childhood setting.

Observe and Decide What to Teach

Ask the following questions as you watch a child's response to your setting. The suggestions will help you formulate a plan to ease her concerns and help her become fully engaged in your early childhood setting.

Does This Child Become Upset, Cry, or Fuss
When She Is Left at the Early Childhood Program?

Crying, fussing, or being upset are normal initial reactions to being left at an early childhood program until a child adjusts. Help a new child and her parents get off to a good start by easing them into your program. Create a website that shows prospective parents and children what their new program will look like. Highlight staff photos and qualifications, the facility, learning centers, and different types of activities (Stephens 2004). Parents and their child can virtually tour your program to learn what to expect.

Offer an orientation and phase-in period during which the parent and child can visit your program. If a parent isn't available, perhaps a grandparent or other trusted adult could substitute. The first visit can be quite short. On following days, the child and parent can attend together and gradually lengthen their stay. The parent should play near the child at first and then move to the side of the room to serve as a safe base. Once the child seems comfortable, the parent should say good-bye and take a short walk or read a book in the car. The length of time spent away from the child can be increased each time until the child is able to stay for the whole program day. Try to time the parent's return when the child is having fun. The length of the phase-in period depends on the individual. With this type of orientation, the child is much more likely to approach daily separations positively.

Entice the child to participate in activities by learning about her interests. Have these available when she arrives and gently try to engage her in activities. During initial contacts with her, avoid quick movements and physical contact (unless the child requests it). Allow the child to watch others and learn about your setting from the corner of the room or the sidelines of a game, or by peeking from behind the easel. If she does engage with materials, play next to her. Describe what you are doing, but do not expect a response. Try sharing a material with her without talking. Follow the child's lead in play. Once she is ready to talk with you, let her direct you verbally or with her actions.

If the child is crying, reflect what she might be feeling. Say, "It's sad when Mom has to go." Reassure her that her parent will return. If she wants comfort, offer it. Try to distract her with engaging toys. Do a puppet play in which the puppet is frightened by being in the early childhood setting. Show how the teacher can help the puppet and how the puppet meets others and finds things to do.

Set a consistent daily routine. This helps a child gauge when her parent will return and helps reduce fear of the unknown. Make a pictorial schedule. Talk about what will take place so she knows what to expect. Talk about the specific time someone will pick her up (for example, after snacktime or after games). Allow her to carry a security item, such as a blanket, a cuddly toy, or a picture of her family.

Some children who feel they can't stop their parent from leaving may try to control what they can. They may hoard toys or insist on a certain chair. Understand the underlying need to hold on while gently introducing the concept of sharing toys with others. Many of these behaviors are transitional. Guide the child's behavior with care and understanding. It is important to build a positive relationship at this time. Let her settle in before you become overly concerned.

On his first day of preschool, Seng, a four-year-old boy for whom English is his second language, slumped against the door. He cried and called out to his father in his home language. The teacher cautiously approached with a clipboard and drawing paper. She drew a picture of a boy who was crying. She drew a picture of a boy with a truck, followed by a picture of his dad in the doorway. Next, she drew the boy with a happy face. The teacher went on to draw a family and house. Seng named his family members and corrected the drawing so it depicted his family. The teacher handed him the clipboard and marker. She stayed with him while he drew.

Before too long, the teacher announced, "In five minutes, we'll go see what toys there are." When the time came to tour the room, Seng refused. The teacher took the clipboard and marker and began to draw and label the toys in the room. Just minutes later, they were moving around the room together. The teacher showed Seng a pictorial schedule of their day and explained again when his father would return. Seng began to play with a toy that caught his eye. Before long, other children joined him. Another child was overheard saying, "Don't worry. Your dad will be back soon. It will go fast. I promise."

Does the Child Become Fussy at Naptime or Mealtime?

Naptime and mealtime can remind children of home. At naptime, a child might miss family routines like reading a book or cuddling with a parent. To help a child who is having difficulty, find out about her naptime routine and repeat as much of it as possible. Encourage her to bring a familiar blanket or cuddly animal. Play quiet, soothing music to provide a distraction as well as help to create a calm atmosphere. Consider if the child is overtired from first exposures to a group setting. If so, allow additional rest periods earlier in the day, or move naptime ahead a few minutes. Perhaps this child does not nap at home and is upset by the request. Strike a compromise, such as a short rest time or time to read books. At mealtime, plan meals that are familiar to the child. If possible, include her in food preparations. Explain any mealtime routines. Encourage the child to eat without forcing her; she may be too nervous to eat much.

Has This Child Been in Your Program for Some Time and Is Now Tearful or Upset at Drop-Off?

Some children seem to adjust well the first few weeks of attendance and then fall apart. It is as if they realize that school is here to stay. That's what happened with Anna at the beginning of the chapter. Her early childhood program was fun at first, but when she realized it was going to be most every day, she wasn't so sure she liked it. Staff at her program recognized her need for support. They made attempts to greet her, helped her find toys that sparked her interest, and guided her toward peer relationships. They worked with her parents to develop a morning routine. Before long, Anna had made the adjustment and was able to enter the program with smiles each day.

Children will sometimes become upset when they have to separate after a terrific weekend at home, a family vacation, or a special celebration. Typically, these adjustment periods are short and easy for a child to overcome. If a child you are working with seems to have periodic separation issues, see if there is a pattern. Do they follow special family times? Use appropriate suggestions listed under the first question above. Build your relationship with the child. Greet her daily. Find something special to share, such as a joke, a way she can help, or a common interest. Consider sources of anxiety. Has there been a change at home or in the early childhood setting? Was there an upset with another child or adult? Is she upset because she was disciplined for something? Has a special friend or teacher left the program? Support this child while she learns to cope with changes and her feelings.

Does This Child Fully Engage in Program Activities?

The work of separation is not complete until a child is fully engaged in the early childhood program. Watch to see if a child who has had difficulty is now participating and not just going through the motions until it is time to go home. Identify any of her favorite activities. Affirm her involvement in these by saying, "It's fun to paint at school" or "You really listened to story today." Preview things to look forward to the next day. Say, "Next time you come, we'll read the book you were looking at." Be sure you do.

Plan dramatic play themes that involve a lot of children and that are highly motivating. If the children are riding a bus to your program, set up a bus in your classroom and let children take turns being the driver and the passengers. Add some humor by pretending to have a toy dog try to get on the bus. Plan group activities that are highly participatory and motivating. Perhaps each child can hold a toy animal or a picture of an animal in the book you are reading. Ask them to hold up their animal as you read about it. Plan tabletop activities that are engaging, such as playdough. Assign a child to the newcomer to act as a buddy and help her through routines. Recognize the times in which she is actively engaged in play or with friends, and whisper affirming messages like, "Helen likes playing with you." Plan small-group activities that help her learn the names of the other children. For example, play a simple game in which the children sit in a circle and roll the ball to each other. When the ball rolls to each child, she says her name before rolling it to someone else.

Is Leaving the Early Childhood Setting or the Reunion with the Parent Difficult?

Some children have so much fun or are so involved in activities that when their parent arrives to pick them up, they cry or behave inappropriately. This might also happen when a child has been working to control her emotions all day—and she finally releases them. Help a child who has difficulty at the end of the day by warning her that her parent will be arriving soon. Wait until after this child leaves to start an involved or lengthy activity. Assure the child that the toys she is playing with will be available next time. Encourage the parents to allow enough time for pickup in case the child needs to finish a project or game. Reduce the amount of time spent in conversation between adults so the parents can focus on the child. Share necessary information in writing or over the phone. Be clear about who is responsible for guiding the child's behavior at pickup time. Sometimes each adult is waiting for the other to do something.

When to Seek Assistance

Adjustments are individual. Some may take three hours; some, three days; and others, three months. If a child attends your program sporadically or is shy in all settings, separation may be an issue for a long time. If a child cries regularly for more than ten minutes every day for several weeks, she may need additional help. A child experiencing this level of distress may require a longer orientation period or a shorter day in your program, or her parents may need the counsel of a parent educator or counselor who specializes in working with families of young children (Brodkin 2003).

Work with the Parents

As you talk with a family that is interested in your program, let them know about your flexible orientation policy. Expect and accept the stress that separation causes parents. Encourage them to spend time easing their child into your setting even if they think their child will be all right. Talk with them about how important it is to prepare their child for coming to your program. Offer them the information for parents on the following pages. Work with them to develop a good-bye strategy to use when their child is ready to begin her regular schedule. The plan might include special time at home before getting in the car, one quick tour of the room to decide what to play with first, and then a kiss and a hug before leaving. Let the parents know of progress their child makes in participating in your program. Reassure them that you are doing everything you can to help their child feel comfortable.

A Plan for Action

To develop your Plan for Action, choose or modify one of the suggested goals to best match your situation. Add how well or how often you expect the skill or behavior to be demonstrated. Remember: you are looking for growth, not perfection. Keep in mind that you want to move the child from where she is currently by increasing your expectations slightly. Next, determine three or four actions that teachers and parents will take. Choose additional actions specific to the early childhood setting and home. Write your choices on the planning form found at the end of the book.

Sample goals for a child having difficulty separating:

- Separates without upset

- Leaves child care without protest

- Engages in _____ and _____ each day (list an activity or two)

- Settles in to naptime without crying

- Fully participates in early childhood program

Sample actions parents and teachers can take:

- Participate in a phase-in period

- Accept this child's fear

- Consider other sources of anxiety

- Reassure this child her parent will return

- Reduce adult conversation at pickup time

Sample actions teachers can take:

- Greet this child daily
- Be responsible for the child's behavior once this child enters
- Allow a security item from home
- Have activities of interest available when this child arrives
- Offer foods this child likes to eat
- Build relationship with this child
- Play next to this child
- Follow this child's lead in play
- Avoid quick movements and physical touch (unless requested by the child)
- Reflect the feelings this child may be having
- Put on a puppet play about separation
- Assign another child as a buddy
- Talk about the specific time this child will be picked up
- Repeat as much of the family's naptime routine as possible
- Compromise about the need for nap or the length of rest time
- Do not start an involved or lengthy activity just before this child is picked up

Sample actions parents can take:

- Pretend-play about going to your child's early childhood program
- Spend time with your child prior to drop-off
- Bring a security item
- Create a routine around leaving and returning
- Plan what you will do together when you get home
- Say good-bye before leaving, and then leave promptly
- Allow adequate time for pickup
- Be responsible for your child's behavior whenever you are with the child
- If your child continues to exhibit separation difficulties, talk with a parent educator or counselor; share pertinent information with your child's teacher

Information on Separating

WHAT IS IT?

Children are typically upset the first few times a parent leaves them at an early childhood program. There is a lot for them to learn about and adjust to in this new setting. The intensity, however, varies from child to child. Some children approach a new setting enthusiastically. Others become upset or cling to the parent. Others don't cry but still miss their parent. A few children withdraw and refuse to engage in activities.

Observe and Respond

Help your child adjust to a new program by arranging an orientation period. If you aren't available, ask a grandparent or other trusted adult. The first visit can be short, followed by gradually longer visits. Play near your child at first, and then move to the side of the room. Once your child seems comfortable, say good-bye and take a short walk or read a book away from the child care program. The length of time spent away from your child can be increased each time until your child is able to stay for the whole program day.

Prepare your child by reading books like *The Kissing Hand* by Audrey Penn or *Will You Come Back for Me?* by Ann Tompert. Pretend going to preschool or child care. Take turns being the one who leaves and the one who is left behind. Be honest about your own feelings about leaving your child, but be careful those feelings don't rub off.

When you and your child are at home and relaxed, create a positive mental image of the new setting. Emphasize that you will be back. Talk about things that may take place and how your child will fit in. Find another child going to the same program, and get together a few times. Talk with the teacher about letting your child carry a security item, such as a cuddly toy or a picture of your family.

It is best to say good-bye before leaving rather than sneaking out, even if your child becomes upset. Sneaking out teaches your child to be wary about when you may leave. Once you say good-bye, leave promptly. The teacher will do everything possible to help your child become involved and make a positive adjustment. Most likely, your child will shut off the tears and begin to play happily soon after you close the door.

Sometimes children become upset after a few weeks of attendance or after a special family time. Look to see if there is a pattern to the upsets (for example, every Monday after a terrific weekend at home). Consider if your child is anxious about something. Has there been a change at home or in the early childhood setting? Was there an upset with another child or adult? Is your child upset because he or she was disciplined for something? Your child needs support while learning to cope with changes and new feelings.

The work of separation is not complete until your child is fully engaged in the early childhood program. Ask the teacher if your child is wholeheartedly participating or just going through the motions until it is time to go home. Look at newsletters or lesson plans so you can ask questions about specific activities and preview things to look forward to the next day. Say, "Tomorrow you're going to do a pretend car wash on the playground."

Some children cry or behave inappropriately when their parents arrive to pick them up. Children who fall apart at the end of the day may be releasing emotions they have worked to control. They may have been involved in an interesting activity, or they may have been having so much fun that it's hard to leave. Help your child respond to pickup time more positively by setting a regular time to arrive. Make sure there's enough time for your child to finish activities. Highlight something fun that you have planned to do at home. Focus on your child at this time rather than talking with the teacher. Be clear about who is responsible for guiding your child's behavior at pickup time. Sometimes each adult is waiting for the other to do something.

CONNECTING WITH SUPPORT

Adjusting to a new setting is highly individual. It may take your child three hours, three days, or three months. If your child attends the program sporadically or is shy in all settings, separation may be an issue for a long time. A child who cries daily for more than ten minutes for several weeks may need additional help. If your child is experiencing this level of distress, consider a longer transition period or a shorter day in the program, or talking with a parent educator or counselor who specializes in working with families of young children.

3 ◆ "Watch This!" Attention Getting

FOR TEACHERS

Brady wants me to watch his every move. When I spend time with him, it never seems to be enough. I feel like he demands so much attention that I don't have enough time for the other children.

❖ **Standards**

Demonstrates confidence in own abilities.

Interacts and plays with others.

Regulates own emotions and behaviors most of the time.

What Is It?

Everyone wants attention. Children especially like to have adults spend time with them, notice the things they are doing, and comment on what they are learning. Some children require more attention than others, and some seem to have an insatiable need for attention. It is easy to tire of their pleas to play with you or to watch them, yet it is essential to respond in ways that support their growth. In working with a child who requires a high level of attention, recognize the important role you play. Be sure to watch this child carefully and try to identify what he needs to learn. A child who requires a great deal of attention can often benefit from more than one standard. Many children benefit from gaining confidence. Other standards that may apply include interacting and playing with others and regulating emotions and behaviors most of the time.

Observe and Decide What to Teach

Watch a child who requires a great deal of attention to see if there is a pattern to his behavior. Ask yourself the following questions to help you determine which standard to use as a goal. Use the suggestions to formulate a Plan for Action.

Does This Child Call Your Attention to His Activities?

"Watch this," "Watch me," and "Look," are favorite phrases of a child who is excited about newfound skills. Some children, however, call your attention to their activities in order to boost their confidence. They look for confirmation of their skills from others rather than feeling assured of their own abilities. Help a child begin to feel good about himself by teaching him to be proud of his own work. Model words for him to use by saying something like "I see colorful lines and circles." Help him praise his work by asking, "What is your favorite part of your picture?" or "Which part did you work on the hardest?"

Help a child gain confidence in his skills by ensuring that he is often successful. Make sure materials are displayed at his level so he can access materials he needs. Check to see if the level of difficulty of toys and materials are appropriate for this child. If he seems bored, add items that are more difficult or that he hasn't seen in some time. Set out easier toys for a child who may feel he cannot do the activities available to him. Try to provide the right level of challenge by offering activities he can do with just a little assistance from you. Once he can perform activities with your help, he can soon perform the task independently. Notice when he tries his best. Accept mistakes. If he feels free to try new things without worry of ridicule, he gains confidence. Help him focus on his efforts or the progress he is making rather than on the end product.

If this child calls your attention to his activities time after time, you may need to set a limit on how many times you will watch him. Say, "I will watch you one more time, and then I must watch one of the other children."

At times, a child will exaggerate his abilities in order to gain recognition or favor. Help him feel proud and competent in many areas. Bolster his confidence by commenting on times when he is strong, making good decisions, or running fast. De-emphasize competition. Play cooperative games, such as musical mats, where mats are taken away when the music stops, and children share a space on a mat rather than leaving the game. Plan activities in which children work together, such as making a fruit salad or telling a group story.

Does This Child Ask You to Play with Him All the Time?

A child who has a high need for attention may read books with you for ten minutes and then ask you to play a game with him. Brady, in the example at the beginning of the chapter, never seemed to get enough attention. His teacher watched him for a number of days and found that he really hadn't developed friendships with any of the other children. She decided to encourage him to play less often with her and more often with other children.

Some children who call for an adult's attention have difficulty playing alone or may not have satisfying peer relationships. Help a child having difficulty move from being dependent on you to being more independent and involved in relationships with other children. Structure your day so that there are times when he is asked to play independently, he has special time with you, plays next to you, and plays with other children. Be firm but fair about the amount of time you have to spend with him. Spend time with this child early in the day before he searches for ways (possibly inappropriate) to get your attention. In addition, schedule a special time together. Talk about your special time and when it will take place. Make it clear how long you will be able to play with him. Draw the play session to an end after five to ten minutes. Promise to play with him again later or the next day. Once your time together is over, explain in a kind but firm way that you have other things you must do and that he must do something on his own. Help him decide what activity he will engage in and get him started. When he is playing alone, look for a break or pause in the action. Comment on his independence.

Arrange times when you and this child can work side by side. Set him up with an activity that he can do next to you. Continue with your work while he does his. Your nearness will help him feel valued. Occasionally give him a nonverbal signal, such as a wink or the okay sign, to let him know you appreciate his efforts to play independently.

Encourage relationships with others by playing with this child and inviting another child to join in. Once they have begun to play together, step away, but remain close enough to offer suggestions or help solve problems. You can also foster relationships with other children by arranging partner activities or asking this child to work on a classroom job with another child. Encourage the child you are working with to ask another for help. For example, if he needs help with something on the computer, you can say, "Tamara is good at that. Ask her to show you." Include time and space for children to play in small groups. Dramatic theme play areas usually bring children together as they pretend to play house, restaurant, or car wash. For more information on children playing in groups, see chapter 4, "I Want to Play Too!" Joining a Group of Players. Recognize when this child is cooperating with others and comment on it.

Does This Child Interrupt or Ask Questions Frequently?

Most children find it difficult to wait for their turn to talk. A child who requires extra attention is more likely to interrupt others or ask questions in order to draw attention to himself. You can help him learn to regulate this aspect of his behavior by helping him learn to wait for a turn to talk. Make a rule for all children that only one person talks at a time. Explain confidentially to this child that he needs to wait for his turn. Tell him, "I'd like to hear what you have to say, but someone else is talking. You need to wait until she is done." Ask him to tell you one word of what he has to say so you can both remember what he is going to tell you. Then he must wait. Be sure to ask him about what he wanted to tell you at an appropriate time. If he interrupts frequently during group time, talk with him about being quiet. Give him the thumbs-up or okay signal when time passes without interruption as a way to pay attention to him without disrupting the activity.

Does This Child Look at You and Then Break a Rule?

At times, children feel as if the only time they get attention is when they are being reprimanded for doing something wrong. Adults inadvertently play a role in helping children develop this feeling if they do not comment when children are behaving as expected or if they ignore appropriate behaviors. A child who seeks attention through inappropriate behavior may look to see if you're watching and then break a rule. To turn this behavior around, pay attention to this child early in the day and often. Be sure he is behaving appropriately and say something like "Thanks for helping set the table for breakfast" or "I see you are being careful so the blocks don't fall over." Let him know you appreciate his hard work to follow the rules.

He may not need to seek your attention inappropriately as often if you teach him some simple phrases to use to ask for your attention. He can say, "Sit by me," or "Hold my hand." If this child is imitating inappropriate behaviors of others, let him know he has good ideas of his own and doesn't need to copy other people.

When he does break a rule, pay as little attention as possible. State simply that what has been done is not acceptable, and then move him to another part of the room or require him to choose a quiet activity for a short time. Do not engage in discussion or argue with him at this point. If he argues with you, he may be attempting to keep you involved. Instead, let him know what he needs to do before you will attend to him again. For example, you might say, "I will come and sit by you when you have stopped kicking the table."

Work with the Parents

Talk with this child's parents about his need for attention. Describe his behavior in your program and how challenging it can be to deal with in a group setting. See if they have similar concerns. It may be easier for them to meet their child's need for attention at home, or they may be frustrated with his attention-seeking behaviors too. Find out if there have been any changes that may have led this child to seek extra adult support. Work with the parents to develop a Plan for Action. Establishing consistency between the home and the early childhood setting will help him become more confident, learn to build peer relationships, and develop self-regulation skills.

> **When to Seek Assistance**
>
> By attending to a child many times a day and letting him know when his behavior is appropriate, you can help most children to get their need for attention met. However, if a child's bids for attention are dangerous or self-injuring, refer the family to a counselor who specializes in working with young children.

A Plan for Action

To develop your Plan for Action, choose or modify one of the suggested goals to best match your situation. Add how well or how often you expect the skill or behavior to be demonstrated. Remember: you are looking for growth, not perfection. You want to move the child from where he is currently and increase your expectations slightly. Next, determine three or four actions teachers and parents will take. Choose additional actions specific to the early childhood setting and the home. Record your choices on the planning form found in the appendix.

Sample goals for a child requiring a high level of attention:

- Compliments his own work
- Works next to you for _____ minutes each day (choose a time that is slightly longer than his current performance)
- Plays alone for _____ minutes each day (choose a time that is slightly longer than his current performance)

- Plays with another child for _____ minutes each day (choose a time that is slightly longer than his current performance)
- Waits to talk until it is his turn
- Asks for attention in appropriate ways
- Follows simple rules _____ percent of the time (choose a percent that is slightly greater than his current performance)

Sample actions parents and teachers can take:

- Arrange toys and materials so the child can help himself
- Provide toys that challenge him but with which he can be successful
- Focus on his efforts
- Spend time one-on-one with this child early in the day and often
- Firmly draw a play session to a close
- Comment on this child's independence
- Be specific as you comment about this child's work
- Ask this child to praise his own work
- Pay attention to this child with nonverbal signals when you can't talk with him
- Set limits on how many times you will watch this child
- Arrange times to work side by side
- Make it clear that only one person is to talk at a time
- Pay little attention to this child when he breaks a rule
- Restate the rule that has been broken and tell this child his behavior is unacceptable
- Move this child to another part of the room and ask him to choose a quiet activity for a short time
- Teach him to ask for attention appropriately

Sample actions teachers can take:

- Spend a few minutes of special time together each day
- Structure group activities, partner activities, and independent playtimes
- De-emphasize competition

Sample actions parents can take:

- Alternate between doing things together and independently
- Plan cooperative activities
- Talk with a counselor if your child does things that are extremely dangerous or self-injuring, and share pertinent information with your child's teacher

Information on Attention Getting

WHAT IS IT?

Children like to have adults spend time with them, notice the things they are doing, and comment on what they are learning. However, some children require more attention than others, and some seem insatiable. It is easy to tire of their pleas to play together or for you to watch them, yet it is essential to respond in a way that supports their growth.

Observe and Respond

Help your child feel more confident, play alone more often, and follow simple rules to reduce dependence on your attention. "Watch this," and "Look," are favorite phrases of a child looking for confirmation of newfound skills. Help your child feel proud of work by modeling words of praise by saying something like "I see colorful lines and circles." Help your child praise his or her work by asking, "Which part did you work on the hardest?"

Help your child gain confidence by ensuring success. Check to see if your child's toys are difficult enough to be challenging but not frustrating. If your child seems bored, add items that are more difficult or that haven't been used for some time. Set out easier toys if your child seems unable to do the activities with just a little assistance. Notice when your child is trying hard. Accept mistakes. Focus on your child's efforts or on progress made rather than on the end product. Bolster your child's confidence by complimenting actions like making good decisions and running fast.

If your child continually calls your attention to activities, you may need to set a limit on how many times you will watch. Say, "I will watch you one more time, and then I need to get my work done."

Help your child move from being dependent on you to being more independent. Be firm but fair about how much undivided attention you can give. Schedule special times together each day. Talk about your special time and when it will take place. Make clear how long you will be able to play. Draw the play session to an end. Promise to play with your child again later. Once your time together is over, explain in a kind but firm way that you have other things you must do and that your child must do something independently. You can help your child decide and then get the activity started. Once your child is playing alone, look for a break or pause in the action. Commend your child for how independent he or she is.

continued

Arrange ways to work side by side. Continue with your work while your child does too. Your nearness will help your child feel valued. A nonverbal signal, such as a wink or the okay sign, lets your child know you appreciate his or her efforts to play independently.

Some children crave attention most when you are talking to others. Help your child learn to wait for a turn to talk by making a rule that everyone must take a turn or interrupt politely. Tell your child, "I'd like to hear what you have to say, but someone else is talking. You need to wait until she is done." Teach your child to put a hand on your shoulder or wait for a break in the conversation and then say, "Excuse me."

Occasionally a child will feel as if the only way to get attention is to be reprimanded for doing something wrong. A child who feels this way may seek attention through inappropriate behavior. Turn this type of behavior around by paying attention when your child is behaving appropriately. Say something like "Thanks for helping set the table." Teach your child some simple phrases to use to ask for your attention appropriately, such as "Sit by me" or "Hold my hand."

When your child does break a rule, pay as little attention as possible. Simply state that what has been done is not acceptable. Do not engage in discussion or argue with your child at this point. Instead, explain what needs to happen before you will attend to him or her again. For instance, you might say, "I will come and sit by you when you stop kicking the table."

CONNECTING WITH SUPPORT

Talk with your child's teacher. Work together to develop a plan to meet your child's need for attention. Establish consistency between the home and the early childhood setting to teach your child to be more confident and independent and to develop self-regulation skills. If your child does things for attention that are dangerous or self-injuring, see a family counselor who specializes in working with young children.

4 ◆ "I Want to Play Too!" Joining a Group of Players

FOR TEACHERS

I feel bad when Mackenzie stands on the fringe and watches other children play. One day, I watched as she found the toy the others were searching for. She handed it to James and then ran off. It was as if she was scared to join them.

❖ **Standard**
Enters group and plays with others.

What Is It?

Many children are highly motivated to be a part of group play. Children usually learn to join play by watching and copying those in the group. These children join right in and seem readily accepted. Others find it difficult to join already established play groups. They stand on the outskirts and look in, or they are excluded from play. When a child appears anxious or as if she does not know how to join in, it is time for you to offer support. Children need a number of entrance strategies that do not call undue attention to themselves and are not too disruptive. Asking, "Can I play?" is often answered with a resounding, "No!" Adults working with children can help them learn other ways to enter play that may be more readily accepted.

Observe and Decide What to Teach

Ask the following questions while you watch a child who is having difficulty joining group play. The suggestions that accompany each question will help this child learn to enter groups and play with others.

Does This Child Play Alone Most Often?

It is common for infants, toddlers, and young preschoolers to play alone. Children of all ages play by themselves when they do not know each other very well, are feeling shy or cautious, or need some time to themselves. They may also play by

Common Reasons Children Are Rejected

All children, even highly skilled children, are rejected at times. Children reject others for many reasons. Assess the reason and respond appropriately. Reasons that children are rejected include the following:

- To protect a limited number of play materials rather than share
- To protect a role they are enacting and don't want someone to take from them
- To limit the number of players (sometimes, children are not socially skilled enough to see how one more person would fit into the space or story line)
- To feel as if they are a part of a group
- To feel powerful by including and excluding players
- To exclude someone who has a reputation for being disruptive or aggressive (they don't want to face the upsetting behaviors again)

To reduce the chances of a newcomer being rejected, do this:

- Foster a sense of belonging, inclusiveness, and caring for others
- Teach the child entrance strategies that do not call attention to herself or disrupt the play
- Teach her to play near the other children and imitate their actions
- Join the play yourself and then invite the newcomer in; help to resolve conflicts
- Give the child a prop to bring to the play that supports the story line
- Watch to find a role that isn't already taken; provide the newcomer with ideas about how to act her part
- Teach the child any social skills she may be lacking
- Offer support for a child who is rejected once in a while; say, "I think she needs some time to herself. Let's play over here for a while until she is ready to play again."

If one child is rejected frequently, intervene on her behalf. Take her by the hand and join the group together. Help the children recognize her good ideas. Help her solve any problems that arise. If you insist that the group includes this child without your support, you may build resentment that leads to further rejection of her.

themselves because they enjoy it. When children have the skills they need to join others in play but choose to play alone, respect their decision. However, a preschooler can use your help if she appears upset, looks as if she doesn't know how to join in, or is always on the outside of play. Encourage a child who doesn't know how to join in by offering materials that support group play, such as dramatic play or building with blocks. If she tends to play with toys that are for one person at a time, like puzzles, books, or an easel, find ways to bring these materials into group activities. Set up a dramatic play theme of a library. This child can play with others while they read books, pretend to check them out, and help to straighten the library displays. Offer structured small-group activities so that she gets to know others while you are there to direct the activity. Play games that help this child learn the names of those in the group. Comment on things that she has in common with others. Say, "You and Kayla both like to pretend about the movie you saw."

Does This Child Have Trouble Playing with You or Another Adult?

Most children who are successful with their peers have had good relationships with adults. To help a child who is having difficulty playing with peers, first develop your own relationship with her. Find out what she enjoys and engage in those activities. Spend time listening to and talking with her. Share a joke or an innocent secret. Learn about her family and what she does outside of your program. Get down on the floor and play with her. Follow her lead, letting her direct the play scenario. Occasionally become a member of group play in which she would be interested. Invite this child to join you. Encourage but don't force interactions. If she doesn't respond to your invitation, place a positive expectation that she will join you soon. Even after she is playing with others, she may need to return to you at times as a safe base from which to operate.

Does This Child Find It Difficult to Play with One Other Child?

At about three and one-half years of age, children generally spend more time with peers than with teachers (Poole, Miller, and Church 2003). If a child you are working with is not playing with at least one other child, suggest a playmate who is similar to her in development, temperament, and level of impulsiveness (Gower et al. 2001). Choose a slightly younger playmate if you want to boost her confidence and give her practice with leadership skills. It may be easier for her to include someone in her play than for her to join others, so bring a child to her. Offer materials that encourage interaction and plan paired activities, such as fingerpainting, errands, and puppet plays. Change pairings periodically to give her practice with others. Allow this child to feel comfortable playing in pairs before expecting her to join larger groups. Read books about friends, such as *Will I Have a Friend?* by Miriam Cohen or *My Best Friend* by Pat Hutchins.

Does This Child Play with Only One Other Child?

Occasionally a child has a best friend who offers support and friendship from which she learns many things about trust and intimacy. However, if a child's best friend is absent, interested in other people, or attracted to activities that do not include her, the child may experience difficulty. Help a child who is feeling left out build additional relationships by looking for ways to connect her to new people. Weave her play together with the play of others. If she is cooking and others are making a house, suggest that she take her neighbors some dinner. Join the play yourself, and then find ways to include more players. For example, if you are pretending to go to the movies, include a ticket seller, usher, the concession stand cashier, as well as the audience.

Does This Child Stand Near a Group of Children Who Are Playing but Does Not Join Them?

When children begin to show an interest in joining others, they may play on the fringes of a group. Sometimes this is enough to become included, because the play wraps around them. If a child remains on the edge of the group, help her participate more fully by teaching her to imitate the actions of the rest of the group. Play next to her and draw her attention to what the others are doing. Encourage her to practice their activity before entering the group. For example, if others are feeding grass to plastic dinosaurs, hand her some grass and suggest she feed hers too. When she has an idea that goes along with the play, help her make her suggestion to another child in the group. Teach her to say the name of one child or to get their attention before making her comment. This increases the chances her idea will be acknowledged. She can say, "Chloe, let's say the dinosaurs run away from the hot lava."

Does This Child Try to Join Play in a Way That Is Disruptive?

Children who disrupt play or draw undue attention to themselves by being aggressive, barging in, criticizing, or being bossy are not as likely to be accepted in play (Kostelnik et al. 1998). For example, if a child wants to play firefighter with children who are rocking babies to sleep, she is likely to be rejected. Instead, help her find a group in which her idea fits. In this case, the children building with blocks and then knocking them down may be willing to join her in pretending to be firefighters.

Some children initiate play by slapping another child's shoulder, bulldozing their way into a group, or knocking over the toys of others. This ill-fitted attempt is upsetting to adults as well as children. Watch a child who behaves this way to see if her actions seem meant to gain entry into the group. Interpret this child's intentions for others by saying, "I think Aubrey is trying to squeeze in this spot to join your game." If this child is aggressive at other times, too, teach problem-solving skills (see chapter 9, "Whack!" Aggression).

Join the play yourself to help work through difficult situations. A reputation for being aggressive or disruptive can live long after the behavior. In addition to helping this child learn more appropriate behaviors, work to change the image children hold of her. Praise her ideas and recognize her when she is helpful. Assign this child important classroom tasks that she can succeed at (Brodkin 2006).

Consider if this child is using physical initiations because her verbal skills are limited. Suggest she take a less verbal role, such as that of the person washing the baby, pretending to be the family pet, or busing dishes at a restaurant. If she seems stuck in using a single approach to join play, encourage her to experiment with a number of different entrance strategies. Offer a suggestion, and then add, "If that doesn't work, come back, and we'll think of something else."

Does This Child Interrupt Play as She Enters?

Sometimes children try to join others but interrupt the existing play with their own idea. Teach this child to join play more successfully by offering a prop, material, or comment that supports the ongoing play. Help her learn to watch the play of others. Then suggest that she offer a prop that is related to the play. Mackenzie, in the example that begins this chapter, found the coffeepot for those who were playing house. She would have been even more successful if she had said, "Here's the coffee," and then offered to pour.

Watch to see that a child joining the play of others is not trying to take a role someone else has already claimed. Children have difficulty making room for two teachers or two babies. For example, if children are playing bakery, rather than becoming another baker, suggest that she be the taxi driver who takes people home. Help a child think of things she can do in the role she is to take. Make sure she is able to act out the role. For example, it may be difficult for a child with limited language skills or a dual-language learner to take on a role that requires her to be highly verbal.

A child who makes comments related to play has learned to add to play rather than try to change it or call undue attention to herself. Help a child who is not yet making comments related to play learn to do this by standing with her and scanning the room to see what play is taking place. Coach her on how she can fit into existing play. Help her plan what she wants to do and how it fits into what others are already doing. Ask, "What can you do to let them know you want to play? What can you bring to help them? What can you say to let them know you want to play?" Model words she can use to join the existing play. To increase her chances of being accepted, help her get the attention of one other person and suggest that she make her comment directly to that person. For example, if she says, "Here's a bag to put the groceries in," encourage her to say, "Dylan, here's a bag to put the groceries in."

Work with the Parents

Share with parents what you see in your setting. If they don't have an opportunity to see their child with other children, they may not be aware of the struggle she faces when learning to join others. Perhaps they have seen their child have difficulty with other family members or play groups. Some parents and teachers become concerned when a child is not interacting with other children or making friends. They may

Support Dual-Language Learners in Joining Play

Playing in groups is highly motivating for most children. When dual-language learners join groups of English-speaking children who are playing, they have the opportunity to learn new vocabulary and practice putting phrases together. Many dual-language learners become skilled observers and easily join play by following the lead of the other children. Others communicate non-verbally, indicating through gestures, facial expressions, or behaviors that they want to play. If a dual-language learner is having difficulty joining a group of players, there are a number of things that you can do to support her efforts.

- ◆ Use puppets to demonstrate entrance strategies

- ◆ Draw simple pictures of entrance strategies, such as stand near and watch, offer a prop, or copy what the other children are doing

- ◆ Suggest that a dual-language learner take on a nonverbal role

- ◆ Speak on behalf of a dual-language learner so she is not ignored

- ◆ Model simple phrases for this child to use

A child whose language is lagging in development may not be able to keep up with the verbal demands of group play. Other developmental lags, such as motor skills that are not yet developed or difficulty understanding pretend play, may cause a child to remain on the outskirts of play. Watch such a child and record your observations for three to four months. Does she play by herself most often? Does she respond negatively to the invitations of others? Is she consistently rejected by others? Is her behavior disruptive? Does she avoid contacts with others by choice? Does she have difficulty joining others at home as well as in the early childhood setting? Are her language skills lagging? Does she seem overwhelmed by the noise, sights, and activities of the group?

If the child you are concerned about demonstrates a pattern of worrisome behaviors or if you answered yes to many of these questions, encourage her parents to get her skills screened by her school district.

fondly remember their own childhood friends and want a similar experience for their child, or they may remember painful rejections of their own. Work with parents to help a child who does not have the skills needed to join others, who feels anxious about joining others, or who is frequently rejected by other children. Give the parents the accompanying information and create a shared Plan for Action. You might also suggest they join a parent discussion group.

A Plan for Action

To develop your Plan for Action, choose or modify one of the suggested goals to best match your situation. Add how well or how often you expect the skill or behavior to be demonstrated. Remember: you are looking for growth, not perfection. You want to move the child from where she is currently and to increase your expectations slightly. Next, determine three or four actions teachers and parents will take. Choose additional actions specific to early childhood setting and home. Record them on the planning form found in the appendix.

Sample goals for a child who has difficulty joining group play:

- Plays with an adult
- Plays with one other child (can be the same child)
- Plays one-on-one with different children
- Imitates behavior of group
- Offers a prop that supports the play of the group
- Makes a comment related to the play
- Gets attention of one of the children before making a comment related to play
- Enters group and plays with two or more children

Sample actions parents and teachers can take:

- Get down on the floor to play with this child each day
- Follow this child's lead in play
- Notice and comment on things this child has in common with others
- Help this child connect with someone who is similar

- Join the play to facilitate relationships
- Encourage but don't force interactions
- If the child ignores your invitation, express a positive expectation that she will join you soon
- Help this child watch and imitate the play of others
- Weave this child's play together with that of others
- Build relationships with more than one child
- Hand this child props she can bring to the existing play
- Help this child think of a role that complements what others are doing
- Teach this child to get the attention of one player before presenting an idea
- Encourage this child to try a number of entrance strategies
- Suggest appropriate roles for a child who is less verbal
- Join the play to coach this child through conflict situations
- Teach problem-solving skills
- Teach social skills
- Praise the child's ideas and acknowledge her when she is helpful
- Intervene on behalf of a child who is rejected
- Interpret this child's actions for others
- Read books about friends and friendship skills

Sample actions teachers can take:

- Foster a sense of belonging, inclusiveness, and caring for others
- Offer materials that support group play
- Work to develop an adult-child relationship
- Learn about this child's family and what she likes to do outside of the early childhood program; offer similar experiences
- Play games that will help this child get to know the other children
- Offer small-group activities led by the adult
- Plan paired activities
- Help this child look for appropriate groups to join
- Teach appropriate play behaviors
- Comment on the child's strengths and improvements in behaviors

Sample actions parents can take:

- Invite other children for play dates
- Direct and support play when children come to your home
- Arrange for a developmental screening; share pertinent information with your child's teacher

Information on Joining a Group of Players

WHAT IS IT?

Many children are highly motivated to become part of group play. Children usually learn to join play by watching and copying others. Others find it difficult to join already established play groups. It isn't necessary to expect your child to play with others at all times. Children of all ages play by themselves when they do not know each other very well, are feeling shy or cautious, or need time to themselves. When children have the skills they need to join others in play but choose to play alone, respect their decision.

Observe and Respond

If your child appears anxious or doesn't seem to know how to join in, it is time to offer support. You can help your child learn effective ways to enter play. Most children who are successful with their peers have had good relationships with adults. Be sure your child knows how to play with you by playing together each day. Get down on the floor and follow your child's lead. Your child will want to play with you even after learning to play well with other children.

Look for children who can be playmates for your child in your neighborhood, early childhood program, or place of worship. Set up play dates. Try neutral settings like playgrounds first, before inviting another child to your home, where your child must share toys. When another child comes to your home for the first time, the visitor may need time to explore. Once the children settle in, join the play too. Find ways to solve any problems that may come up.

Children who disrupt play or are aggressive, critical, or bossy are not as likely to be accepted by a group of children who are playing. If your child tries to take over play, such behavior is likely to result in rejection. If your child's play idea is too different from what is already taking place, the group is likely to reject her or him. Help your child develop ideas that fit in with what others are already doing.

Some children initiate play by slapping a child's shoulder, bulldozing their way into a group, or knocking over toys. These behaviors are upsetting to other children. See how your child tries to gain entry into a group. Consider if your child is being physical because of limited verbal skills. If that's the case, suggest your child take a less verbal role, such as pretending to be the family pet or busing dishes at a restaurant. If your child uses only one approach to join play, offer a different suggestion, and then add, "If that doesn't work, come back, and we'll think of something else."

One successful strategy for joining group play is to offer a prop that supports play. Your child can bring coffee to those who are playing house or be the pizza delivery person. Watch to see that your child is not taking a role that someone else has already claimed. Children have difficulty making room for two teachers or two babies. Help your child think of how to act out a role before actually playing it.

A child who makes comments related to play has learned to add to play rather than try to change it. Help your child watch play and then decide where to fit into it. Ask, "What could you bring that would help them? What can you say to let them know you want to play?" To increase your child's chances of being accepted even further, suggest getting the attention of one other person before making a comment. For example, encourage your child to say, "Dylan, here's a bag to put the groceries in."

CONNECTING WITH SUPPORT

Talk with your child's teacher to determine what the adults are doing to encourage your child to enter group play and what you can do to support their efforts. Seek additional assistance by having your child's skills screened by your local school district if the verbal expectations of group play seem too demanding or if your child seems to be on the outskirts of play because of difficulty in understanding the pretend aspect of it.

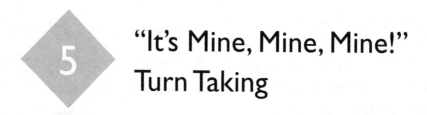

"It's Mine, Mine, Mine!"
Turn Taking

FOR TEACHERS

Cameron sits on the floor, spreads his legs, and dumps a bucket of blocks between them. He never really plays with them. He just keeps guard over them to make sure no one else takes them.

❖ **Standard**
Shares materials when appropriate.

What Is It?

Learning to take turns isn't easy for preschoolers. It wouldn't be a problem if there were enough materials and attention for all the children in a group. However, in most group settings young children are expected to take turns with toys, adult attention, and to wait for their turn to talk. Turn taking includes learning to give up materials once a child is done, asking to play with a material someone else is using, and waiting for a turn when there aren't enough toys to go around. Some children learn to take turns by watching others and experiencing give-and-take with adults. Some children require adult guidance in order to learn this important skill.

Observe and Decide What to Teach

Watch a child having difficulty learning to take turns. After you observe, consider the suggestions that follow and develop a plan to help him learn to share materials when it is appropriate.

Does This Child Refuse to Give Up a Toy?

Children show their refusal to take turns in a number of ways. They may dissolve into tears, vehemently reject the idea, or leave the area in a huff if required to give up a toy. A child who responds in this way will need help in learning to take turns with toys and materials. Before the age of three and one-half, many children may not be developmentally ready to share. Cameron, in the example at the beginning of this chapter, is a young three-year-old. His teacher encourages him to take turns with materials but doesn't require him to. She has found that if she forces him, he becomes very upset. But if she shares toys with others when Cameron is close by, he sometimes imitates her.

If you are working with a child who refuses to share, don't demand it. This can cause additional stress for a child who may not be sharing because he feels anxious. Instead, place positive expectations for future turn taking (Heidemann and Hewitt 2010). Say within this child's hearing, "I'm sure he'll give it to you when he is done." Allow this child plenty of time with a material. He needs to feel as if he has possessed something before he willingly shares it with others. Be sure to provide a place for this child to put personal belongings. Offer ample materials and duplicates of toys that are favorites of the group. Most important, lay the groundwork for turn taking by being a generous role model.

Determine if there are certain times of the day when it is more difficult for this child to take turns. If he is especially tired before naptime or hungry before snacktime, steer him toward materials that are typically used by one person at a time. Or teach him to take materials he wants to use by himself to a private area of the room. Teach him to say, "I want to play alone right now." Respect his need to use the materials on his own for a time. Do not lecture or reprimand him.

This child may be more willing to take turns with a toy that has multiple pieces. When he is playing with a toy like blocks, join his play. Draw his attention to other children who want to play too. Ask this child, as well as others playing with the material, to give a portion to a newcomer. Thank him for whatever he is willing to share, even if it is only a pinch of playdough or a few blocks.

Another reason a child may refuse to take turns is because he is worried that the toy he is lending will not be returned or will be ruined by the borrower. He may ask to have the toy back right away to see if the other child is trustworthy. Let the child who is giving up the material put some limits on its usage. He can say, "You may look at it if you give it right back." Let him describe how it is to be used by saying something like "You may use my car, but don't smash it into any walls."

If you must structure turn taking for this child, let him know when his turn will be over. Some teachers use a timer. Although some object to this strategy, claiming it doesn't allow the child to finish on his own, most often when this type of warning is provided, children begin to make plans for their next activity.

Does This Child Refuse to Take Turns with an Adult?

Many children need to learn first to share with an adult. To help a child having difficulty with turn taking, teach him to take turns with you. Play games that have a back-and-forth rhythm. Roll a car back and forth, bounce a ball to each other, or talk on a toy telephone. Pause expectantly while you wait for the child to return the toy or take his turn. Emphasize the term *turn* by saying, "Your turn" and "My turn" each time. Or give this child a toy and ask to have it right back. Then ask him to give you something. Return it right away. This type of back-and-forth play suggests to the child that if he shares something it will come back (Kutner 2011). After you practice with him a number of times, you should include one other child in your play.

Call attention to daily situations in which people share or sharing scenarios depicted in books. Read stories like *The Doorbell Rang* by Pat Hutchins or *Connie Came to Play* by Jill Paton Walsh. Point out the benefits of sharing.

Does This Child Leave a Toy Yet Won't Allow Others to Play with It?

Some children put aside a toy but protest if another child plays with it. Help a child who does this learn that if he leaves a toy, others may use it. Watch him carefully so you can go to him when he changes activities. Remind him that if he leaves a toy, someone else may use it. Ask him if he is finished or if he wants a few more minutes with the toy. Tell him you can't save it for him (unless he is just going to the bathroom). Take a photograph or draw a picture of it and let him save the paper. Reassure him that he can have another turn at some point. When a child abandons a toy, ask if he is finished or if he wants it a few more minutes. If he decides to return to the toy, or if you must call his turn to an end before he is done, ask, "May Claire have it now or in two minutes?" This helps him feel as if he has some control of when his turn ends. Children are more willing to give up a toy if they are done with it or if it isn't their favorite. Play a game about turn taking when he is not in the middle of a turn-taking situation. Make up a vignette: "What if Blake is on the swing, Jason is waiting, and Blake gets off. Whose turn is it?"

Does This Child Have Difficulty Waiting for a Turn?

There are many times a child needs to wait for a turn in an early childhood setting. He needs to wait if the computer is in use, if it is too crowded in an interest area, or if he has asked for a turn and has been told no. Teach a child how to wait for a turn by creating routines for situations in which turns must be taken. Place chairs at a table or hang badges in an interest area to indicate how many children may participate in an activity at one time. If all the badges for the area are being worn or all the chairs are taken, this child will need to come back later. Make a sign-up sheet for certain areas. When one child leaves, he needs to let the next child on the list know that it is his turn. Place a waiting chair near a popular area like the computer: one is for the child who is using the computer, and the other is for the child who is waiting for the next turn. Usually the child in the waiting chair is very involved in the play too.

If a child needs to wait for a turn, help him find something interesting to do. Scan the room with him to see what he finds interesting; get him started. Give this child concrete information about how he will know when it is his turn. He can watch the first child to see when he puts the toy down, when he finds a new toy, or when he goes to play with something else. If the waiting period becomes extraordinarily long, help this child go to the one using the toy and say, "I've been waiting for a really long time. When will you be done?" Comment favorably when this child is waiting patiently, such as for a snack or a turn at the drinking fountain.

Practice waiting and turn taking in the dramatic play area by setting up a doctor's waiting room or a bakery with numbers for the customers to take. Read a social story for this child that focuses on waiting for a turn (see the accompanying box for information about social stories).

Does This Child Ask for a Turn and Grab the Toy at the Same Time?

Some children grab materials others are using without asking for a turn. Others see what they want, and while they may have learned to ask for a turn, they may not have learned to wait for a response (Bedrova and Leong 2007). If you are working with a child who asks for a turn but doesn't wait for a response, supervise his turn taking closely. Move next to him before a problem occurs. Encourage him to ask for a turn. Then help this child pause and wait for a response.

Watch your own response if you see this child take a toy away from another child. Remain calm. If you go to him and take the material he has just taken, you may inadvertently model grabbing. Slow the process down by saying, "Meng was using that." Try the problem-solving strategies mentioned on the next page. If he does not return the toy, direct him to give it back. Say, "You need to give it back. Can you do it by yourself, or shall I help you?" If he doesn't return the item at this point, you can gently return it.

Confidentially explain the consequences of taking toys that others are using to him (others get angry or may not want to play with you). Put on a puppet play in which two puppets have difficulty sharing. Let the children decide a number of ways the puppets can work out the problem. Act out their solutions and the possible consequences. End with the puppets taking turns.

Teach this child to make trades. Help him think of something the other child may want, and encourage him to take it to the other child. Practice making trades by having the children do role plays. Collect a number of popular toys. Have one child play with a toy. Ask

Teach Turn Taking with a Story

Social stories are tools that have been found helpful in working with children with autism. They can be helpful in teaching social skills to children who are developing typically too. Social stories usually

- Are written for an individual
- Are written at the child's developmental level
- Are written from the child's perspective, using first person ("I")
- Focus on one behavior and provide positive expectations
- Describe what the child is to do
- May be strengthened for young children with pictures
- Should be read or told at times other than in the middle of situations the child is trying to negotiate
- Are read daily
- Help children better understand social situations

(Early Childhood Services Team: Community Living Toronto 2011)

Social stories are available online or may be offered through your school district's early childhood special education program. If you contact your school district, be careful not to share information about a child if you don't have parental permission. Sample stories should be tailored to meet each child's needs. One sample story follows.

Waiting for My Turn
I like to play with toys at school.
Sometimes someone else is playing with the toy I want.
When I see a toy I want, I feel like taking it.
When I take a toy someone else is using, it makes the other child sad.
When I feel like taking a toy someone else is using, I can say, "May I have a turn?"
I can look for another toy just like it.
Or I can play at the water table until the other child is done with it.
When I wait for my turn, the other children are happy.
I will get a turn when they are done.

another child to choose a different toy from the collection that he thinks the first child will like. Help him make a trade (Heidemann and Hewitt 2010).

Does This Child Complain to You When He Has Trouble Taking Turns?

When children tell you that someone won't take turns, they are usually asking for help to solve this problem. (See chapter 6, "I'm Telling on You!" Tattling, for more information.) Teach a child who is complaining to say, "I want a turn. Can you help me ask?" Use your professional judgment to determine how much help he needs. Some children may need you to provide words for them to use, others will need your physical presence to work through the situation, and others will need a reminder to use skills they have learned in the past. Model words to ask for a turn, such as "I like trucks too. May I use the blue one?"

In other situations, a child may need you to give him words to say politely that he isn't done with his turn. Teach this child to say more than "No" if someone asks for a turn with a toy he is using. Help him explain why the other child must wait. For example, he can say, "No, I only have one, and I'm using it right now" (Greene 1998). Support this child as he tries the words you model.

Help him learn to problem solve turn-taking situations (see Steps in Problem Solving in chapter 1). Describe what you see happening. Say, "It looks like you both want to use this tractor." Ask a "What?" question to help them begin to think about ways to solve their problem. Say, "What can you do to work this out?" or "What should you do about that?" or "What can you do that will make you both happy?" Offer a solution if they are unable to come up with one. Say, "One of you can have it first, and then it will be the other person's turn." Draw simple pictures of possible solutions; teach the ideas to the whole group; post the pictures on the wall. Pictures might show children playing a back-and-forth game or making a trade. Ask the children to suggest solutions and add pictures of their ideas. After this child has lots of experience with problem solving, remind him to use the pictures on the wall for ideas. Another turn-taking strategy is using a turn taker. To make a turn taker, cut a circle from cardboard. Put a different color on each side of the circle. One child flips the turn taker; the other calls out one of the two colors while the disc is in the air. If it lands on the color called, it is that child's turn first.

Does This Child Sometimes Agree to and Suggest Turn Taking?

Children need to be able to suggest that they take turns as well as to agree to the turn-taking suggestions of others. Eventually, all your modeling and teaching will pay off and you may notice a child to whom you have been teaching turn-taking skills spontaneously agreeing to take turns. The challenge is to keep this positive behavior going. Pay attention to the efforts of this child when he is proposing or agreeing to turn taking. Comment positively on the growth he has made in this area. For example, you might say, "Taking turns is a good idea. That way, you and Griff will both get a turn with the steering wheel."

Work with the Parents

Let the parents know that turn taking is difficult for their child in your setting. They may experience similar problems with turn taking at home. But they may not see this behavior if they do not see their child in a group setting or if he is an only child. Whether or not they have similar concerns, you will want to work with them to develop a Plan for Action. Give them the information for parents and arrange a time to discuss what steps you will take to work with this child. Establishing consistency between the home and the early childhood setting will help this child learn appropriate skills more quickly.

When to Seek Assistance

Turn taking is a skill that develops over years. Even children who share most of the time have difficulty occasionally. Look for patterns of difficulty. If a child is unable to share for a number of weeks despite your best efforts to help him learn this skill, consider if he is feeling especially stressed. If so, talk with his parents and do what you can to reduce stress he feels in your setting. If a child three and one-half years of age or older rarely takes turns or is repeatedly upset by instances in which he must share, talk with his parents and develop a Plan for Action. If the child uses aggression to get the materials he wants, see chapter 9, "Whack!" Aggression.

A Plan for Action

To develop your Plan for Action, choose or modify one of the suggested goals to best match your situation. Add how well or how often you expect the skill or behavior to be demonstrated. Remember: you are looking for growth, not perfection. Children should not be expected to take turns every time they are asked. Move the child from where he is currently and increase your expectations slightly. Next, determine three or four actions that teachers and parents will take. Choose additional actions specific to the early childhood setting and the home. Record your choices on the planning form found in the appendix.

Sample goals for a child having difficulty taking turns:

- Takes turns with an adult
- Leaves a toy and allows others to play with it
- Waits patiently for a turn
- Asks for a turn and waits for a response
- Takes turns when coached by an adult
- Asks for a turn
- Asks for help in turn taking
- Agrees to and suggests taking turns with others

Sample actions parents and teachers can take:

- Be a generous role model
- Call attention to situations in which people share

- Describe the benefits of sharing
- Read books about taking turns
- Allow this child plenty of time with a toy
- Allow this child to play without sharing in a private area
- Teach this child to say, "I want to play alone"
- Don't lecture or reprimand if this child doesn't take turns
- Place positive expectations that this child will take turns in the future
- Help this child find something to do while waiting for a turn
- Comment on times when this child is waiting patiently
- Play games that have a back-and-forth rhythm
- Include one other child in turn-taking games
- Remind this child someone else may use a toy if he leaves it
- Warn this child when his turn will be over
- Teach this child to say more than "No"
- Allow this child to decide if he will give up the toy "now or in two minutes"
- Reassure him that he can have another turn at some point
- Move close to this child before turn taking becomes a problem
- Structure turn taking for this child
- Give this child concrete information about how he will know when it is his turn
- Teach this child to describe how something he is lending is to be used
- Teach this child words to use when asking for a turn
- Teach this child to make trades
- Help this child problem solve
- Ask a "What?" question to aid in problem solving
- Comment positively when this child shares spontaneously

Sample actions teachers can take:

- Provide plenty of materials
- Provide a place for personal belongings
- Provide duplicates of favorite materials
- Put on a puppet play about turn taking
- Practice turn taking in dramatic play situations
- Create routines that help the child take turns
- Read social stories

- When someone joins a group and materials must be divided, let this child decide how much he will share

- Draw a picture of a toy or project to "save" it

- Post ideas for turn taking

- Use a turn taker

Sample actions parents can take:

- Practice turn taking with your child

- Include one other child in your play

- Ask your child to identify things he is not able to share with a visitor; put these away

- Supervise play time carefully and provide help when needed

- Bring a bag of toys and books to occupy your child during times when he must wait

- Play guessing games during waiting periods

- Play board games; emphasize when your child's turn will come

Information on Turn Taking

WHAT IS IT?

In most families (especially those with more than one child), children need to learn to share toys, materials, and adult attention. Some children learn to take turns by watching others and experiencing give-and-take with adults. Some children require adult guidance in order to learn turn taking. Before the age of three and one-half, many children may not be developmentally ready to share. If your child is this age or younger, don't expect turn taking with toys every time your child is asked. Allow plenty of time for using a material when possible; your child may need to feel the fullness of possession before he or she willingly shares something with others. Lay the groundwork for sharing by being a generous role model.

Observe and Respond

Determine if there are certain times of the day when it is more difficult for your child to take turns. If your child is especially tired before nap or hungry before dinner, activity or material that can be used alone is a good choice. You can teach your child to play with cherished materials alone in his or her room. Teach your child to say, "I want to play alone right now."

Your child may refuse to take turns from fear that the toy being lent will not be returned or will be ruined by the borrower. Your child may ask to have the toy back right away. It's okay if your child says, "You may look at it if you give it right back," or "You may use my car, but don't smash it into any walls."

Teach your child to take turns by playing games that have a back-and-forth rhythm. Roll a car back and forth or bounce a ball to each other. Pause expectantly as you wait for your child to return the toy or take the next turn. Emphasize turns by saying, "Your turn" and "My turn." Play board games. Emphasize when your child's turn will come by saying, "It's almost your turn. As soon as Mom is done, it will be your turn."

Include one other child in your play. Learning to take turns with one other child at home may set the stage for sharing more widely with others. If your child's friend is coming to your home, put away new or favorite toys. Taking turns with favorites may prove too difficult.

Help your child learn that toys that aren't being used can be used by others. When your child abandons a toy, ask if he or she is finished or wants it a few more minutes. If your child decides to return to the toy or you must call your child's turn to an end, ask, "May Claire have it now or in two minutes?"

There are many times your child may need to wait for a turn, such as when you are in line at the grocery store. Help your child learn to wait by finding something interesting to do. Play simple guessing games while you are in line. Or bring a bag of small toys to the waiting room at the doctor's office. Comment favorably on the times your child waits patiently.

If your child takes toys from others, play alongside and explain the consequences of taking toys that others are using (others get angry and may not want to play with you). Give your child words to use, such as "May I have a turn on the swing?" or "I like trucks too. May I use the blue one?" Help your child learn to wait or find things to do while waiting.

For other situations, your child may need to learn how to politely say he or she isn't done with a turn. Teach your child to say more than "No" if someone asks for a turn with a toy your child is using—for example, "No, I only have one, and I'm using it right now."

CONNECTING WITH SUPPORT

While taking turns may be difficult for your child at home, the difficulty can be magnified in a group setting. Talk with your child's teacher to determine what steps you should take to teach this important skill. Establishing consistency between the home and the early childhood setting will help your child learn appropriate skills more quickly.

"I'm Telling on You!" Tattling

FOR TEACHERS

Brooke tells on everybody. She doesn't even try to take care of problems herself.

❖ **Standard:**
Seeks assistance from an adult when needed.

What Is It?

Children today are faced with many difficult situations. They must feel free to tell trusted adults when someone is hurting or bothering them or when someone else is in danger. When they are older, children must feel free to tell adults when someone is using drugs or carrying a weapon. In many situations, seeking support from an adult is the right thing to do.

However, many people feel that telling an adult about the behavior of others, complaining about their actions, drawing attention to infractions of rules, and telling about another person's wrongdoings is tattling. Some adults frown on tattling because they view it as attending to someone else's business, they are concerned that the child who tattles will lose friends, and responding to tattling requires a great deal of their time and attention. Children also oppose tattling, seeing it as disloyal and weak. Words such as *tattletale*, *snitch*, or *rat* suggest the negative attitudes toward this behavior.

Reframe your thinking about tattling by renaming it so you do not view it negatively. Many have begun referring to it as *reporting*. Children need to feel free to report any concern they have. How you respond to a report needs to be tailored to the individual. Handle the serious situations children face. Guide them as they learn how to handle everyday challenges on their own. As children gain problem-solving skills, their need to seek adult assistance usually decreases.

Observe and Decide What to Teach

Many adults believe the reason children tattle is to get another in trouble. While this may be one motivation, other reasons exist as well. Watch a child who tattles frequently. Ask the following questions, and consider what reason the child may have for reporting. Then think about how you will match your responses to fit each situation and teach a child to seek adult assistance when needed.

Does This Child Tell on Others in Order to Draw Attention to Herself?

Some children report behaviors and actions of others in order to gain a teacher's attention. If you are working with a child who seems to call attention to herself when she tells on others, listen to what she is saying. Decide if the complaint is reasonable. Determine if this child has the skills to handle the situation herself. If so, send her back to cope with it. If not, provide alternatives for her to try. Consider if this child seeks attention in other ways as well. Prevent the need for getting attention through tattling by giving her plenty of attention at other times. Build or rebuild your relationship with her. Spend a few minutes with her early each day. Talk with her often about subjects in which she is interested. Recognize her strengths, and comment positively on what she does well.

Is This Child Telling You about Behaviors of Others Because You Sometimes Want to Know?

In some cases, you may be grateful to a child for bringing a dangerous situation to your attention. At other times, you may be aware of what is taking place. For example, you need to know about times when someone is hurt, crying, or being bullied. Or you may have asked an older child to help look after younger ones. The older child may feel a sense of responsibility to tell an adult if something that is not permitted is taking place. Allow a child to tell you, but let her know that unless you ask, she doesn't need to be in charge. Say, "Thanks for telling me" or "I'll take care of it."

Is This Child Seeking Emotional Support Because She Appears Nervous about the Actions of Others?

Some children may come to you with wide eyes and concern in their voices as they describe the daring acts of others. Be patient and responsive when a child who is truly concerned tells you about the behavior. Reassure her by saying, "I can see you are upset. I'm watching. She is climbing very high, isn't she?" Having adult contact and knowing that you are attending may be enough to reduce her fear and allow her to return to her own play. If this type of reporting is persistent, you might add, "It's my job to keep her safe, and it's your job to play."

Does This Child Tell about Infractions of Rules to Understand Them Better Herself?

In *Tools of the Mind*, Bedrova and Leong (2007) talk about how children are often aware of the times other people break the rules before they recognize that they are breaking the same rules. They describe how children apply the rules to others before they apply them to themselves. This seems to be a necessary step before young children can regulate their own behavior and stay within the rules themselves. Brooke, with whom we began this chapter, reports the behaviors of others frequently. She is likely to be at the stage Bedrova and Leong are describing.

Help a child at this stage of development by limiting the number of rules you have. State those rules positively. Be consistent in your rules and the consequences for them. When she reports to you that someone is breaking the rules, she may be looking for affirmation that she knows the rules. Acknowledge her comment by saying, "I'm glad you know the rules." Reassure this child that you will take care of a problem if needed.

Does This Child Tell You about Problems She Doesn't Know How to Solve on Her Own?

Some preschool children share their concerns when they don't know how to resolve a problem on their own. Problem solving is a complex skill that involves identifying a problem, thinking of ways to solve it, choosing the best idea, and trying it out. Teach all of the children the steps to problem solving during group time. Use a picture of a stoplight to remind them of the steps involved. Red means to stop and identify their problem. Yellow reminds them to think of ideas to solve the problem. Green stands for "try the best idea." Over a number of days or weeks, conduct role plays and puppet plays to demonstrate solutions to different problems. For example, do a puppet play in which one puppet is trying to color a picture where another puppet is driving a car. The puppet trying to draw keeps getting bumped until the puppets stop to think about what they can do to solve their problem. Have the puppets think of a number of ideas. Ask the puppets to choose the best idea. Finally, show how the puppets decide the one who is drawing should take her paper and crayons to the table.

After introducing problem solving to the group, when a child brings a concern to you, go with her and help her work through the conflict. Listen to what each child says is taking place. Ask a "What?" question to help them think of solutions. Say, "What could you do so you are both happy? What could you do to share this toy? Or what could you do to work this out?" Ask them to choose their best idea. Then help them get started.

Has This Child Tried to Problem Solve on Her Own but Has Been Unsuccessful?

Children seek adult backing to make their words work and help them to get what they want. You might overhear a child say, "I'm going to tell!" as a way to enhance her power and stop an unwanted action. Avoid rushing in as the enforcer or the problem-solver for a child who feels powerless. Instead, listen to what she has to tell you. Paraphrase what she says. This gives her the chance to tell you more and to correct any misunderstandings you may have. You might say, "It seems like you are having trouble getting Sophie to listen." Be sure you have observed this child frequently enough to have a sense of her problem-solving skills.

Determine if she has the skills to handle the situation on her own. If so, let her know you believe she can manage by asking, "What could you do?" Or say something like "Oh" or "I'm sorry you're not getting along. You're very good at figuring out ways to solve problems. I'm sure you'll find a way to work this out." This may be all she needs to go back and try again. When this child solves problems independently, comment positively on her success.

If you think she needs some help in resolving the issue, provide alternatives for her to try. Suggest an alternative like "How about letting her play with one of your old dolls?" If the child still seems unsure of herself, offer to go with her while she works to solve the problem. Ask, "Can you talk with her by yourself, or do you want me to go with you?" Your presence will inspire confidence and show your support for her. Help the other child listen to her suggestions. The other child does not have to agree to the suggestions made but does need to politely acknowledge what has been said.

Help a child who uses only one problem strategy or a strategy that is unsuccessful to think of more than one solution. In a dispute about sharing, ask, "What can you do to get your toy back?" Encourage her to think of more than one idea. Ask, "What else could you do?" or "What's another idea?" Help her decide which solutions are the best and which are unacceptable by asking, "What would happen if you did that?" Make a suggestion. Say, "If that doesn't work, come back and we'll think of something else."

A child who has limited language skills may come to you for assistance in being understood by others. She may tug on your sleeve, gesture, or tell you to come. Go with this child and talk on her behalf. Doing so serves as a model for the language she can use in the future. Say, "Pa Ying doesn't like it when you take the toy she is using. She says, 'Please give it back!'"

Work with the Parents

Talk with the parents of a child who is tattling excessively about the importance of allowing children to tell adults anything that concerns them. Share examples of problems their child has brought to you but then solved on her own as well as those she was unable to solve. Anticipate the types of situations in which she may need help and how you will both respond. Develop a shared Plan for Action. Establishing this type of consistency between the home and the early childhood setting will help the child get the message that she can tell adults anything and that you will help her learn to handle various situations.

> **When to Seek Assistance**
>
> When tattling is persistent despite your efforts, observe again. Look to see if this child is having difficulty interacting competently or fitting into the group. If she is, work with her on the social skills that are essential to successful group play. See chapter 4, "I Want to Play Too!" Joining a Group of Players. Also consider if this child's needs for attention are being met. See chapter 3, "Watch This!" Attention Getting for additional information.

A Plan for Action

To develop your Plan for Action, choose or modify one of the suggested goals to best match the situation. Add how well or how often you expect the skill or behavior to be demonstrated. Remember: you are looking for growth, not perfection. You want to move the child from where she is currently and to increase your expectations slightly. Next, determine three or four actions teachers and parents will take. Choose additional actions specific to the early childhood setting and the home. Record your choices on the planning form found in the appendix.

Sample goals for a child who reports on the behaviors of others:

- Seeks attention in appropriate ways
- Is responsible for her own actions (knows you will take care of other situations)
- Seeks assistance in problem solving from an adult when needed
- Uses problem-solving strategies
- Experiments with more than one solution to a problem

Sample actions parents and teachers can take:

- Comment on this child's competencies
- Limit the number of rules; be consistent in rules and consequences
- Affirm this child when she is following rules
- Listen to complaints and reports
- Tailor responses to fit each situation
- Reassure this child that you are aware of what is taking place
- Paraphrase what this child says when she complains
- Teach the steps in problem solving
- Ask "What?" questions to help this child think of solutions to problems
- Provide ideas about ways this child can handle a situation that concerns her
- Encourage experimentation with more than one problem-solving strategy
- Offer to go with this child when she tries to work out a problem
- Give the responsibility for solving the problem to this child
- Give this child confidence that she can manage the situation on her own
- Avoid rushing in to be the enforcer or to solve the problem for her
- Act as a mediator in disputes; listen to both sides
- Acknowledge this child's complaints in a noncommittal way

Sample actions teachers can take:

- Build or rebuild your relationship with this child
- Let this child know she doesn't need to be in charge unless you ask
- Do puppet plays and role plays to teach problem solving

Sample action parents can take:

- Avoid asking your child to be responsible at certain times but not at others

Information on Tattling

WHAT IS IT?

Children today are faced with many difficult situations. Some are too dangerous or too challenging for them to handle on their own. They need to feel free to tell trusted adults when someone is hurting or bothering them or when someone else is in danger. In many situations, they need support from an adult in order to learn to handle a situation on their own.

Unfortunately, many people feel that telling an adult is tattling. Although tattling can be annoying, it is important not to discourage children from seeking adult guidance. Try to think of tattling as reporting. By responding effectively, you may be able to help your child gain problem-solving skills.

Observe and Respond

Many adults believe the reason children tattle is to get another in trouble. While this may be one motivation, other reasons exist. Some children tattle in order to draw attention to themselves. Prevent your child from needing attention through tattling by paying attention to him or her at other times. Spend time each day cuddling, talking, and playing.

Sometimes a child will report because he or she has been asked to help look after others. Or he or she feels an adult needs to know when someone else is hurt, crying, or being bullied. Your child may become confused and think he or she should always tell you if something is wrong. Avoid giving your child mixed messages. Allow your child to tell you, but when a situation is not dangerous, help your child learn to handle upsets on his or her own.

Your child may come to you with wide eyes describing the daring acts of others. In such situations, your child may be truly concerned about another child. Reassure your child by saying, "I can see you're worried. She is climbing high, isn't she?" Knowing that you are paying attention may be enough to reduce your child's fear and allow him or her to return to his or her own play.

If your child seems to be reporting about others who are breaking the rules, he or she may be trying to understand them better. Or your child may be looking for affirmation that he or she knows the rules. Acknowledge your

continued

child's comment by saying, "I'm glad you know the rules." Reassure your child that you will take care of a problem if needed.

Some children report upsetting behaviors when they don't know how to solve a problem on their own. Help your child learn to solve problems independently by teaching him or her the steps in problem solving. Use the colors of a stoplight to remind him or her of the steps: Red means stop and identify the problem. Yellow reminds your child to think of ideas. Green stands for "try the best idea." Help your child use the steps when he or she brings a concern to you. Ask "What?" questions to help your child think of ideas. Say, "What could you do to work this out?" Encourage your child to think of more than one idea. Ask, "What's another idea?" Help your child choose the best one; then help your child try out his or her idea. Say to your child, "If that doesn't work, come back and we'll think of something else."

Sometimes children will report behaviors to you as a way of seeking support. You might overhear your child say, "I'm going to tell!" as a way to enhance his or her power. Avoid rushing in to solve a problem for your child. Instead, listen to what your child has to tell you. Then say, "It sounds like you're having trouble getting Sophie to listen." If your child has the skills to handle the situation without adult help, let your child know you believe he or she can manage. Say, "I'm sorry you're not getting along. I'm sure you'll find a way to work this out." This may be all your child needs to go back and try again.

If you think your child needs some help resolving the issue, offer to go with him or her. Ask, "Can you talk with her by yourself, or do you want me to go with you?" If your child chooses to have you go with, your presence will inspire confidence.

CONNECTING WITH SUPPORT

If reporting persists, talk with your child's teacher. Anticipate the types of situations in which your child needs help and decide how you and your child's teacher will respond. Developing consistency between the home and the early childhood setting helps your child get the message that telling adults his or her concerns is okay and that the adults will help him or her learn to handle most situations independently.

"##@&!!" Inappropriate Language and Swearing

7

FOR TEACHERS

Austin has been using a lot of bad language lately. The worst part is he knows how to use it. Some of the other children are copying him. I've even had a parent complain about it.

❖ **Standard**

Uses words to express feelings that are appropriate to the situation.

What Is It?

Young children are just learning to express their emotions by using words instead of crying or acting on those feelings. They need adults to help them learn to label their varied and sometimes strong feelings in acceptable ways. They need help learning to regulate their emotions and to express themselves in ways that are appropriate to the situation.

Some children use inappropriate language like swearing when they are upset. They usually learn swear words from other children, their siblings, parents, the community, or the media. Hearing other people swear gives young children the message that it is acceptable. Sometimes they are only being silly or experimenting with language. Help a child who happens upon an unacceptable word continue his fun with sounds by making up silly or rhyming words. You can say, "What rhymes with *crackle*? With *pow*? With *padiddle*?"

Children may swear without knowing the meanings of the words they are using. Although they may not understand what they are saying, they usually have a sense that these words are not a part of pleasant conversation. Many children, especially four-year-olds, explore this kind of out-of-bounds talk. They may be curious about the reactions these words get. Adults hearing a young child talk like this usually react in one of two ways: with laughter or shock. The child may try to elicit the response again through continued use of the words. People working with young children need to help them learn that this type of language is not to be used and to teach them other ways to express themselves.

Observe and Decide What to Teach

Observe the child who is using inappropriate language. Find out when he swears, under what circumstances, and, if possible, what reaction he gets when swearing. This will help you determine how to curb the use of inappropriate language and how to teach him to express his feelings in ways that are appropriate to the situation.

Is This Child Imitating Others Who Swear?

Children imitate what they see and hear. They try out inappropriate words they have heard because it makes them feel grown-up or powerful and because doing so usually gets a reaction. Deal with swearing or foul language when you first hear it. If you ignore it the first time, you may unintentionally give the message that using these words is okay.

If you are working with a child who uses inappropriate language, respond in a matter-of-fact manner. Overreacting may cause a child to look for the same reaction in the future. Make it clear that swearing is not acceptable in your setting. Say, "That's not a word we use here." Model the kind of language that is okay, such as, "Oh shoot! My building keeps falling down."

If a child is swearing because that kind of language is used in his home, in his community, or by his playmates, eliminating the practice may be difficult. In the story at the beginning of this chapter, Austin was hearing people swear, and he imitated the words he was hearing and used them to express anger and frustration. Unfortunately, he did not know other words could be used to describe his emotions.

If you are working with a child who hears swearing and knows how to use it, focus on teaching him more acceptable words. Talk with this child confidentially. Say, "That sounds like something a grown-up might say. It's not okay to say that here." Don't talk negatively about the setting in which the child hears it or the person or people from whom he may be learning to swear. Instead, clearly state the expectations for your setting. Let him know of some of the consequences for continuing to use this type of language: it upsets other people; others may not want to be around him when he talks like that; he may hurt someone's feelings; and he may be embarrassed if he says that in front of some people (like his grandmother or teacher).

Does This Child Become Frustrated Frequently or Easily?

Young children need help learning to recognize the signals that they are becoming upset and what to do then. Observe a child who has difficulty expressing feelings in appropriate ways in order to recognize the signals that he is becoming upset. His face may become flushed; his voice may get louder, higher in pitch, or change in quality (that is, become whiny); more arguments over toys may erupt. Intervene before he becomes so frustrated that he swears. Teach him to recognize that he is becoming frustrated. Talk about how his stomach may get tight, he may start breathing fast, or he may clench his fists.

If he is becoming frustrated, offer your support. Give him ideas about how he can handle his frustration. He can get an adult, leave the area, or say, "This is too hard for me." Recognize that he has attempted a difficult or complicated task and

Teach a Feelings Vocabulary

Below are a few suggestions for teaching children to express their feelings:

◆ Model using words to express your feelings

◆ Label this child's emotions for him: "You look frustrated."

◆ Look at magazines and books to see how the people who are pictured are feeling, and then label the feelings pictured and explain how you can tell: "I think he might be happy. He has a big smile."

◆ Examine pictures of people and try to determine why they are feeling a certain way; if a problem is pictured, think of possible explanations

◆ Recognize sounds that indicate how someone is feeling: "I hear someone crying—I wonder if she is sad."

◆ Make a feelings cube: place a picture of someone showing a different feeling on each side of a large cube. Role the cube: imitate or label the expression shown on the top picture.

◆ Play a game in which you describe a situation and ask the child how he would feel: "How would you feel if you scraped your knee? If you couldn't watch your favorite TV show? If you climbed to the top of the climber?"

◆ Play a guessing game in which you describe a brief situation and then ask, "How am I feeling?" "Pretend I am riding my bike really fast and fall down; how am I feeling?"

help him with it. Lower your immediate expectations for this child and substitute activities that are easier so he can be more successful. Reduce competition in activities. Change toys that cause problems or acquire duplicates. Consider if your environment is overstimulating for him so he has difficulty calming down on his own. Make changes to reduce the stimulation. Offer spaces where he can settle down with a book or in a comfy chair.

Does This Child Swear Because His Needs Aren't Being Met or He Is Experiencing Chronic Stress?

Some children swear as an expression of unmet needs or stress in their lives. Recognize that the emotions this child is feeling are big and that he may be unprepared to cope. A child experiencing this level of stress may feel out of control. Begin to address unmet needs by developing a strong, nurturing relationship with him. Help him feel safe in your setting by offering a predictable routine and consequences that are fair and consistent. Make sure that the activities you offer are challenging yet achievable. Adjust your schedule to assure that his basic needs are met rather than having him wait.

Teach this child to deal with anger and other negative emotions in more appropriate ways. Make sure he knows that swearing is not acceptable. If he is feeling upset, he can get help, stamp his feet, walk away, or use problem-solving techniques. Give him words to use when he is angry. Say, "I know you are angry. You can tell me, 'I'm so mad.'" Replace swear words with those that are more acceptable like *shoot*, *darn it*, or *I can't stand it*. Expand his vocabulary for expressing feelings. Include a range from *upset* to *furious*.

If it is necessary for this child to leave an upsetting activity for a short time, require him to choose a quiet activity to do by himself. When he regains control of his emotions, he can rejoin the others. You will need to assist with this reunion in order for it to be successful.

Does This Child Seek Attention by Swearing?

Often a child receives a great deal of attention for swearing, whether it is laughter or lecture. The attention that encourages the behavior may come from you, from the other children, or from outside your setting. If a child receives attention for swearing, you can reduce the amount he receives when he is in your care, but you won't be able to control the attention he gets elsewhere. This may make it harder to eliminate the swearing you hear. Reduce the amount of swearing in your setting by making your expectations clear. Then ignore the swearing. If this child does swear, keep a straight face and teach more appropriate words to use.

Increase the amount of positive attention this child receives at times when he is not swearing. Make a point of going to him early in the day and often. Talk with him and pay attention to him when he is behaving appropriately. Say something like "I noticed you told Brady you were upset he knocked down your building." Point out positive things about him in front of other children. Say something like "Timothy is really creative when he paints." (For more information on attention getting, see chapter 3, "Watch This!" Attention Getting.)

If one child reports that another is using inappropriate language, tell him to let the other child know he doesn't like it. Let the child who reports know that he can move away from the one who is swearing. Help the other children refocus their attention. A child who swears immediately after someone else may need to learn better ways to get attention. Whisper to him, "You have good ideas of your own. You don't need to copy Josh's words."

When to Seek Assistance

If swearing does not decrease after three to four months despite your efforts to reduce it, this child may not understand this or other rules. If he has difficulty understanding all types of rules, has a number of emotional outbursts, or consistently has difficulty getting along with peers, encourage his parents to contact their local school district and set an appointment to have his skills screened. If he expresses anger that seems out of proportion to a situation or if his anger is prompted by a chronic stressor in his life, suggest that the parents talk with a family counselor to help him learn coping skills.

Work with the Parents

Children hear swearing from many people and in many places. When a child swears, parents sometimes assume inappropriate language is being learned in the early childhood setting. In turn, teachers often assume that parents are permitting swearing or modeling it. Most parents use appropriate language in front of their children. Occasionally a swear word will slip out, and this may be the one word the child imitates. It can be frustrating to the adults when the child repeats the one mistaken word many times. Some parents use this type of language as a way to express themselves. Whether the language is only an occasional word, the typical language of a parent, or something learned from someone else, let the parents know that their child is swearing in your setting. Suggest that they help their child learn other ways to express himself, reduce his exposure to swearing by limiting time spent with others who swear, or reduce his exposure to television, movies, and music in which inappropriate language occurs. Give the parents information on swearing, and meet to discuss your Plan for Action. Establishing consistency between the home and the early childhood setting will help the child learn appropriate language more quickly.

A Plan for Action

To develop your Plan for Action, choose or modify one of the suggested goals to best match the situation. Add how well or how often you expect the skill or behavior to be demonstrated. Remember: you are looking for growth, not perfection. You want to move the child from where he is currently and to increase your expectations slightly. Next, determine three or four actions that teachers and parents will take. Choose additional actions specific to the early childhood setting and the home. Record your choices on the planning form found in the appendix.

Sample goals for a child who swears:

- Uses appropriate words to express anger and frustration
- Seeks attention in appropriate ways
- Expresses feelings that are appropriate to the situation

Sample actions parents and teachers can take:

- Model appropriate language
- Respond in a matter-of-fact manner when this child swears
- Make it clear that swearing is not acceptable
- Divert the child to a more appropriate activity
- Intervene before this child gets frustrated
- Help this child with difficult tasks
- Expand the child's vocabulary of words for expressing feelings
- Replace swear words with *shoot* or *nuts*
- Praise this child for controlling his anger
- Talk with this child about the consequences of continued swearing (for example, loss of friends, embarrassment)
- Have this child choose a quiet activity if he must leave an upsetting activity for a short time

Sample actions teachers can take:

- ◆ Point out positive things about this child in front of others
- ◆ Create fun with sounds through silly rhymes
- ◆ Reduce stimulation in the environment
- ◆ Reduce competition

Sample actions parents can take:

- ◆ Monitor television programs your child watches
- ◆ Encourage friendships with people who do not swear
- ◆ Arrange for your school district to conduct a developmental screening; share pertinent information with your child's teacher
- ◆ Talk with a family counselor; share pertinent information with your child's teacher

Information on Inappropriate Language and Swearing

WHAT IS IT?

Young children are just learning to express their emotions using words instead of crying or acting on their feelings. Some children swear when they are upset. Children usually learn swear words from other children, family members, people in their community, or the media. Hearing other people swear gives young children the message that it is acceptable. If your child is swearing, you can help him or her learn more acceptable ways to express himself or herself.

Observe and Respond

Although your child may not understand the meaning of swear words, he or she probably has a sense that these words are not acceptable. Many children, especially four-year-olds, explore this kind of out-of-bounds talk. Adults hearing young children talk like this usually react with laughter or shock. Your child may try to get this type of response by repeating the words.

Make it clear that using this type of language isn't okay the first time you hear it. Respond in a matter-of-fact manner. Say, "That's a word we don't use." Model the kind of language that is okay, such as, "Oh shoot!" or "Nuts." Let your child know some of the consequences of swearing: it upsets other people, others may not want to be around when he or she talks like that, or he or she may hurt someone's feelings.

Teach your child words that describe feelings at times when he or she is not upset. Look at pictures to see what people are feeling. Label the feelings and explain how you can tell: "I think he might be happy. He has a big smile." Try to determine why the person might be feeling that way. If a problem is pictured, think out loud of possible solutions. Listen for sounds that indicate how someone is feeling. "I hear someone crying; I wonder if she is sad." Play a game in which you describe a situation and ask your child how he or she would feel. "How would you feel if you scraped your knee? Or if you couldn't watch your favorite TV show?"

If your child becomes frustrated, offer your support before he or she swears. Teach your child to ask for help or to say, "This is too

continued

hard for me." Find a substitute toy or activity that is easier so your child can be successful, or help your child settle down with a book in a comfy chair.

Recognize that some emotions feel big for your child, and he or she may feel unprepared to cope with them. Help your child feel supported by spending time each day in pleasant conversation and cuddling together. Help your child feel safe by offering predictable routines and consequences that are fair and consistent. Adjust your schedule to ensure your child's needs are met rather than having him or her wait.

Teach your child to deal with big emotions in appropriate ways. Your child can ask for help, stamp his or her feet, or use problem-solving techniques. Give your child words to use when he or she is angry. Say, "I know you are angry. You can tell me 'I'm so mad.'" Teach your child that feelings range from upset to furious.

If your child needs to leave an upsetting activity for a short time, ask him or her to choose a quiet activity to do alone. When your child regains control of his or her emotions, he or she can try again.

Children hear swearing many places. Monitor the television programs your child watches and the music he or she listens to. Ensure that appropriate language is used. Find ways for your child to socialize with people who do not swear. Be sure to use words you are willing to have your child repeat.

CONNECTING WITH SUPPORT

If you believe that your child is learning swear words from someone in the early childhood setting, talk with the teacher about it. Develop a Plan for Action. Work to establish consistency between your home and the early childhood setting to teach your child more acceptable behavior. If swearing does not decrease after three to four months despite your efforts to reduce it, your child may not understand this or other rules. Contact your school district for a skills screening to see whether your child is developing skills at an age-appropriate rate. If your child expresses anger that seems out of proportion to the situation or if the anger is prompted by a chronic stressor in your child's life, talk with a family counselor who can teach coping skills.

8 ◆ "I'll Kick and Scream Until I Get My Way!" Temper Tantrums

FOR TEACHERS

Angelique threw a huge tantrum when I took away the paper she was holding. She had picked up Andrea's by mistake and was convinced it was her own. When I gave her the right one, she started screaming. She ripped up the paper, threw it on the floor, and stomped on it. I gave her some paper to make another one at home, but she kept screaming.

❖ **Standard**

Demonstrates increasing use of words instead of actions to express emotions.

What Is It?

Children have temper tantrums for a variety of reasons. They may throw themselves on the floor when they do not get what they want or when they become extremely frustrated. They may also have temper tantrums when someone asks them to do something they don't want to do. Sometimes children become overstimulated by activities or feelings. Occasionally they are overwhelmed by anxiety and don't know how to calm themselves. These emotional outbursts are easily recognized if a child kicks, cries, screams, throws things, bangs about, or throws herself to the floor. Other children may replace physical demonstrations of emotion with loud, angry verbal protests.

Tantrums reach different levels of intensity depending on whether children receive attention, have language skills to express their needs and wants, and have effective coping skills. Some children have learned they will get what they want when they cause a fuss. Other young children may not have the language needed to express how they feel and can become anxious about their overwhelming feelings. Children of all ages can get locked into a tantrum and not know how to stop the rush of emotions. You can help children learn to express their feelings and support them when they lose control.

Observe and Decide What to Teach

To better understand how to help a child who has tantrums, observe carefully what leads up to the outburst. Watch the child in a variety of situations. Use the suggestions that follow while you decide how you can best help her learn to use words instead of actions to express her emotions.

Does This Child Have Tantrums More Frequently When She Is Tired, Sick, or Hungry?

Most people find it difficult to cope when they are tired, sick, or hungry. Children are even more prone to outbursts under these circumstances. Angelique, in the story on the previous page, lost control when she had the wrong paper fifteen minutes before nap. She was tired and found it very difficult to cope.

Help reduce the risk and frequency of tantrums by meeting children's basic needs. Vary your schedule to accommodate a child who may be overtired or hungry. Avoid new or challenging activities when this child may be fatigued. Late afternoon and just before nap or lunch are particularly taxing times for children. Understand that emotions are close to the surface the day before a child becomes ill. If possible, anticipate other situations that may cause this child to have tantrums. Common triggers include playing with other children when she needs alone time; being asked to perform a chore that appears overwhelming; having too many changes in activity; having too much going on at one time; and experiencing stressful family changes, such as a new sibling, a move, or a death in the family.

Does This Child Express Frustration When She Is Challenged by a Task?

Some children become frustrated when they try to perform a task they do not yet have the skills for. You can reduce frustration for such a child by providing many activities with varying skill levels from which she can choose. Steer her toward the choices that best match her abilities. Teach her to avoid those that are too hard for the time being. Say, "Let's look for a puzzle with about six pieces." Intervene when this child is becoming frustrated. Help her learn to recognize her own tolerance level. Say, "It looks like you're getting frustrated; take a break, count to ten, or take a few big breaths." Encourage her to ask for help. Point out that you need help cleaning the room and that someone else needs help tying his shoe. Teach her safe ways to express herself when she is angry. She can stamp her feet, yell, crumple paper, talk with someone about it, or pound playdough. When she is patient, comment positively on it. Teach her self-calming skills, like deep breathing or finding a quiet place to take a break. Read *Calm-Down Time* by Elizabeth Verdick with her and talk about the suggestions while you read.

Young preschoolers are often frustrated by difficult tasks, and they lack the language to express their frustration. They can usually be distracted by new activities, going outside, or even inviting a new person over to visit. Older preschoolers are not distracted quite as easily, but distracting or redirecting them can often defuse tense situations.

Does This Child Imitate Others Having Tantrums?

Many young children imitate the behavior of those around them. A child you are working with may throw tantrums when she sees others do so. To avoid having a child imitate the tantrums of others, be sure to pay attention to her many times a day when she is behaving appropriately. When she watches someone else who is having a tantrum, let her know the other child is having a hard time. Get her interested in some other activity. Praise her for having ideas of her own.

Be careful not to model emotional outbursts yourself. Recognize your own need to take a break. Use words to name your feelings. Demonstrate how to calm down by listening to music, looking at a book, singing, drawing, or playing. Avoid demanding that things be done now. This child may think she has the right to demand what she wants now too.

Does This Child Have Tantrums When You Set a Limit or She Doesn't Get Her Way?

Some children throw tantrums when they are asked to join a group activity or to pick up toys and they don't want to. Avoid angry outbursts when you set limits for a child by establishing routines and procedures in which she can be as independent as possible. Place coat hooks at eye level, arrange materials so she can choose from what is available, and clearly mark where things go so she can put them away by herself. Provide choices when possible. When you must set a limit, be firm. Remember not to take outbursts personally. Do not let her outbursts sway you. Offer a choice: "Do you want to do it by yourself, or shall I help you?" Encourage her to use her words rather than her behavior to tell you, "I want help." For more help coping with outbursts, see chapter 14, "I'm Not Listening!" Following Directions and Power Struggles.

If you aren't able to give this child something she wants for a good reason, do not give in. Detach yourself from the situation by focusing on something else or by walking away. Don't try to explain or talk with her while she is upset. Ignore her outburst. Listen for a break in crying and watch for signals that she is calming down. Move close to her to offer comfort and support. Let her know you are there by staying close and holding her if she is ready. When the tantrum is over, do not lecture. Help her become engaged in an activity. If she brings up the difficult situation, problem-solve how to handle it. Give her the words to use next time. Resist the temptation to ask her, "Why did you get so upset?" Very few children have sufficient verbal skills or understanding of their own behavior to explain it.

Books about Feelings and Tantrums

Read books about feelings and tantrums to help children learn more appropriate responses to frustration. Here are some suggestions:

Chocolate-Covered-Cookie Tantrum by Deborah Blumenthal

Llama Llama Mad at Mama by Anna Dewdney

No Biting! by Karen Katz

A Boy and a Bear: The Children's Relaxation Book by Lori Lite

When I Feel Angry by Cornelia Maude Spelman

Sometimes I'm Bombaloo by Rachel Vail

Calm-Down Time by Elizabeth Verdick

Is This Child Destructive or Hurtful During a Tantrum?

If a child you are working with is destructive or hurtful during a tantrum, you may need to respond in ways that will protect people and property. Make sure you remain calm. If you respond by yelling or becoming upset yourself, you may escalate her tantrum, and it will be more difficult for everyone to calm down. Help other children move away. If another child is hurt, attend to him (rather than the one who is having a tantrum). Tell the hurt child you are sorry it happened. Do not use the other child's name or blame her in any way. Stay near the child who is having the tantrum. Be aware of what she is doing while you pretend to attend to something else. Once the tantrum stops, go to this child and sit near her without talking. When she is ready, help her clean up anything disrupted during her outburst. Then get her started in an activity. Some children want to be physically held once they have calmed down. Others fight it. Respect her choice.

Focus on teaching this child words she can use to express herself. Read books about feelings. Play a game in which you ask her to name "How would you feel if _____?" Fill in different situations, such as there is a thunderstorm, someone has given you a present, or someone has taken your toy. Find pictures in magazines of people expressing different emotions, and talk about the feelings they are showing. Listen for people laughing, crying, singing, or yelling. Guess how each person might be feeling from the sound you hear. Teach her a variety of feelings words. Teach vocabulary such as *angry, mad, frustrated, sad, upset, surprised, happy,* and *frightened.* Recognize that not every event is tragic. Talk with her about the intensity of her feelings. Is she feeling really, really mad or just a little bit?

Does This Child Have a Tantrum When She Becomes Overstimulated or Anxious?

Children often become overwhelmed by anxiety or overstimulating activity. Watch to see if the child you are working with is in the middle of a lot of activity, worried about her performance, or picking up anxiety from other children before she has a tantrum. If so, try to moderate the stimulation in your environment. For example, look around your setting to see if you have too much on the walls, too many toys out, or too many activities. Note when certain classroom routines, such as transitions or whole-group times, become overwhelming to her. Teach her how to recognize when situations are becoming too much for her and how to give herself a break before she loses control. If she seems anxious, encourage her to tell you she needs a break, and then help her engage in physical activity rather than a tantrum.

Children's tantrums may increase when they are under stress. Family changes, such as moves, new babies, divorce, separation, or deaths in the family, can be beyond the coping skills of young children. If you think a child you are working with is experiencing such a stressor, stay firm and kind while setting limits. Set aside special quiet times to talk with her about her feelings. Be supportive and encouraging when she is patient and expresses her feelings in words. Your goals are to encourage her to use words rather than actions to express her feelings and to help her adjust to the changes.

Occasionally a child can become locked in a tantrum and may not know how to calm down on her own. In this situation, she will need your help to stop. If she gets stuck in tantrums frequently, you may need to intervene differently than previously recommended. Move to this child. Let her know you understand she is upset. Distract her with another activity. If her tantrum lasts more than ten to fifteen minutes, tell her, "It's time to stop now." Help her take deep, relaxing breaths and engage her in a new activity.

> *Sophia was a very bright and energetic child who seemed to love school and enjoyed playing with the other children. Because Sophia was so enthusiastic about school activities, Leah, her teacher, was surprised by Sophia's behavior during large group. Almost every day in the middle of reading a story, Leah would have to stop to comfort Sophia, who would begin to cry, shake her hands and arms, and hit other children. Sometimes Leah would have to remove her from the group. She began carefully observing when Sophia fell apart. She noticed that occasionally Sophia fell apart during free play as well, especially when there were several children crowded together doing an activity. Leah wondered if having children sitting so close together during large group was overwhelming Sophia. Leah made her circle a little bigger and encouraged Sophia to pull herself away from the group slightly when she started to feel overwhelmed. During the next few weeks, she noticed Sophia was pulling herself back during the story, and the tantrums decreased dramatically.*

Work with the Parents

Many parents teach their children to use words to get their needs met. A few, however, give in to their child's demands and accidently reinforce a tantrum. You will not be able to control all the factors that keep temper tantrums going. Do what you can in your setting to be consistent and firm. Help parents understand the variety of reasons children have tantrums. Give the parents the information that follows. Use the Plan for Action to discuss how you can work together. Consistency between the home and the early childhood setting will give a child a clear message that she can express her feelings, needs, and wants through words and that adults will respond.

When to Seek Assistance

Suggest the child's parents contact a parent educator or a family counselor who specializes in working with young children if their child throws tantrums each time she is in a stressful situation or is denied her way, if her tantrums seem filled with extreme anger or distress, if her tantrums consistently last beyond fifteen to twenty minutes, or if you do not see a significant decrease in tantrums despite your efforts. Consider contacting an early childhood consultant who may be able to provide suggestions for ways to work with this child in your setting. Be sure to obtain parental permission before contacting a consultant.

A Plan for Action

To develop your Plan for Action, choose or modify one of the suggested goals to best match your situation. Add how well or how often you expect the skill or behavior to be demonstrated. Remember: you are looking for growth, not perfection. You want to move the child from where she is currently and to increase your expectations slightly. Next, determine three or four actions that teachers and parents will take. Choose additional actions specific to the early childhood setting and the home. Record your choices on the planning form in the appendix.

Sample goals for a child who has temper tantrums:

- Uses words to express frustration or anger
- Uses self-calming strategies like deep breathing when upset

Sample actions parents and teachers can take:

- Offer developmentally appropriate activities for this child
- Intervene when this child is becoming frustrated
- Encourage this child to ask for help
- Teach this child safe ways to express anger
- Model words to use when you express your own emotions
- Avoid challenging or new activities at times of the day when this child is tired
- When this child is being patient, comment on it positively
- Be firm, fair, and friendly when setting limits
- State the limit and the reason why one time only; do not argue
- When limits are set for good reason, remain firm even if the child has a tantrum
- Ignore emotional outbursts
- Remain calm by detaching yourself from the situation
- When there is an outburst, listen for a break in crying
- Move close to this child after an outburst; offer comfort and support
- Help this child take deep, relaxing breaths
- After the outburst, help this child clean up anything she disrupted
- When she is calm, help this child engage in an activity
- If the tantrum lasts more than ten to fifteen minutes, tell this child it is time to stop

Sample actions teachers can take:

- Help other children move away from a child who is having a tantrum so they do not get injured
- Learn more about how to help this child; share pertinent information with the parents

Sample action parents can take:

- Talk with a parent educator, counselor, or pediatrician; share pertinent information with your child's teacher

Information on Temper Tantrums

WHAT IS IT?

Children have temper tantrums for a variety of reasons. Some throw themselves down on the floor when they do not get what they want, when they are asked to do something they don't want to do, or when they become frustrated. Sometimes children become overwhelmed by activities, anxiety, or feelings.

Tantrums reach different levels of intensity depending on whether children receive attention, have the language to express their needs and wants, and have effective coping skills. Sometimes children have learned they will get what they want when they cause a fuss.

Observe and Respond

Children are prone to outbursts when they are tired, sick, or hungry. Help reduce the risk and frequency of tantrums by adjusting your schedule to avoid your child becoming overtired or hungry. Stay away from challenging activities when your child is fatigued. Watch for symptoms that your child may be getting ill; emotions can be close to the surface the day before he or she comes down with something. Other common triggers include too many changes in activity, too much going on at one time, or stressful family changes, such as a new sibling or a move.

Help your child learn to recognize when he or she is becoming frustrated. Say, "It looks like you're getting frustrated. Take a break or count to ten." Encourage your child to ask for help; teach safe ways of expressing anger. Your child can stamp feet, yell, or talk with you about it. Teach your child to take deep, calming breaths.

Be careful not to model emotional outbursts yourself. Recognize your own need to take a break. Use words to name your feelings. Demonstrate how to calm down by listening to music, looking at a book, or taking a walk.

Provide choices when possible. When you must set a limit, be firm. Remember not to take outbursts personally. Do not let your child's outbursts sway you. Offer a choice: "Do you want to do it by yourself, or shall I help you?" Encourage your child to use words rather than behavior to tell you, "I want help."

continued

If you can't give your child something for a good reason, do not give in. Ignore any outburst. Detach yourself from the situation by focusing on something else or by walking away. Don't try to explain while your child is upset. Listen for a break in crying and watch for signals that your child is calming down. Move close to offer comfort and support. When the tantrum is over, do not lecture. Help your child become engaged in an activity. If your child brings up the difficult situation, problem-solve how to handle it. Offer the words to use next time.

Focus on teaching your child words to use to express feelings. Read books about feelings. Find pictures in magazines of people expressing different emotions, and talk about the feelings they are showing. Listen for people laughing, crying, or yelling. Guess how each person might be feeling from what you hear. Teach your child a variety of feelings words. Teach vocabulary such as *angry*, *mad*, *frustrated*, *sad*, *upset*, *surprised*, *happy*, and *frightened*. Explain that not every event is tragic. Talk with your child about how the intensity of feelings can vary from really, really mad to just a little bit frustrated. Set special quiet times aside to talk more about your child's feelings.

Occasionally children become locked into tantrums. If your child gets stuck, move in close and acknowledge the feelings. Distract your child with another activity. Once a tantrum has lasted more than ten to fifteen minutes, say, "It's time to stop now." Help your child take deep, relaxing breaths.

CONNECTING WITH SUPPORT

Work with your child's teacher to develop consistency between the home and the early childhood setting. If your child has a tantrum in every stressful situation or when denied his or her way; if the tantrums seem filled with extreme anger or distress; if the tantrums consistently last beyond fifteen to twenty minutes, talk with a parent educator or a family counselor who specializes in working with young children.

9 ◆ "Whack!" Aggression

FOR TEACHERS

I've got to watch Colton all the time. Anytime he doesn't get the toy he wants, he hits whoever is playing with it.

❖ **Standard**
Uses problem solving to resolve conflicts.

What Is It?

Unfortunately, aggressive behaviors can be common when children come together in group settings and don't yet know how to solve problems. Typically, aggressive behaviors are those that injure people or property. Hitting, kicking, slapping, scratching, throwing toys, and destroying materials in anger are all aggressive behaviors. When young children are asked to share materials and toys, they are more likely to experience frustration that can cause aggression. Occasionally children will demonstrate aggressive behaviors in a group setting but not at home. More typically, children who haven't yet learned to problem-solve are aggressive regardless of the setting.

Problem solving is a complex skill that requires a lot of guidance and practice. It involves identifying a problem, thinking of ways to solve it, choosing the best idea, and trying it out. To learn how to solve problems, children need to observe others as they successfully solve problems. They also need the assistance of adults when they first try problem solving and many opportunities to practice problem solving on their own. Problems that arise out of conflict are part of everyday life for children. Protecting them from challenges or solving conflicts for them robs them of the chance to learn important skills. Through conflict, children learn to articulate their ideas about how to solve problems. They broaden their repertoire of solutions when they listen to the ideas of others.

Classrooms in which children are fully engaged in meaningful, challenging learning activities tend to have fewer conflicts. When conflicts do occur, help children reach the standard "uses problem solving to resolve conflicts." Focus your efforts on teaching a child who is aggressive what to do when he feels angry, frustrated, or overwhelmed and to resolve conflicts without hurting others. Usually aggression decreases as children learn to problem-solve.

Observe and Decide What to Teach

Knowing that aggression can be common doesn't make it easier to deal with. Observe the situations in which a child may become aggressive. The following questions and suggestions will help you formulate your plans as you teach a child to problem-solve.

Was a Behavior Misinterpreted as Aggressive?

Some aggression is accidental and is not intended to hurt others or to ruin their things. For example, when children are crowded, they are likely to bump into each other or knock things over. If this is the case, you may need to quickly describe the situation as unintentional. Say something like "Sarah accidentally knocked down your blocks when she tried to get to her building." Help the children brainstorm ways to avoid the problem. Say, "Your buildings are so close together that they are getting knocked down. What can you do so this won't happen?"

Other situations in which children misinterpret actions include bumping into one another in line or trying to make space for themselves when they are crowded together. Help children understand the situation by saying, "Devon pushed you over because he wants to sit next to you." Then ask Devon, "What can you do to let him know you want to sit next to him?" Teach him to say, "Move over, please." Or avoid crowding altogether by marking each child's personal space with a carpet square, tape mark on the floor, or a chair.

Occasionally children try to make contact by poking, pushing, or slapping someone on the back in a way that is interpreted as aggressive. Watch to see if a child is trying to be friendly. Teach ways to make contact, such as tapping a child's shoulder or gently rubbing a friend's back. Comment when you see this child make contact or get another person's attention appropriately. Help him learn to greet another child or ask him to play by offering an appealing play idea. (For more information on initiating play with others, see chapter 4, "I Want to Play Too!" Joining a Group of Players.)

Does This Child Have Limited Vocabulary, or Is He Hard to Understand?

Children who use few words or who are difficult to understand may become frustrated when their words don't work. Some may try to get what they want with aggressive behavior. You can help a child who is having difficulty learn a few important words to use, to come and get you for help, or to yell rather than hit. Once you are aware this child needs help, move close to him. Walk him through the steps in problem solving. Model words for him to use. Keep these words very simple. "Stop," "That's mine," or "Help" are examples. When this child is ready, teach more complex statements, such as "I was using that" or "When can I have a turn?" Comment on it when he uses words. Repeat what he says if another child doesn't understand him. Make sure the other child responds to his words, even if the answer is "No."

Teaching Problem Solving to Young Children

◆ Make a poster listing the steps in problem solving. Use simple phrases or a picture of a stoplight to help children remember the steps.

  1. Red = Stop. What's the problem?
  2. Yellow = Think of ideas to solve the problem.
  3. Green = Try the best idea.

◆ Use puppet plays, roles plays, modeling, coaching, and children's books to demonstrate the process. For example, perform a puppet play in which one puppet is trying to color a picture in the area where another puppet is driving a car. The puppet trying to draw keeps getting bumped until the puppets stop to think about what they can do to solve the problem. Have the puppets think of a number of ideas. Ask them to choose the best idea. Finally, show how the puppets decide that the one who is drawing should take her paper and crayons to the table.

◆ Draw simple pictures of things children can do if they have a problem. For example, they might take turns, ask an adult for help, walk away, stamp their feet, pound playdough, yell, or scribble on a piece of paper. Post the pictures in your room to use as a reminder.

◆ Practice brainstorming by playing games in which you think of all the things you need to pack for a trip, list all of the things you could do in the snow, or try to move in different ways to get from one place to another.

◆ Establish an environment in which it is safe to state an idea and try it out without being laughed at.

◆ Let children make choices in foods, activities, open-ended art projects, and books to read.

◆ Encourage children to think of something else if their first idea doesn't work.

◆ Teach them to problem-solve in all sorts of situations, not just when they are experiencing conflict. Use problem solving when deciding how to fix a broken toy, how to build a fort out of blankets, or what to do about the noise level.

◆ Expect that problems will be resolved. When you experience a challenge or difficulty, say something like "I wonder how I can work this out. Maybe I could try . . ."

◆ Use a problem you are experiencing to show children how to think of many different solutions. If you try to make something and it doesn't work, say something like "My first idea isn't working. I'll have to come up with another idea."

Is This Child Trying to Engage Another in Physically Active Play? Does the Play Turn Aggressive?

Many children love to roll around and physically engage in play with others. Guide their energy by providing indoor and outdoor movement opportunities each day. (For ideas, see chapter 21, "I Can Run, Hop, and Gallop!" Large-Motor Skills.) Consider having a gym mat for a child who especially needs this type of play. Have a group discussion to decide on rules for roly-poly play (Gartrell and Sonsteng 2008). Limits might include stopping when someone says, "Stop," only two children at a time, and only wrestling. Be sure to supervise closely.

Help this child transition to a calming activity after this type of play. Try sensory experiences like playdough, water, sand, and fingerpainting. Offer this child opportunities to be powerful in other ways by having him help make rules, run errands, and plan activities. Comment on times he uses his strong muscles to help rearrange furniture or to climb to the top of playground equipment. Meet his need for physical play by offering exciting dramatic play themes like race car driver or escaping dangerous animals.

Is This Child Using Aggression to Express Anger or to Get What He Wants?

All children feel angry from time to time. Anger is often caused by feelings of frustration. Children are likely to be frustrated when they feel their needs aren't being met or they aren't getting what they want, whether it is attention, a toy, or an activity. How intensely children react is influenced by temperament, age, maturity, culture, and gender (Honig, Miller, and Church 2007). If you are working with a child who is aggressive, try to learn the triggers and the signs that he is becoming frustrated. Are there certain times of the day he is more likely to become aggressive? Perhaps a change in schedule would better meet his needs. Are there certain activities that are frustrating? Simplify activities for the time being. Is there a certain child he has trouble getting along with? Separate them whenever possible.

Colton, the child described at the beginning of the chapter, gave many signals that he was becoming frustrated. His voice began to rise and became shrill; his face became flushed; he had tussles with others. Once his teacher learned his signals, she could move close to him and help him figure out how to get what he wanted without hurting others. With her guidance, he eventually learned to work problems out on his own. As you learn the signals that a child's frustration level is escalating, move close to him. Your presence may help to calm him. Reduce the tension by labeling his feelings for him if he doesn't yet know the words to use.

After introducing problem solving to the group, if the child you are working with is involved in a conflict, walk him through the steps. Ask each child involved to describe the problem. Then ask, "What can you do that will make both of you happy?" If the children are unable to come up with any solutions, suggest a few for them or remind them to use the pictures described earlier. Ask them to choose their best idea. Then help them try it.

Read books in which a problem is presented, such as *Bailey Goes Camping* by Kevin Henkes, *Geraldine's Blanket* by Holly Keller, or *The Little Mouse, the Red*

Ripe Strawberry, and the Big Hungry Bear by Don Wood and Audrey Wood. Stop before the end of the story. Discuss the problem and how it can be solved. Find out what the characters in the story do to solve the problem.

Is This Child Hitting Many Times a Day or for a Number of Months?

A child who is frequently aggressive risks having the other children begin to dislike or avoid him. To help him learn to interact more appropriately and to keep the other children safe, you will need to be watchful and stay close by. Build or strengthen your relationship to increase the chances that he wants to please you and to earn your approval.

Controlling Impulses

Young children who engage in aggressive behaviors need to learn to control their impulses and regulate their behavior. When they are able to do this, it is because they can think about acting, stop themselves from doing so (instead of acting on their impulses), and make another choice. This requires that a child pause between his immediate reaction and a more thoughtful action. Learning to stop emotional reactions and control impulses takes time. By four or five years of age, children have developed some impulse control, but many people work on this into early adulthood. Age-appropriate ideas for helping a child develop impulse control follow.

- Tell a child you will count to three, and then tell him what part of his body to shake. Say, "One, two, three, shake your hands/head/toes with me." Then try asking him to keep each part still. Say, "One, two, three, keep your legs/ears/fingers still with me." Games that require a child to freeze help him learn to control himself.

- Tell this child you want him to pretend to do something but he is not to start until you give a signal. Give the direction but wait for a few seconds before giving the signal. For example, this child can pretend to eat a sandwich, tie his shoe, or ride a bike but only after the signal. Waiting like this helps develop self-regulation.

- Ask a child to plan what he wants to do during dramatic play and have him stick to it. Once he has stated his intention, he should think about ways he can act out his role. If he begins to wander, remind him of his plan and help him reengage. Staying in character requires a child to practice controlling his physical actions, social behaviors, and language (Bedrova and Leong 2007).

- Encourage this child to use words to remind himself how to behave (Bedrova and Leong 2007). For example, when he is angry and feels like hitting, teach him to cross his arms over his chest and say out loud, "Stop. Don't hit. Do something different." This reminds him to do something more appropriate and helps him regulate his behavior.

Play stop-and-freeze games that help this child learn to control impulses. If he learns to stop and freeze when you call his name, you can move close to him and coach him through upsetting situations. It may also help to teach him to take a few deep breaths to relax. Have him pretend to blow up a balloon with slow deep breaths. As he does so, have him stretch up and stand on his tiptoes. Pretend all the air escapes when he blows air out and sinks to the floor.

Teach this child to recognize when he is angry. Do his fists get tight? Does he purse his lips? Do his eyebrows scrunch up? Make a personal book for him to carry in his pocket with pictures of things he can do if he has trouble. Rehearse the steps when he is not upset. Walk him through the steps when he is upset.

If this child needs to leave an upsetting activity, help him choose a quiet one by himself for a time. When he is in control of his emotions, he can rejoin the others. Assist with this reunion to ensure that it is successful.

Demonstrate and comment on examples of cooperation that take place around him. Encourage children to work cooperatively by saying, "How can you work together to build that tower?" Be sure to recognize him when he is playing well with others.

Alyssa, a family child care provider, ran across her living room when the fists began to fly. By the time she got to the girls, both Hayley and Maddie were frantic. Alyssa took each girl by the hand and moved to the side of the room. Maddie was sobbing, unable to stop. Both girls looked really scared.

Alyssa thought she first needed to help the girls calm down. Alyssa said to Hayley, "Tell me what happened." Hayley couldn't explain much except, "Maddie kept hitting me." It appeared that Hayley no longer knew what had happened or couldn't put it into words. While still holding the hands of each girl, Alyssa turned her attention to Maddie. Maddie was still crying but not as uncontrollably. Alyssa asked if Maddie was hurt, and she shook her head no. Alyssa asked Maddie to tell her what had happened. Her response was much like Hayley's: "Hayley was fighting me."

Alyssa decided that whatever had brought on the dispute had been lost in the girls' flood of emotions. Both were still breathing hard, and Alyssa thought it was important for them to continue to relax. She asked the girls to choose between playdough and coloring. Hayley chose playdough, and Maddie slunk down in a chair by the coloring materials. Before long, Hayley had cooled off and could rejoin the group of players. It took a little longer and a little more support before Maddie regained her composure. Alyssa sat near her and colored a picture too. Occasionally Alyssa commented on her own picture. Eventually Maddie joined the conversation.

Work with the Parents

Let the parents of a child who is using aggressive behaviors know early on there is a problem. Most parents will do all they can to help decrease it. However, some parents may not know how to curb it or may have different feelings about how children should respond to conflict. It is not productive to blame the parents for a child's aggression. Instead, let the parents know that in your setting, you need to help their child learn other responses. Tell them it is your job to keep children safe, including preventing children from hurting each other. Talk with the parents about steps to take, using the Plan for Action. Consistency between the home and the early childhood setting will help this child learn to problem-solve more quickly.

A Plan for Action

To develop your Plan for Action, choose or modify one of the suggested goals to best match your situation. Add how well or how often you expect the skill or behavior to be demonstrated. Remember: you are looking for growth, not perfection. You want to move the child from where he is currently and to increase your expectations slightly.

> ### When to Seek Assistance
>
> Learn more about working with a child who is aggressive by taking a class, attending a workshop, or reading about agression. If you do not see a decrease in aggressive behaviors after trying what you learn and the suggestions listed here for a number of weeks, have an early childhood consultant observe and give suggestions specific to your situation.
>
> Aggression in young children tends to peak during toddlerhood and declines over time. Persistent high levels of aggression may require specialized instruction (Chacko et al. 2009). Log how often this child is aggressive. This information can help when you talk to specialists about the behavior. Seek assistance if the child is frequently aggressive toward himself or others, doesn't seem attached to you or other adults, or rarely follows directions (Tomlin 2011). Recommend that his parents contact a parent educator, family counselor, or behavior specialist to help this child learn more effective interaction skills.

Next, determine three or four actions teachers and parents will take. Choose additional actions specific to the early childhood setting and the home. Record your choices on the planning form found in the appendix.

Sample goals for a child who is aggressive:

- Uses gentle touch in approaching others
- Keeps hands to self when close to other children
- Engages in roly-poly play at appropriate times and in appropriate spaces
- Expresses anger without aggression
- Brings problems to an adult for help in solving
- Actively helps in problem solving
- Problem-solves independently

Sample actions parents and teachers can take:

- Teach gentle touch
- Teach ways to greet others
- Provide sensory activities
- Provide indoor and outdoor movement opportunities

- Make sure there is adequate space for an activity

- Give opportunities for this child to be powerful

- Be clear that aggression will not be permitted

- Teach safe ways to express anger

- Help this child recognize angry feelings, stop, and think

- Teach words to use when upset and to express wants and feelings

- Teach problem solving

- Label accidental situations

Sample actions teachers can take:

- Define personal space

- Teach this child and others to say, "Move over, please"

- Separate those who are having difficulty sitting next to each other

- Play stop-and-freeze games to teach self-control

- Ask this child to choose a quiet activity to do alone when he needs to calm down

- Assist this child in joining other children

- Provide a space where it is okay to wrestle

- Learn more about working with aggressive behaviors; share pertinent information with parents

- Gain parental permission, and then have an early childhood consultant observe your interactions; share pertinent information with parents

Sample actions parents can take:

- Comment on examples of cooperation

- Comment on times when your child solves problems without aggression

- Set limits on roughhousing

- Reduce the amount of aggressive television your child views

- Arrange for a developmental screening to be done by your health care provider or the early childhood screening program in your school district; share pertinent information with your child's teacher

- Talk with a parent educator or counselor; share pertinent information with your child's teacher

Information on Aggression

WHAT IS IT?

Unfortunately, aggressive behaviors can be common when young children come together in group settings. When young children are asked to share materials and toys, they are more likely to experience frustration and conflict, which can cause aggression. Aggressive behaviors include hitting, kicking, slapping, scratching, throwing toys, and destroying materials in anger. Children who are aggressive need to learn to express their frustration and solve problems without hurting others or ruining things.

Problem solving involves identifying a problem, thinking of ways to solve it, choosing the best idea, and trying it out. Children learn to problem-solve by observing others, direct instruction, and trying out a solution on their own. Usually aggression decreases as children learn to problem-solve.

Observe and Respond

Some aggression is accidental. For example, when children are crowded, they are likely to bump into one another or to knock things over. When this occurs, you may need to quickly say something like "Sarah accidentally knocked down your blocks when she tried to get to her building."

Occasionally children try to make contact by poking, pushing, or slapping someone on the back in a way that is interpreted as aggressive. Watch to see if your child is trying to be friendly. Teach your child to tap other children's shoulders or gently rub their backs to get their attention. Children who use few words or who are difficult to understand may become frustrated and act out when their words don't work. If this is the case, teach your child a few simple words to use: "Stop," "That's mine," or "Help." When your child is ready, teach more complex statements like "I was using that" or "When can I have a turn?"

Many children love to engage in roughhousing. If you wrestle with your child, establish a few rules, for example, stop when someone says "Stop," and wrestling only—no hitting. Help your child transition to a calming activity after this type of play. Try sensory experiences like

continued

playing with playdough, helping to wash the dishes, or taking a warm bath.

Everyone feels angry from time to time. Anger is often caused by feelings of frustration. Children are likely to become frustrated when they feel they aren't getting what they want, whether it is attention, a toy, or an activity. Learn your child's triggers and the signs of building frustration. Is your child more aggressive when tired? Perhaps a nap is needed before playing with a friend. Are certain activities usually frustrating? Try easier activities for the time being. When you see a sign your child is becoming frustrated, move close by. Reduce the tension by labeling your child's feelings.

Teach your child to recognize his or her signs of anger. Perhaps these are tight fists, pursing lips, or scrunched eyebrows? Teach your child to stop and think, "Don't hit. Do something different." Effective possibilities include getting help, yelling, pounding playdough, or scribbling a picture.

When a problem arises, walk your child through the steps in problem solving: identifying the problem, thinking of solutions, choosing the best idea, and trying it. Ask each child involved in an upset to describe the problem. Then ask, "What can you do that will make both of you happy?" If the children are unable to come up with any solutions, suggest a few. Ask them to choose the best idea. Then help them try it.

CONNECTING WITH SUPPORT

Use the suggestions listed here, and work with your child's teacher to formulate a Plan for Action. Consistency between your home and the early childhood setting will help your child learn appropriate behaviors more quickly. Persistent high levels of aggression may require specialized instruction. Seek assistance if your child is frequently aggressive, doesn't seem attached to you or other adults, or rarely follows directions. Contact a parent educator, family counselor, or behavior specialist to help your child learn more effective interaction skills.

Part 3

Approaches to Learning

All children approach learning in unique ways. Their temperament, experiences, families, and culture help shape how they approach new experiences and activities. The approaches to learning domain include children's attitudes toward learning, acquiring information, and inventiveness in putting information together to formulate new understandings. Children need to be interested, engaged, enthusiastic learners. They need to be motivated to try new experiences and have opportunities to initiate their own learning. These important attitudes play a role in later learning and educational experiences.

In early childhood settings, teachers set a foundation for learning by arranging a safe and comfortable space to explore. They act as resources who can find a needed prop or tool to help children extend their learning. They give children the time to direct their own learning in ways that match their preferred learning styles. They help those who need encouragement to take appropriate risks; help others organize their play by asking, "What do you want to do next?"; and help some settle into activities or persist in completing them.

Parents set the stage for children to develop the skills to approach learning when they share their child's awe. They help their child try something new by providing a safe base from which to explore and then return for reassurance. They introduce or show their child more than one way to play with a toy, like patting playdough into a circle, rolling it into ropes, or pushing cookie cutters into it to make shapes. Their acceptance of frustration helps their child stick with a challenging task.

All children are capable learners. They benefit from hands-on learning experiences and time spent with people who share their enthusiasm for new discoveries. When children develop positive attitudes toward learning, they approach new situations with confidence, are interested in and take initiative to learn new things, and are creative in their approaches to problem solving.

As in all the developmental domains, states may have more standards than those included in this book. Three early learning standards are incorporated in part 3, Approaches to Learning. These standards, or ones very similar, are found in the standards of many states. The following standards are included:

- ◆ Shows ability to attend to and persist at a task, chapter 10
- ◆ Is curious about and willing to try new things, chapter 11
- ◆ Tries pretend roles in play, chapter 12

10   "Let's Go, Go, Go!" Activity Level

FOR TEACHERS

Tamara comes in running and doesn't stop. She wiggles and bothers others while I try to read a story. She never really finishes anything during free play. I need to take vitamins just to keep up.

❖ Standard
Shows ability to attend to and persist at a task.

What Is It?

Children grow increasingly active until three to four years of age, when their activity level peaks. This activity level means most children won't attend to any one thing for very long. Depending on the activity, a two-year-old child can usually sit and be engaged for two to three minutes, and a five-year-old child for fifteen to twenty minutes. Young children need to pay attention to and persist at tasks to learn from activities. Teachers can help children learn by accepting where each child starts from and slowly increasing the expectation that the child pay attention.

The wonderful amount of energy that young children possess becomes problematic when a child is unable to focus her attention long enough to learn. Children with high activity levels may be easily distracted, have trouble finishing projects, and act without considering the consequences of their behavior. Because a child who is always on the move usually hears a number of messages about her behavior, it is especially important to protect her self-esteem while helping her learn to focus her energy.

Observe and Decide What to Teach

Observe and record the length of time a child is able to concentrate on activities she chooses, on adult-directed activities, and in play with others. Pick another child of about the same age and temperament, and record her attention span for similar activities. Compare their records and use this information to gain perspective, identify trouble spots during the day, and consider influences on activity level.

Your observations and the suggestions that follow will help you learn how to work with a child who needs to learn to attend to and persist at a task.

Does This Child Prefer Materials That Allow Her to Move?

Children with high activity levels are often drawn to materials and activities that allow them to move. Let a child who needs to move release energy by getting outside at least once each day. Provide many ways for her to move indoors too. Include large-motor equipment, such as an indoor climbing structure, rocking boat, or a Sit 'n Spin as regular parts of your environment. Plan additional movement activities, such as throwing foam balls into a basket, jumping across parallel tape lines on the floor, dropping pegs into a plastic jar, carrying cotton balls on a spoon, or dancing to music (see chapter 21, "I Can Run, Hop, and Gallop!" Large-Motor Skills).

Tune in to the nonmobile activities that interest this child in your setting. Join her when she is enjoying one of these activities. Often your presence helps expand the time she is able to stick with an activity. When she seems ready to move on, ask that she do one more thing, such as feed the doll or park the toy car in the garage. As you discover the child's other interests, be sure to include them in your environment too. Help calm or soothe the active child by offering sensory activities like pouring sand, water, or potting soil and manipulating playdough. Plan movement and music activities that combine moving and learning during whole-group times.

Does This Child Quickly Move from One Activity to Another during Free Play?

Some children with high activity levels wander from activity to activity without settling into play. If this is the case for a child you are working with, consider how your environment may be affecting her. Make sure activities are simple enough for her to be successful, yet difficult enough to challenge her. Plan traffic patterns so others are not walking through her play and distracting her. Arrange your space so that quiet activities are not next to loud ones. Eliminate runways or wide open spaces that invite running. Reduce noise by adding soft materials that absorb sound or teaching children to use quieter voices. Look at your space to see if it might be overstimulating. Cut back on or rotate the number of materials available at one time. Reduce the decorations or displays on the wall without making things look sterile. Display toys and materials attractively so it is easier for children to see what is available and to make choices.

Ask this child to choose what she will play with. Stay with her while she gets started. If she begins to wander without purpose, ask her what she will do next. Be sure to notice and comment on her behavior when she is engaged in an activity. To help her focus, offer sensory motor materials, such as water, sand, and playdough. Offer interesting toys, such as funnels, measuring cups, and sand molds. Play next to her and encourage her to try new ways of interacting with the materials. If other children join you, ask her to show them what the toys do. Determine if she is wandering because others are excluding her from play. If so, see chapter 4, "I Want to Play Too!" Joining a Group of Players.

Does This Child Act Impulsively without Considering the Consequences of Her Behavior?

Some children are moving so quickly and without thinking that they don't realize the consequences of their actions. Teach a child who behaves in this way to control her actions. Play stop-and-freeze games ("Red Light, Green Light") in which the child stops in response to a drum, bell, or word from you. Practice many times so she learns to stop when you call her name. When she behaves impulsively, move close to her. Confidentially state the rule. For example, you might say, "It's not okay to open the guinea pig's cage. What can you do instead?" Provide alternative actions from which she can choose. If needed, offer choices like "You can open and close the doors on this shape box or draw a picture of the guinea pig." At other times, play "What if?" games with the child. Ask, "What if you were trying to get to the sink but you were moving so fast you bumped into someone?" Brainstorm appropriate solutions to each situation you pose. Evaluate the solutions and choose the best one.

Does This Child Have a Hard Time Transitioning from One Activity to the Next?

Children who have high activity levels seem to do best with predictable schedules and routines. If a child you are working with needs help moving from one activity to the next, pay attention to the rhythm of the day. Pattern your schedule so that opportunities to move come before and after activities that require the child to sit. Provide a balance between adult-directed and child-directed activities. Make a pictorial schedule of the day, and teach this child what comes next.

Give a warning a few minutes before an activity comes to an end. Be specific about what the child is to do and where she is to go during changes in activity. Tell her to stand by her cubby, sit on her carpet square, or line up at the back door. Reduce the number of times children must wait by planning your schedule carefully. For example, young children engage in more sophisticated levels of dramatic play if they have a block of forty to fifty minutes to play rather than shorter periods of time. Be well prepared for each activity. Be sure to gather the materials you need before gathering the children. When a child must wait, help her be successful by asking her to be a helper, singing songs, or asking her to do slow, repetitive actions to help her relax.

Does This Child Have Difficulty Attending to Story or Group Time?

Some children wander away, fidget inattentively, or pester others during group time. If a child is having a great deal of difficulty concentrating during group, consider other activities this child (and others) might do while some are listening to the story. Tamara, the child described at the beginning of the chapter, was having so much difficulty attending to the story when she sat close to others that her teacher decided that very few children were getting anything out of story time. She decided to let Tamara look at books in a comfy chair in the library corner during story time. After a few days, she found that Tamara was watching the group and listening from where she was. Eventually she moved the chair to the back of the group, and Tamara participated from there.

Be sure that group times are highly motivating and engaging. Sing songs, do fingerplays, put on puppet plays, act out stories, or tell flannel board stories. Pique the interest of this child by beginning the group activity with a short demonstration, using a prop, wearing a costume, or posing a riddle or mystery question. Keep group times short. Plan a seating arrangement that places the active child in the center at the back. There she can see well but won't block the view of others if she is wiggly. Place children who are able to ignore her on either side of her. Mark her spot with tape or a carpet square. Talk about personal space as if it is a bubble that surrounds each person. During group, children should keep their hands and feet inside their bubble. Reinforce this child when she is looking at you and participating in the activity by giving her the thumbs-up or okay signal. When you do need to draw her attention to the activity, touch her gently or ask her a multiple-choice question. Say something like "Do you think the boy in the story will run home or run to school? Let's find out."

When to Seek Assistance

It is sometimes difficult to determine when a child's activity level lies outside the norm. Before becoming overly concerned, put the suggestions into action for three to four months. Then consider if the child is still in constant motion; has difficulty sticking to an activity for more than a few minutes; acts without considering the consequences; continues to have difficulty following routines. If necessary, suggest the parents contact resources in your community that may be of help. These may include the child's health care provider, an early childhood screening program in the school district, or a family counselor specializing in working with young children.

Work with the Parents

Share with her parents examples of what the child is interested in, her strengths, and the steps you are taking to build on those. Give the parents the family information and arrange a meeting to discuss difficult situations. Use the Plan for Action that follows to determine steps to take at home and in the early childhood setting. Establishing consistency will help the child learn how to slow down and become more attentive to the people and materials around her.

A Plan for Action

To develop your Plan for Action, choose or modify one of the suggested goals to best match your situation. Add how well or how often you expect the skill or behavior to be demonstrated. Remember: you are looking for growth, not perfection. You want to move the child from where she is currently and to increase your expectations slightly. Next, determine three or four actions teachers and parents will take. Choose additional actions specific to the early childhood setting and the home. Record your choices on the planning form in the appendix.

Sample goals for a child with a high activity level:

- Engages in activities of choice for _____ minutes (choose a time that is slightly longer than the child's current performance)

- Sits at snack or a short group activity for _____ minutes (choose a time that is slightly longer than the child's current performance)

- Moves from one activity to the next independently

- Attends a short, interactive group time

- Stops actions when an adult calls her name

Sample actions parents and teachers can take:

- Take the child outside at least once a day

- Provide indoor movement activities

- Offer sensory activities

- Cut back on the number of materials available and rotate them

- Display materials and toys so choices are easier to make

- Notice and comment on the child's behavior when she is engaged in an activity

- Sandwich a passive activity between two that allow the child to move

- Be specific about behavioral expectations during changes in activities

- Move close to the child or whisper when you need to talk to her about her behavior

- Play "What if?" games to help the child learn consequences of her actions

- Help this child focus on the responses of others to her behaviors

- Teach this child to recognize accidents

Sample actions teachers can take:

- Plan things that especially interest the child

- Reduce waiting times; fill those that cannot be eliminated

- Plan traffic patterns to reduce disruption and runways

- Help this child make activity choices during free play

- Stay with this child while she starts an activity

- Watch to see if the child is excluded from play by others

- Keep group time short

- Start group with an attention grabber

- Place this child where she can see and hear well at group

- Mark the child's spot with tape or carpet square

- Teach this child about personal space

- Reinforce this child for paying attention to the group activity
- Regain this child's attention with a touch or a multiple-choice question

Sample actions parents can take:

- Offer balanced meals
- Make sure your child gets adequate rest
- Develop a consistent bedtime routine
- Encourage your child's interest in reading
- Commend your child when she is concentrating
- Take things for your child to do when she may need to wait during outings
- Limit the amount of time your child watches television or plays computer games
- Consult with another professional about your child's activity level (for example, pediatrician, early childhood assessment program, or family counselor)

Information on Activity Level

WHAT IS IT?

Young children need to pay attention to and persist at a task in order to learn from their activities. They also learn through hands-on exploration. They have high activity levels, and most don't attend to any one thing for very long. Depending on the activity, a two-year-old child can usually sit and be engaged for two to three minutes, and a five-year-old child for fifteen to twenty minutes. While a high amount of energy is normal, some children with high activity levels may be easily distracted, have difficulty finishing projects, and act without considering the consequences of their behavior.

Observe and Respond

You can help your child learn to focus his or her attention and persist at tasks. Let your child move and release energy by getting outside at least once a day. Provide ways for your child to move indoors too. Throwing rolled up socks into a basket, jumping across parallel tape lines on the floor, dropping pegs into a plastic jar, or dancing to music helps burn off youthful energy. It may be tempting to sit your child in front of the TV or computer, but these activities may increase the amount of energy and restlessness your child exhibits. Limiting these activities increases your child's ability to focus.

Join your child in playing with a favorite toy. Often your presence helps expand the length of play time. Be sure to notice and comment when your child engages in an activity, and offer positive attention for time spent concentrating. When your child seems ready to move on, ask for one more action with the toy, such as feeding the doll or parking the toy car in the garage.

To help calm or sooth your active child, offer sensory activities, such as pouring sand, playing in water, or working playdough. Reduce noise and cut back on the number of toys available at one time. Displaying toys attractively makes it easier for your child to make choices.

If your child is moving too quickly to analyze the consequences of an action, move close by. Confidentially state the rule by saying something like "It's not okay to open the guinea pig's cage. If you open the door, he will get out, and we may not be able to find him. What can you do instead?" If necessary, offer

continued

choices like "You can open and close the doors on this shape box or draw a picture of the guinea pig."

Many children who have high activity levels do best with predictable schedules and routines. Arrange your child's day to include an opportunity to move before and after sedentary activities. Provide a balance between things you must do and things your child wants to do.

Give notice a few minutes before an activity needs to end. This gives your child a chance to complete an activity or mentally prepare to take a break from it. When you must wait for an appointment or in line at a store, bring a bag of books and toys or play a simple guessing game. Keep your child occupied with appropriate things to do.

Reading books together helps your child learn to focus his or her attention. Pique your child's interest in the story by posing a riddle or question before beginning to read. Keep the book short so your child can successfully focus on it. When you need to draw your child's attention back to the book, ask a question like "Do you think the boy in the story will run home or to school? Let's find out."

CONNECTING WITH SUPPORT

With your child's teacher, work to teach your child to slow down and become more attentive. Consistency between home and school will help your child learn more quickly. Determining if your child's activity level is outside of the norm can be difficult, so try some of the suggestions listed here for three to four months before becoming overly concerned. Then consider if your child is still in constant motion, has difficulty sticking to an activity for more than a few minutes, or continues to have difficulty following routines. If necessary, contact your pediatrician; have your child's skills screened through the school district; or talk with a family counselor specializing in working with young children.

"Hey, What's This?"
Curiosity and Questioning

11

FOR TEACHERS

Dominic loved to push the large yellow dump truck around the room. Every day when he arrived at school, he ran to the shelf and grabbed the truck. He rarely showed an interest in anything else.

❖ Standard
Is curious about and willing to try new things.

What Is It?

From very young ages, children are driven to learn about the world around them. They are curious about the people, places, and things they see and experience. Through their explorations, they learn vocabulary, how things work, and whether they can effect changes. Their explorations help them acquire knowledge that they will build on throughout their lifetimes. They use this knowledge to make sense of what they read, solve a scientific problem, or resolve a conflict with a peer.

When children are curious about something, they become engrossed in exploring it. They lean in to get a closer look; focus their attention; show surprise, wonder, or glee; spontaneously describe what they see; ask questions; or mess around with an object to see what else it can do or if it works in another way.

Sometimes experiencing new things can be stressful for children. Supportive relationships with adults provide a secure base from which to operate. Children who have supportive relationships feel safe and are willing to risk new experiences. Some children are secure enough to try new things just knowing that an adult is nearby, just in case. Other children may want to stand by a parent or teacher for a few moments to scan new surroundings. Once a child who does this feels comfortable, he can move away from the adult to explore. He may return a few moments later to describe a new discovery or garner some additional support. After he has checked in, he feels ready to go out and investigate some more. Still other children may need an adult to support their exploration by engaging in the new experience with them.

Teachers can support a child's curiosity by sharing his wonder, providing a safe environment, introducing him to new experiences, and providing ways for him to delve into things that capture his interest. Children who are encouraged to be curious learn how to learn and discover the world around them.

Observe and Decide What to Teach

As you observe a child, ask the following questions and consider the ways you can support his natural sense of curiosity and willingness to try new things.

Does This Child Lack a Sense of Wonder?

Children often demonstrate a sense of awe while they learn about the wonderful things around them. Each new thing they encounter is something to explore. It may look to some as if the child is just playing with an object when he engages all of his senses to learn about a new material. Actually, he is taking in a great deal of information about it. He may turn an object to examine it from all angles, touch it, poke it, pinch it, or sniff it. Encourage a sense of wonder in the children you are working with by taking sensory walks, such as a walk to listen to all the sounds you hear or a walk following a spring rain to smell how fresh it is. Go on field trips to new places. Create a sense of wonder by making predictions about what you might see. Before going to the zoo, say, "I wonder if there will be a giraffe." Or create a chart on which the children answer the question "What do you think we will see at the zoo?" Create anticipation by making a list of things you think you will see at the zoo. Write their ideas down and then check the predictions when you return. It doesn't matter if their predictions were correct as long as the list helped build their curiosity about the event.

Feed an incurious child's interest by collecting things like old radios, sewing machines, or tape recorders (be sure to remove electrical cords). Give him a screwdriver and let him take the items apart to discover what's inside. Grab this child's attention by creating suspense. Tiptoe to a closet together to find a surprise, such as a toy animal hidden there. Stop reading a book before the end to create suspense; finish it at another time. Place an object in a mystery box. Give simple clues about what it is. Ask this child to guess. Wonder out loud about things that you see, read, or hear. Show enthusiasm for what this child learns. Model your excitement about things you see or hear by commenting on the colors you see when the light shines through a prism or your delight at the way the pattern changes when you look through a kaleidoscope.

Once a child shows curiosity about things he sees, he may begin to ask questions. Respond to his questions. If you don't know the answer, find out together. Encourage this child to describe what he wants to know and then determine how he can find out. Help him get answers by looking together for information in books, online, talking to someone who knows, or by experimenting, so he can discover answers on his own. If you get stuck, try turning the question back to him. Ask, "What do you think might happen? Why do you think it would be that way?" This will not only get you off the hook for an answer but will give you insight to his current level of understanding. Ask questions of your own, such as "How did you learn that? What did you do first? What happened next? What will you do next time you try it?" Allow this child time to think before expecting an answer or asking another question.

Does This Child Resist Trying New Things?

Children have a natural urge to explore their surrounding, toys, and materials. A problem exists if a child tends to choose the same type of toys or materials instead of a wider variety of activities and materials, because he is not gaining the broad base of understanding that comes from exploring a variety of things. Encourage him to expand what he plays with by selecting toys, materials, and projects that build on his interests. For example, if this child tends to choose building materials, expand his interest by adding books about construction to the library area or adding cars to drive on the roads he builds. Dominic, the boy mentioned at the beginning of the chapter, was encouraged by his teacher to paint with small trucks, put sand in the back of the yellow dump truck, use plastic tools to pretend to fix the truck, and build a garage for it with large wooden blocks.

Be sure that you offer materials that are sufficient in number, variety, and accessibility. Display them on low shelves so a cautious child can select what he wants to do. Rotate materials regularly so he will find them interesting again when you put them out the next time. Provide a variety of books in your reading area, including reference materials, fiction, nonfiction, and picture books. Make room for a number of interest areas in your setting, including science, sensory, dramatic play, building, art, and writing center. Be sure your environment appeals to all senses and learning styles.

There are a number of different ways that children approach new situations. Some children watch before joining, some join with teacher support, others join when they are invited by a friend, and some jump right into a new activity. Respect individual differences in the way a cautious child approaches new situations. Help him join new activities, but don't force his participation. For instance, if this child is reluctant, encourage him to join a circle game of Duck, Duck, Goose by saying, "I'll say the words, and you can run." Persuade him to try a new approach to learning by saying something like "Let's go listen and see what we can find out" or "Let's go try it and see what we can learn." Talk about his discoveries. Ask him to show you what he has learned in different media: for example, he can draw a picture, make a graph, make a recording, or dictate a description. When he explains what he has learned to others or represents it in some way, he deepens his own understanding.

Encourage this child to try new things by arranging activities that can be done in more than one way. For example, set up an obstacle course and ask him to move through it in different ways. Place plastic cones in a line a few feet apart from each other and ask, "Show me one way you can move through the cones. Is there another way?" The child may decide to crawl, walk backward, or slither like a snake. Count or list all the ways he thinks of to spur even more creativity. Offer a balance of open-ended materials, such as blocks and art materials, in addition to toys that are made for a single purpose, such as puzzles. Open-ended toys support children of varying abilities, allow them to be creative, and encourage them to experiment with using materials in new ways. Find a way for the reluctant child to try something new even when he is uncomfortable. For example, modify a finger-painting activity by allowing him to use a cotton swab. Comment on new things he is trying in order to increase his feelings of success and encourage his future explorations.

Work with the Parents

Parents and teachers alike will probably be concerned about a child who does not demonstrate an interest in the people and things he encounters. Talk with the parents to find out if they know what sparks this child's interests. Try additional activities to see if any pique his curiosity. Find ways to build on his interest.

A Plan for Action

To develop your Plan for Action, choose or modify one of the suggested goals to best match your situation. Add how well or how often you expect the skill or behavior to be demonstrated. Remember: you are looking for growth, not perfection. You want to move the child from where he is currently and to increase your expectations slightly. Next, determine three or four actions teachers and parents will take. Choose additional actions specific to the early childhood setting and the home. Record your choices on the planning form found in the appendix.

Sample goals for a child who is not yet trying new things:

◆ Shows a sense of wonder

◆ Shows an interest in new things

◆ Tries new things

◆ Asks "wh" questions: what, why, and who

◆ Seeks answers to questions

Sample actions parents and teachers can take:

◆ Take sensory walks

◆ Go on field trips

◆ Create a sense of wonder by making predictions

◆ Create suspense

◆ Wonder out loud about things that you see, read, or hear

◆ Model your excitement about things you see, hear, or learn

◆ Encourage this child to choose from a wide variety of activities and materials

- Offer toys, materials, and projects that build on this child's interests
- Offer plenty of materials
- Offer a variety of materials
- Display toys and materials on low shelves so this child can select for himself
- Rotate materials regularly
- Provide a variety of books, including reference materials, fiction, nonfiction, and picture books
- Respect individual differences in the way this child approaches new situations
- Invite the child to join an activity, but don't force participation
- Find a way for this child to try something new even when he feels uncomfortable
- Comment on new things he tries
- Respond to this child's questions
- Work with the child to find answers to his questions
- Read books that answer this child's questions
- Turn questions back to the child
- Ask questions of your own
- Allow this child time to think before expecting an answer to your question or asking another question

Sample actions teachers can take:

- Make room for a number of interest areas
- Be sure your environment appeals to all senses and learning styles
- Ask this child to use a variety of media to show what he has learned
- Offer activities that can be done in more than one way
- Offer open-ended materials, such as blocks and art materials

Sample actions parents can take:

- Let your child take old machines apart and discover what's inside
- Show enthusiasm for things your child learns
- Visit the library and check out reference materials, fiction, nonfiction, and picture books

Information on Curiosity and Questioning

WHAT IS IT?

From very young ages, children are driven to learn about the world around them. They are curious about the people, places, and things they see and experience. Through their explorations, they learn vocabulary, how things work, and whether they can effect changes. This helps them acquire knowledge that they can build on throughout their lifetimes.

When children are curious about something, they become engrossed in their exploration of it. They lean in to get a closer look, focus their attention, show surprise, spontaneously describe what they see, or ask questions about it. Support your child's curiosity by sharing wonder, providing a safe environment, introducing new experiences, and offering ways to delve into things that capture your child's interest.

Observe and Respond

It may look to you as if your child is just playing with an object, but playing engages all of a child's senses in learning about a new material. Encourage your child's sense of wonder by taking walks to listen to sounds you hear or to smell how fresh it is following a spring rain. Go new places together. Make predictions about what you might see before you go. It doesn't matter if your child's predictions prove correct, as long as they build curiosity about the event.

Encourage curiosity by letting your child take apart items you no longer use: an old radio, sewing machine, or tape recorder and screwdriver can stimulate new discoveries (be sure to remove electrical cords). Grab your child's attention by stopping before the end of a book; finish it later. Wonder out loud about things you see, read, or hear. Model your excitement about new things by commenting on a plant breaking through the soil or a spider web strung between two branches in a tree.

If your child tends to choose the same type of toys or materials, encourage other choices. For example, if your child plays with blocks most of the time, expand on this interest by suggesting toy cars, which can drive on roads built from blocks. Keep toys organized so your child can easily find them. Put some toys away for a while. When you bring them out again, your child may have a renewed interest. Learn about new things by reading books. Check out a variety of books from your local library.

Invite but do not force your child to join a new activity. Your participation may encourage your child to try it. Say something like "Let's go listen and see what we can find out" or "Let's go try it and see what this is about."

Around the age of three years, children begin to seek answers to more and more questions. They ask "Why?" about most everything. While the number of questions can sometimes be unsettling, it is good to know that your child is curious about new things. Take the time to respond to these questions; remember that no question is stupid, even when you are tired of answering. If you are in the middle of something and can't take a break, keep a list of questions to answer later. Be sure to come back to your list. If you don't know an answer, find out together—first,

your child can describe the question, and then the two of you can determine how the information can be found. Get answers by looking together for information in books, online, from someone who knows, or by experimenting to discover answers. If you get really stuck, try turning the question back to your child. Ask, "What do you think might happen? Why do you think it would be that way?" Ask questions of your own, such as "How did you learn that? What did you do first? What happened next?" Allow your child time to think before expecting an answer or asking another question.

CONNECTING WITH SUPPORT

If you notice that your child is not very inquisitive, doesn't try new things, or doesn't ask questions about new things or experiences, talk with your child's teacher. Seek additional assistance if your child usually wanders around without becoming occupied by activities other than TV or electronics, shows little interest in nearby people and things, is so fascinated by something that you cannot draw away his or her attention, or is so fearful of trying new things that your child's learning seems to be affected.

"Let's Say I Have Special Powers!" Superhero Play

FOR TEACHERS

I have a few children in my group who only want to play superheroes. Just about every day, I hear Addie say, "Let's say I have a special power that makes me fly."

❖ **Standard**
Tries pretend roles in play.

What Is It?

Children who take on pretend roles during play learn essential social and cognitive skills. They also learn self-regulation skills when they stay within roles and to stick to a script (Maxwell et al. 2009). They learn to think creatively and flexibly when they adopt the costumes, voices, and actions of others; they practice language skills as they describe their actions and participate in conversations. When problems arise, children learn to problem-solve and negotiate through role play. They use their imaginations where they create props or use one item to represent another. These skills are important to how children will approach later learning: their ability to think creatively, cooperate with others, and solve problems in new ways are essential to lifelong learning.

Many girls and boys are drawn to the exciting themes of superhero play. As in other types of pretend play, they learn important skills. During superhero play, they take on pretend roles in order to work out their understandings of good and evil, power and control, and real and pretend. Many are also drawn to superhero play because of the action it entails.

Adults sometimes find superhero play difficult to supervise because it has a tendency to become loud and aggressive and may involve violent themes. Banning it doesn't seem to work; children just learn to deny that they are playing it or to play it when adults are not around (Levin 2003). Playing house or post office lacks the same appeal. When teachers look closely at superhero play and become involved in it, however, they can help children understand some of the concepts, expand the learning that is taking place, and help ensure that this type of exciting play remains safe.

Observe and Decide What to Teach

Keep the following questions in mind when watching the child who is most likely to engage in superhero play. Use these suggestions to effectively guide play while allowing her to try out roles within superhero pretend themes.

Is This Child Drawn to Active, Exciting Play?

Children who tend to be active are often drawn to superhero play because it usually involves running, jumping, hiding, and sneaking around. Help a child who is active meet her need to move in other ways too. Be sure to plan many times each day when she can be involved in gross-motor activities (see chapter 21, "I Can Run, Hop, and Gallop!" Large-Motor Skills). Take frequent, active breaks from activities that require her to sit. Find ways to move during group activities by including large-motor games, dancing to music, and participating in stories. Plan other exciting dramatic play themes, such as dinosaur land, space exploration, treasure hunt, submarine adventures, car racing, or forest fire fighting. Include all aspects of the event so that the dramatic theme involves more than racing cars around a track. Have the children build the racetrack, make and sell tickets, set up a concession stand, include a pit and crew, and create awards to give out to all the participants. This helps children learn to develop a play scenario and expand their play; doing so can be as enticing as superhero play.

Children Learn by Pretending to Be Someone Else

Whether a child is pretending to be a mother, shopkeeper, or superhero, she is engaging in key aspects of pretend play that teach valuable lessons.

When a child takes on a pretend role, she	And learns to
Imitates actions, voice, and dress of others	Take the perspective of another person
Stays in character	Plan behaviors and control impulses
Uses objects to pretend	Use representational thought (employ one item to represent another)
Verbalizes about a play scene	Use language to express thoughts
Persists in play	Maintain attention
Takes turns	Coordinate behavior with others
Solves problems	Be flexible in thinking and negotiate

(Heidemann and Hewitt 2010)

Is This Child Attempting to Understand an Issue through Play?

Children use play to work out their understanding of experiences, including their exposure to violence (Levin 2003). Some preschool children may struggle with their feelings about control and power. A child who is working on these issues may pretend to have powers she wishes she had, such as flying like the tooth fairy, becoming invisible so she can go anywhere she likes, being brave and fearless, being strong enough to take care of herself. By pretending to be a superhero, this child has a chance to experience these powers. Help her explore power and control in safe ways. Suggest that she be powerful by pretending to be the queen of the land, ordering monsters around and ridding her kingdom of monsters. She can tell the monsters, "Out of my land right now!" and they must listen. In addition, allow this child to control the play and story line when you play together. Look for other ways she can be powerful in your setting too. Perhaps she can help to make rules, decide what book to read, or show you her strong muscles when she climbs to the top of the playground equipment.

Another child may use superhero play to conquer fears. Watch this child's play to become familiar with her fears. Then work with her to think of ways she can conquer them. Perhaps she can pretend to be a scientist who develops a formula to free the room of scary bugs. Pretend to mix a potion, put it in an empty plant mister, and spray the room. Suggest she put on a cape that makes her invisible. Then she can get close enough to touch a large scary animal (a toy animal). Or suggest that she is brave enough to fight a dragon (scales torn from construction paper glued onto a dragon drawn on butcher paper) with a rolled-up newspaper sword.

> *A three-year-old boy facing surgery was feeling scared and powerless. He was given the opportunity to bring one toy to the operating room with him. Is it any wonder he chose to bring a toy sword?*

Another child may be trying to learn the difference between real and pretend. Identify these feelings by asking, "Some things seem very real, don't they?" Discuss how actors are so good at pretending that it looks real. Give this child an opportunity to be the actor by acting out favorite stories, such as *Where the Wild Things Are* by Maurice Sendak, *Good Night, Gorilla* by Peggy Rathmann, or *Jack and the Beanstalk* by Steven Kellogg. Use costumes and makeup so this child can see how people can transform themselves into characters. Go online to learn about animation.

Does This Child Repeat Story Lines Over and Over?

In dramatic play, children often start with things they have seen or experienced and then create stories that extend beyond their experiences. Expose children to new adventures so they can expand play by reading books; visiting a zoo, museum, planetarium, or IMAX theater; or participating in cultural celebrations, such as an American Indian powwow or Chinese New Year. Then pack a bag and take an imaginary trip to support what they have been exposed to: visit the land of the dinosaurs, go on a photo safari, climb a jungle gym mountain, explore cardboard box caves with a flashlight, cross a river of hot lava on rope spread on the floor, or build a spaceship to escape the slime monster from Mars.

Help a child who is involved in repetitive superhero play create a new story line and stick to it. While planning the story with her, have her describe the scenario. Help her end the story either peacefully (this way, no one dies) or in a

---

Rules to Consider When Allowing Superhero Play

◆ Everyone needs to be safe.

◆ Stop when others say, "Stop."

◆ Everyone gets a chance to be the good guy. (Some might even make a rule that states, "Children are the good guys. At school bad guys are pretend.")

◆ Superhero play takes place only during free play or outdoors.

way that allows the story to continue another day. Have her draw a picture of her idea, or write it down for her. Talk about the materials she will need, including the props and the costumes. Help her start making what she needs, gathering the materials, and then acting out the role. Bring her back to her plan if she starts to become distracted or wander off (Spiegel 2008).

Some of the exciting play themes children create are related to television programs or movies. Watch the programs that influence their play. When you know the story lines and what the characters are likely to do, you can offer viable suggestions that expand the play. Some children seem fixated on television programs and may imitate television scripts rather than expand on them or create their own. If this is the case with a child you are working with, join the play as one of the characters. Expand her ideas by making suggestions that are closely related to the current play. Be careful not to move the story too far from what she is playing, or she may reject your suggestions. For example, if she is playing that the superhero is fighting crime and you suggest that all the superheroes go to a movie, she probably won't see a connection. But if you pretend that you see the villain entering a movie theater and the superheroes need to follow, she may embrace the idea. If she does, help her set up a movie theater, including chairs, a refreshment stand, ticket taker, and a movie acted out by shadow puppets. Preparing the space, making the props, and developing the movie will require at least forty minutes of rich, imaginative play before she may remember to fight the villain. If one suggestion doesn't work, try another. Help her move her story along by commenting on what you observe and asking open-ended questions.

Is This Child Unable to Create Props or Use Toys in New Ways?

Young preschool children first rely on props that look real. Older preschoolers then substitute something similar looking, and eventually they can use imaginary ones. This ability to use one object to represent another is an important step in developing representational thought. Representational thought makes using symbols to represent something else, such as letters to represent sounds, possible.

When choosing play materials, pick items that allow children to use them in a variety of ways (such as blocks for building and plain cars that can become police cars or family cars). Encourage a child who is using realistic objects, such as plastic food items, to use or make a substitute. Addie's teacher, in the story that opens this chapter, was able to work with Addie to assemble an outfit to wear during times it was okay for her to use her special flying powers. Together they found a leotard, made a cape from a silk scarf, and printed a big *A* on a piece of paper, which they secured to the cape. Addie's teacher put the outfit in a special closet and gave it to Addie only during outdoor play. This helped Addie recognize when it was appropriate to play superheroes. Eventually Addie asked for the outfit less and less often and engaged more and more in other types of exciting play.

Some of the toys marketed for superhero play are realistic and are advertised to encourage children to believe they can be used in only one way. Such advertising leads children to believe that they need more toys to perform other functions. For example, a bath time fashion doll is marketed as the only doll that can go in a tub. If a child wants her bath time doll to exercise, marketers want children to believe she must buy another doll for that purpose. Help a child who is using a toy for a single purpose see how it can be used in many different ways.

Does This Child Use Weapons as Part of Superhero Play?

Many people have strong feelings about allowing children to pretend to use weapons in early childhood settings. Yet it seems that no matter what teachers say, someone fashions a weapon, even when it is made out of toast! If you have strong feelings, be careful about the messages you give to children who have loved ones serving in the military or in the local police department—you do not want to belittle the child's feelings for her real-life hero, her parent, or family members. Instead of banning weapons, redirect this child to eat her toast. Encourage a child who is using weapons to create other props for heroes to use. Can she make a radar detector, walkie-talkie, or trap? Ask, "If you were going to track the monster, what would you need? What could you use? What could you make?" Move the focus from fighting people to cooperative efforts to protect the town against a natural disaster such as a forest fire, hurricane, or a dangerous animal that has escaped from the zoo.

> ### Effective Ways to Respond to Superhero Play
>
> When children are stuck in unproductive superhero play, try one or more of the following ideas:
>
> ◆ Suggest a new scene related to the story
>
> ◆ Search for or make a new prop
>
> ◆ Join the play yourself
>
> ◆ Weave a rest time into the play by describing a quiet activity their characters are likely to engage in
>
> ◆ If you allow children to pretend about weapons, put limits on their use; for example, you might decide that weapons must not be pointed at people or that only weapons made by the children can be used
>
> ◆ Draw play to a close with a logical ending to the story or a smooth transition to the next activity

Does This Child Give Signals That Play Is Getting Out of Control?

Some children become so wrapped up in superhero play that they get lost in the excitement and don't realize they can hurt others. Young children engaged in superhero play need to regulate their behavior, control their impulses, and recognize that a karate kick can hurt someone. If you are working with a child who tends to become overexcited by this type of play, supervise her closely. Tune into her signals that play is becoming too chaotic or that she needs help to resolve a problem. Watch for a louder, higher-pitched voice; more arguments about who will do what; or trouble sharing props. Although many teachers are quick to stop the play or redirect it at this point, what the child probably needs is help learning to accept changes in play and to solve problems. Help her learn problem solving by identifying the problem, thinking of ways it can be worked out, deciding on the best solution, and then trying it out. If that idea doesn't work, try another. If the child you are working with is frequently aggressive, see chapter 9, "Whack!" Aggression, for additional ideas.

If you must draw superhero play to a close, do so by ending the story logically. Say, "After trying to find the bad guys all day, the superheroes are very sleepy; let's let them sleep for a while and choose something quiet to do." Have water, sand, or playdough available as calming activities. If needed, have children who have been playing together take a break from cooperative play and play side by side or alone for a while.

It may be helpful to let a child meet her need for exciting play by using action figures for a time instead of physically acting out superhero play. A child can use characters from Lego blocks sets or even wooden figurines. Give her materials to make capes, crowns, or armor out of construction paper. Add other props, such as a cardboard box turned into a mountain or a toy car.

Balance the violence a child may be exposed to with discussions about cooperating and helping others. During superhero play, say, "It seems like the superheroes only know how to solve problems by fighting. What else could they do?" Talk about what superheroes have in common. Discuss real-life superheroes. Describe the characteristics heroes have in common, such as courage and being helpful to others. Point out times when a child is courageous or helpful.

Work with the Parents

Remember: the standard a child is working to reach is to try pretend roles. Be sure to recognize what the child is learning through superhero play as well as the concerns you may have. If the child's play seems stuck in imitating television or is excessively violent, talk with the parents about limiting the amount of violent programming to which their child is exposed. It is unlikely that families who view these programs will eliminate this type of television altogether. However, if there is one particular program that is problematic, perhaps they will be willing to turn it off.

Describe some of the different themes this child has enjoyed in your setting that still allow her to feel powerful. Include some of the creative scenarios the child has developed. Parents may be able to extend this type of play at home. Use the Plan for Action to discuss how to proceed in working with this child.

When to Seek Assistance

If play remains repetitive over a number of months despite your continued efforts to expand it, talk with an early childhood consultant about ways to work with this child. If play is excessively gruesome or violent, especially if the child resists involvement in other types of play, refer the family to a parent educator or counselor who specializes in working with young children.

A Plan for Action

To develop your Plan for Action, choose or modify one of the suggested goals to best match your situation. Add how well or how often you expect the skill or behavior to be demonstrated. Remember: you are looking for growth, not perfection. You want to move the child from where she is currently and to increase your expectations slightly. Next, determine three or four actions teachers and parents will take. Choose additional actions specific to the early childhood setting and the home. Record your choices on the planning form found in the appendix.

Sample goals for a child who plays superhero themes excessively:

- Tries exciting pretend roles other than superhero
- Expands play beyond imitation of television shows
- Creates new story lines
- Creates her own props
- Engages in quiet activity when superhero play is drawn to a close

Sample actions parents and teachers can take:

- Offer gross-motor activities
- Offer exciting play themes
- Visit museums, planetariums, zoos, and cultural celebrations
- Offer open-ended toys and materials
- Have calming activities available
- Recognize and comment favorably on times this child is being strong outside of superhero play
- Allow this child to help set rules and make choices
- Become familiar with television shows influencing play
- Identify feelings that are enacted during superhero play
- Have costumes and materials for props available
- Join the play and help direct it
- Make suggestions that expand this child's play
- Encourage this child to make her own props
- Encourage this child to use a toy in more than one way
- Step in and redirect play before it escalates out of control
- Provide a logical end to the story to end this play
- Practice problem solving when needed
- Introduce play themes that are not related to television

Sample actions teachers can take:

- Give opportunities to move by making group time highly participatory
- Act out favorite stories
- Have children play side by side for a short time after superhero play has disintegrated
- Teach about peacemaking and cooperating
- Plan cooperative learning activities
- Talk with an early childhood consultant; share pertinent information with the parents

Sample actions parents can take:

- Limit the amount of superhero television your child watches

- Read books about other things

- Talk with a parent educator or counselor if play is excessively gruesome or violent; share pertinent information with your child's teacher

Information on Superhero Play

WHAT IS IT?

Many children are drawn to the fast action of superhero play. Whether they are pretending to be parents, shopkeepers, or superheroes, they are learning to take on pretend roles, play with others, sequence a story, and negotiate how play will continue. In superhero play, children work on their understandings of good and evil, power and control, and real and pretend. Adults are sometimes opposed to superhero play because it tends to become loud and may involve violent themes. Banning it doesn't seem to work. Redirecting children to play house lacks excitement.

Observe and Respond

Look closely at your child's superhero play and become involved in it. Then help your child be creative while keeping a lid on this type of powerful play. Children who are active tend to be drawn to superhero play because it usually involves running, hiding, and sneaking around. A child who is active can meet these physical needs in other ways too. Be sure to plan many times per day when your child can play outside or be active indoors.

Some children pretend to have powers they wish they had, such as being brave or strong enough to take care of themselves. Your child can feel powerful by controlling the story line when you play together or showing off strength by climbing to the top of playground equipment.

In dramatic play, children often start by imitating things they have seen or experienced and then creating stories that go beyond. Expose your child to new adventures by reading books or visiting a zoo or museum. Then take an imaginary trip to the land of the dinosaurs, go on a photo safari, climb a jungle gym mountain, explore cardboard box caves with a flashlight, or cross a river of hot lava on rope spread on the floor. Help your child plan a story line. Talk about what materials you'll need, including props and costumes. Help your child get started making props, finding a costume, and then acting out the role.

Some people have strong feelings about allowing children to pretend to use weapons. But no matter what adults say, a child will fashion a weapon—even if it is made from toast! Encourage your child to create other, more creative props. Incredible gadgets like those used by Spy Kids can easily be made. Ask, "If you were going to track an animal that escaped from the zoo, what would you need? What could you make?"

Some children imitate television scripts rather than create their own stories. When this is the case, join the play and expand your child's ideas by making suggestions that are closely related to the ongoing story. If your child is pretending to be a superhero who fights crime and you suggest instead that he or she pretend to go to a movie, your child probably won't see a connection. But if you pretend that you see the villain enter a movie theater and the superhero should follow, your child may embrace the idea. If you must draw superhero play to a close, do so by ending the story logically. Say, "The superhero has been trying to find the bad guys all day, and now she is very sleepy; let her sleep for a while and choose something quiet to do." Direct your child toward a calming activity like playdough.

If your child tends to become overexcited during superhero play, supervise closely. Tune in to signals that play is getting too chaotic or that your child needs help to resolve a problem. Watch for louder voices, more arguments, or trouble sharing props. Help your child learn to solve problems.

If your child's play only imitates television or is excessively violent, limit viewing of violent programming. Perhaps there is one particular program that is problematic and should be turned off.

CONNECTING WITH SUPPORT

If play is repetitive, excessively gruesome, or violent, or if your child resists involvement in other types of play, talk to a parent educator or counselor who specializes in working with young children.

Part 4

Language and Literacy Development

Skills developed in the language and literacy domain allow children to communicate effectively with others. During the preschool years, language skills grow rapidly. In this domain, children learn to listen to and understand what others say as well as learn to speak so that others can understand them. Both listening and speaking skills are learned through interactions with others.

From birth, children listen to and try to repeat the words they hear. The sounds they make start to sound more and more like the ones they are trying to say. They learn that spoken words can be written and that written words can be read. When they see others read and write, they learn that these activities have value. Most children are motivated to communicate in these ways, and by the time they enter kindergarten, they demonstrate emerging reading and writing skills. These foundational skills lead to reading and writing.

In an early childhood setting, children need many opportunities to practice their growing language and literacy skills. They do best when teachers talk with them about their interests and help extend their sentences or explain their own thinking. Children benefit from print-rich environments that include fiction, nonfiction, and wordless picture books. They do well in settings where there are signs and labels, flannel boards, computers, magnetic letters, and song charts. They need writing centers filled with writing tools and writing materials available in all areas of the room so that they can draw pictures of their buildings or write down the number to order a pretend pizza.

At home, children need family members who talk with them from birth, introduce them to new words, and describe their actions. They learn new words when they go places that allow them to experience new things and then discuss their experiences with others. They find the words to express their feelings when adult family members support their developing emotional control. They do best when adults break directions into small parts and provide them with only one or two tasks at a time. Adult family members can help children focus and patiently remind them of directions when they don't listen the first time. Children discover the print around them when people point out signs, write notes to others, or make lists. When adults and older children read books or tell stories, younger children learn vocabulary. When they read books together, children learn how to handle books carefully, and develop a love for reading.

As in all the domains, states may have more standards than those included in this book. Four standards used by many states are included in part 4, Language and Literacy Development. Each standard has one chapter that discusses it in detail. The four standards are

- Uses language to communicate ideas, feelings, and experiences, chapter 13

- Follows simple oral directions, chapter 14

- Shows interest in beginning to read, chapter 15

- Shows interest in beginning to write, chapter 16

In the spring, many of the children in Ms. Carlson's preschool class began to ask questions about going to kindergarten. Ms. Carlson thought she might help prepare them and alleviate some of their fears by doing a class project about going to kindergarten. At group time one day, she mentioned that the children seemed to have some questions about kindergarten. She wondered out loud how they could get some answers. The children offered suggestions like "Read a book," "Ask someone," and "Go see it." She decided to arrange just that.

The first day of the project, she gathered the children and asked what they wanted to know about kindergarten. She wrote the questions on chart paper as the children asked them. They asked questions like "Do you take the bus?" "Do you take a nap?" "Is the teacher nice?" "Do you get to play?" After group time, she transferred each question to a large index card. The next day, she explained to the children that in a few days they were going to have some kindergarten children come to the class to answer the questions they had written. She read the list of questions and asked for a volunteer to read each question to their guest. On the third day, they practiced reading their questions out loud. She encouraged the readers to speak loudly enough to be heard, speak clearly, and wait for an answer. The following day, Ms. Carlson invited three of her preschool graduates to come from their kindergarten class to answer the questions. These kindergartners were eager to offer their expertise. The discussion was a success, with the preschoolers reading their questions and the kindergartners answering proudly.

The next day, Ms. Carlson explained to the children that they were going to a kindergarten class to see what it looked like. They would need to be quiet when they toured the class so the kindergarten children could still do their work. They would take notes and talk about it when they got back to their own classroom. She gave them each a clipboard and pencil and asked them to practice taking notes by writing what they saw in their own classroom. The children busily drew parts of the preschool classroom.

Finally, the day came when they went to the kindergarten room. The preschoolers visited in small groups. They took their clipboards and pencils and spent a few minutes wandering in the kindergarten room while drawing pictures or using invented spelling to represent what they saw. When the children returned to their preschool room, they chatted excitedly about what they had seen. One child drew the rooster puppet he saw on top of the cupboards, another drew the paints at the easel, and one copied her friend's name when she saw it in a pocket chart.

Although she had never tried a project of this sort before, Ms. Carlson recognized that through this activity, the children practiced a number of early learning standards, including the following:

- *Follows simple oral directions*
- *Uses language to communicate ideas, feelings, and experiences*
- *Shows interest in beginning to read*
- *Shows interest in beginning to write*

Mrs. Carlson found the project highly motivating for the children in her group. She also found there was an added benefit in the connection she made to the kindergarten staff in the building.

You can use this same project approach on any topic that interests the children in your group.

Supporting Dual-Language Learners

Many young children live in homes in which a language other than English is being spoken or more than one language is being spoken. Learning a language is complex, and children's capacity to learn more than one language is inspiring. Some children learn two or more languages at the same time. They are exposed to the languages at very early ages and can keep their languages separate. Other children learn a second language after they have a foundation in a home language. In the United States, this usually means a child uses what he knows about his home language to learn English.

Children learn the foundations of language and communication in the context of their family and culture. It is important that children learning English maintain their home language. A child learning a second language builds on what he already knows about his home language; he is not starting to learn about his second language from scratch. A child who can speak the same language as extended family members can engage in rich conversations about values, history, and dreams with others who may not possess expansive English vocabularies.

For many dual-language learners, early childhood settings are the place where they first become exposed to English. Many children are highly motivated to learn English when they attend early childhood programs so that they can play with their peers and be part of the activities. Play encourages children to learn new words and try some of their new vocabulary. Dual-language learners acquire English in a fairly predictable pattern, although they go through the stages at individual rates:

1. Uses home language.

2. Is nonverbal or silent.

3. Uses individual words and short phrases in new language.

4. Uses new language productively.

(Tabors 1997, 39)

For dual-language learners, the standards presented in this book can be considered guidelines rather than firm expectations. It will take time for them to acquire social language skills and can take four or more years to learn the academic language needed for school (NAEYC 1995). To become skilled in one or more languages, children need extended language experiences in the languages they are learning. Parents and teachers can do many things to support the language development of dual-language learners.

What parents and teachers can do:

- ◆ Recognize the value of the home language
- ◆ Understand the stages of dual-language acquisition
- ◆ Provide a language-rich environment in the language you know best
- ◆ Teach vocabulary by labeling objects and describing actions
- ◆ Expand on the child's language with more complex phrases

What teachers can do:

- ◆ Learn a song or rhyme in the child's home language
- ◆ Ask the parents to teach you how to greet the child and speak some common words in his home language
- ◆ Add cues, such as pictures, objects, gestures, props, and routines, to help the child understand what is being said to him
- ◆ Recognize the effort it takes to participate in a setting that uses a language other than the one with which you are most comfortable; allow the child to take breaks from talking and listening at times
- ◆ Label objects in your setting in both languages
- ◆ Have books on tape in the child's home language
- ◆ Play songs sung in the child's home language
- ◆ Avoid correcting the child when he makes mistakes; instead, model the correct way by rephrasing what he has said

- Ask the parents to teach concepts at home that you are working on in the classroom so this child can develop deeper understanding, such as labeling his emotions and the emotions of others

- Locate and use interpreters and translators if the parents are not able to communicate in the same language you use

- Assist this child in joining play so he can practice his language skills in this nonthreatening situation

- Use authentic assessment so this child can demonstrate proficiencies in ways that are not dependent on language (for example, this child initiates play with others using gestures and props)

- Use parent information as a source of data in assessing skill development (for example, "How high can your child count in your home language?")

What parents can do:

- Talk, sing, read, and tell stories to your child in the language that feels most comfortable to you

- Encourage your home language by watching movies and listening to songs sung in your home language

- Visit extended family members and friends who use your home language

- Talk on the phone and let your child talk with others who use your home language

- Encourage your child to use his home language whenever he talks to you; if he doesn't, repeat what he says in English using your home language

People are sometimes concerned when a child is not using "the new" language during the silent phase. At this stage of dual-language development, the child has discovered that the language used at home does not help him in this new setting. He is not yet comfortable enough with his new language skills to risk using words. Usually the child is silent only in a setting where he is not skilled in the language being used. Often it lasts between a few weeks and a couple of months.

People also may become concerned when a child mixes languages and uses a few words of one language in a sentence made up primarily of the other. People sometimes think this is a sign that the child is confusing the languages. Instead, it demonstrates that the child is learning both languages well. He may recognize that there isn't a word in one language that fully explains the concept in the other.

Occasionally a child who is learning English does not pronounce words as a native English speaker would. This can cause people to wonder if he has a language delay or a speech problem. If you are concerned, talk with this child's parents to determine if his speech is developing clearly in his home language. Consider how well he is understood when talking to other native language speakers. For example, you might ask, "How much can his grandma understand of what he says?" or "How well is he understood when he is playing with other children who speak the same language?" Children having problems in their home language or in both languages should be referred for speech and language evaluation.

13 "It's My Turn to Talk!" Speaking

FOR TEACHERS

I can understand Mason most of the time, but others who come into our room seem to have trouble. At times, I need to play by him to help the other children understand what he is saying.

❖ **Standard**

Uses language to communicate ideas, feelings, and experiences.

What Is It?

Children begin to communicate from the time they are born. They cry when they are hungry, tired, or need to be changed. Through interactions with family members, they hear the words of the language spoken in their home and begin to understand that words have meaning. They learn that words fit together to express needs or tell stories. Learning to speak involves listening, comprehension, attention, memory, word knowledge, and grammar. These are the foundational skills for later reading and writing (Decker 2011).

Observe and Decide What to Teach

Keep the following questions in mind when listening to a child talk. Use the suggestions to help a child learn to use language in a variety of ways.

Does This Child Have a Limited Vocabulary?

Children learn an unbelievable number of words when the people around them talk, sing, and read to them. Children as young as three years old may have a vocabulary of about one thousand words (Child Development Institute 2011). If a child you are working with does not have a large vocabulary, help expand the number of words he knows by introducing him to new experiences, labeling objects, and describing actions. Take field trips, when possible, to a corner grocery store, farmers' market, or nearby service station. Talk about the hoist that lifts the car, the wrenches used to change a tire, and the drip pan that catches the oil.

Use self-talk to describe your actions when you sit by this child and paint a picture. Or use parallel talk when you sit by this child and describe what he is doing. Say, "I see you are mixing the red and blue paint. Red and blue mixed together made purple!" Play with him in dramatic play theme areas; talk with and listen to him. Expand this child's single words or short phrases into sentences. In a pretend bakery, he can order "Cookies and doughnuts." Pretend to be a customer too. Say, "Yes, I would like to buy three cookies and a chocolate cake." Strive for five back-and-forth turns in your conversations. Ask open-ended questions to encourage him to use more than one-word responses. Read books in which words are repeated or explained through context.

Do Adults Who Don't Know the Child Misunderstand This Child's Speech?

It takes time for children to perfect the sounds of the English language. Some of the more challenging sounds to produce include: *l, s, r, v, z, y, ch, sh,* and *th* (NIDCD 2000). Usually by the time a child is four years old, his speech is understood by both those who know him and by unfamiliar adults. If a child is mispronouncing words, it is not necessary to correct his speech. Instead, paraphrase what he says using the correct articulation. For example, if a child says, "I have a tat at my house," you can say, "You have a cat at your house! What is its name?"

If you are working with dual-language learners, be sure to learn about second-language acquisition. Children who are dual-language learners are likely to mispronounce words as they learn. Give them plenty of opportunities to hear the new language pronounced correctly. As they practice, they are likely to make closer approximations to the correct pronunciation. Give them breaks from speaking at times. Honor quiet times in which the children can take a break from the pressure of listening to a new language or being asked to respond.

A child who does not articulate clearly may need you to play with him to help others understand what he says. One day, Mason, from the story that opened this chapter, had been frustrated and had stomped out of the block area. His teacher went to him and encouraged him to try again. This time she stayed with him and repeated what he had said: "Mason says, 'Let's build a ramp for a skateboard park.'" Once they understood, the other children said it was a great idea, started searching for the blocks they needed, and talked about how high they were going to make the ramp.

In addition to pronouncing words correctly, children need to catch on to the subtleties of language production. One of these subtleties is using the correct volume for the situation. Teach a child who is always speaking at the top of his voice to modulate his volume of speech. Change your voice and your tone to match those of a character in a story or a puppet in a puppet play. Teach this child to be as quiet as a mouse or to be careful not to wake a pretend baby sleeping in the housekeeping area. Whisper your response to him as a cue to help him bring his own volume down. Teach the appropriate volume for indoor and outdoor spaces.

At times, a child's speech may not be fluent. He may pause, hesitate, or repeat himself. Stuttering will typically first appear in children who are two to five years old (Bernstein 2011). Try not to draw attention to a child's stuttering. Listen attentively. Be patient and give the child time to say what he is thinking. Avoid asking him to slow down.

Is This Child Unable to Use Language for Different Purposes?

Language is used for many reasons, including making requests, asking questions, expressing emotions, making needs known, describing experiences, and providing information. Children need to be encouraged to engage in all types of expressive language. Pretend play is a time when children are highly motivated to use language. In play, they use words to create a scene, agree on what to do next, and take on pretend roles. When a child is pretending to be a mother, you may hear her direct another child using a high-pitched voice to say, "Dear, will you please get the baby ready for bed?"

Besides pretend play, a child who is not using language in a range of ways can be encouraged to sing songs, recite nursery rhymes, and do fingerplays. Ask open-ended questions as part of storytelling or when reading a book. You can ask, "What do you think he was feeling?" or "Why do you think he did that?" Use all of the "wh" questions: who, what, where, when, and why. Model appropriate greetings when people arrive in your setting. Teach a child to ask for help. He can say, "Would you help me . . ." or "I'm having trouble with . . ."

Encourage a child to use words to describe how he is feeling. Teach a variety of feeling words like *angry, frustrated*, and *upset* to express his level of intensity. Show pictures of people with different emotions; ask him to label each feeling. Tune in to sounds that indicate emotions. Point out the sounds of someone laughing, singing, or yelling. Talk about the feelings suggested. Describe physical reactions someone may have when they feel angry or happy. For example, demonstrate how a person may clench his fist, purse his lips, and furrow his brow. Have the child imitate you. Give the child words to use to express his emotions when he feels this way.

Does This Child Only Use Single Words or Short Phrases?

Children begin to string words together to make phrases at a very young age. By the time a child is five years old, he may be able to put eight or more words into sentences (NIDCD 2000). You can help a child expand his sentences by talking to and listening to him frequently. Model the use of complex sentences. Expand his single words or short phrases into lengthier sentences. Add information, explanations, and descriptions to what he says. For example, if he points and says, "More, please." You can say, "Please pass the bowl of peas; they are so good!"

Find many ways to encourage this child to talk throughout the day. Ask him to describe your routines, saying, "What are the steps we do to get ready for snack?" Place an object in a feely box (an oatmeal container with the sole of a tube sock covering the container and the ribbing extending outside the container to provide a sleeve for the child to stick his hand into). Ask him to reach inside and describe what he feels. Take pictures of activities going on in your setting. Ask him to dictate what is taking place. Prompt further description by asking, "What else do you see?" or "What else is going on?" Involve him in group storytelling. Start a story and ask each child in the group to add something. For example, you might say,

"Once upon a time, there was a purple and orange monster who . . ." Let this child finish the sentence. Or cut out a magazine picture and paste it on paper. Have the child draw a background and dictate a story about it.

Is This Child Unable to Engage in Conversation?

Taking part in conversation sometimes involves initiating, while at other times it means responding to someone else's comments. Conversations involve taking turns and listening without interrupting. Children need to learn to add their own thoughts while staying on topic.

When a child has difficulty engaging in conversation, use active listening when you talk with him. To do this, paraphrase what he says. Ask open-ended questions to encourage further conversation. For example, you might ask, "What happened next?" or "What did you do?" Use routines like mealtimes to engage in conversation. Talk about what he is interested in, but have a topic in mind that can spark discussion if he is not very talkative. Possible topics include family pets, trips to the grocery store, siblings, or favorite games he plays. Encourage him to tell you about things that happen outside of your setting as a way for him to practice describing personal experiences.

Teach a child who interrupts to watch for the cues that let him know when it is his turn. Do a role play in which two people engage in conversation and a third person wants to say something. Demonstrate how to put one hand on the speaker's shoulder or arm, and then wait for a turn to talk. Teach this child to recognize when the speaker takes a breath or when there is a pause. Teach him to say, "Excuse me" and wait for a response.

Work with the Parents

Encourage parents to talk with their child frequently and to really listen when he speaks to them. Describe opportunities for conversation that occur naturally during busy days. Involving a child in household chores and using travel time for conversation are two examples. If you or a parent is concerned about a child's language development, work together using the suggestions above and the Plan for Action. After a few

---

When to Seek Assistance

If the child is a dual-language learner, you may find it challenging to determine when articulation errors are matters for concern. Usually articulation errors require further investigation if the child is not understood in his home language by unfamiliar adults who are native speakers. If the child demonstrates any of the following signs in his home language, it is important to seek additional help:

- The child is not easily understood most of the time by three years of age

- The child is not using short (two- or three-word) sentences to communicate by three years of age

- The child's speech is not understandable by unfamiliar adults by four years of age

- The child does not speak sentences that sound almost adultlike by four years of age
(Koralek, Dombro, and Dodge 2005)

If a child is demonstrating any of these patterns, ask his parents to have his skills screened. Start with the child's pediatrician, who is likely to examine records for ear infections and hearing screenings. Ask for a speech and language evaluation. Screening can also be done by the school district in which the child lives. Early recognition and intervention can help this child become better prepared to enter kindergarten ready to succeed.

months of concerted effort at increasing a child's skill level, consider whether it is time to get outside assistance.

A Plan for Action

To develop your Plan for Action, choose or modify one of the suggested goals to best match your situation. Add how well or how often you expect the skill or behavior to be demonstrated. Remember: you are looking for growth, not perfection. You want to move the child from where he is currently and to increase your expectations slightly. Next, determine three or four actions teachers and parents will take. The suggestions listed are appropriate for both teachers and parents. Record your choices on the planning form found in the appendix.

Sample goals for a child who would benefit from additional speaking skills:

- Increases his vocabulary

- Child is understood by others ____ percent of the time

- Uses language to _____ (*Choose from the following and focus on one at a time: ask questions, answer questions, ask for something he needs, express emotions, tell an experience, or provide information.*)

- Uses ____ words in a sentence

- Takes part in conversations

Sample actions parents and teachers can take:

- Introduce the child to new experiences

- Label objects and describe actions

- Describe your actions as you work and play with the child

- Expand on the child's single words and short phrases

- Strive for five back-and-forth turns in conversation

- Paraphrase what the child says, using the correct articulation

- Teach loud and quiet

- Whisper your responses if the child is talking too loudly

- Listen attentively to what the child is saying

- Give the child time to say what he is thinking

- Allow time for play

- Sing songs, recite nursery rhymes, and do fingerplays

- Ask open-ended questions

- Ask "wh" questions: who, what, where, when, and why

- Model appropriate greetings

- Teach the child to ask for help
- Teach the child a variety of feeling words
- Give the child words to use for expressing his emotions
- Model the use of complex sentences
- Expand the child's single words or short phrases into lengthier sentences
- Ask the child to describe routines
- Play guessing games
- Ask the child to describe what he sees in pictures
- Tell a story together
- Use active listening to increase your understanding
- Talk about what the child is interested in
- Teach the child to watch for the cues that let him know when it is his turn to talk
- Teach the child to say, "Excuse me," and wait for a response
- Use routine times to converse with the child

Information on Speaking

WHAT IS IT?

Children begin to communicate from the time they are born. They cry when they are hungry, tired, or need to be changed. Through interactions with family members, they hear the language spoken in their home and begin to understand that words have meaning. Learning to speak involves listening, comprehension, attention, memory, word knowledge, and grammar.

Observe and Respond

Children as young as three years old may have a speaking vocabulary of about one thousand words when people talk, sing, and read to them. You can help increase your child's vocabulary by introducing your child to new experiences. Talk about your experiences. When you are together, describe what you are doing by saying, "I'm going to stir this gravy until all the lumps are gone." Or describe what your child is doing. You can also sing songs and say nursery rhymes. Ask questions that call for more than one-word responses. Instead of asking, "Did you like the movie?" ask, "What was your favorite part of the movie?" Ask all the "wh" questions: who, what, where, when, and why. Encourage your child to use descriptive words like *angry*, *frustrated*, and *upset* to describe feelings.

Expand your child's single words into short phrases or sentences during pretend play. If your child is pretending to order at a restaurant and says, "Pizza," repeat the word but add to it. Say, "Yes, I would like a small thin-crust pizza with sausage and mushrooms, please."

Find ways to include your child in household chores and routines. Use these chances to talk as well as to accomplish some of what you need to get done. You can build vocabulary through everyday activities like cooking together. When you cook you can say: *stir*, *whisk*, *mix*, *measure*, *spread*, and *taste*. Play guessing games while you work. Ask your child to describe something to you. Try to guess what it is. Stop what you are doing when your child initiates a conversation with you. Get down to eye level, paraphrase what your child has said, and then ask, "What happened next?" or "What did you do?"

Help your child build lengthy sentences by taking pictures of things you do together.

When you look at them together, ask your child what was taking place. Solicit more detail by asking, "What else is going on?" Involve your child in storytelling. Start a story and then stop. You can say, "Once upon a time there was a purple and orange monster who . . ." Let your child finish the sentence.

It takes time for children to perfect the sounds of the English language. Some of the more challenging sounds for children to produce include *l*, *s*, *r*, *v*, *z*, *y*, *ch*, *sh*, and *th*. Usually by the time children are four years old, their speech is understood by those who know them and by unfamiliar adults. If your child mispronounces words, it is not necessary to draw attention to the error. Instead, repeat the words using the correct pronunciation.

At times, your child may pause, hesitate, or repeat words. Stuttering usually first appears in children two to five years old. Listen attentively, be patient, and avoid asking your child to slow down. Give your child time.

CONNECTING WITH SUPPORT

Talk with your child's teacher if you are concerned about problems with articulation. Further investigation is usually needed if a four-year-old child is not understood in his home language by people he doesn't know but who are native speakers. If your child demonstrates any of the following problems in your home language, it is important to seek assistance from your primary health care provider or screening through your school district. If your child

- Is not easily understood most of the time by three years of age

- Is not using short (two- or three-word) sentences to communicate by three years of age

- Is not understandable by unfamiliar adults by four years of age

- Is not speaking sentences that sound almost adultlike by four years of age

Early recognition and intervention can help your child become better prepared for entering kindergarten ready to succeed.

"I'm Not Listening!" Following Directions and Power Struggles

FOR TEACHERS

Autumn tries hard to please me, but she never seems to be able to follow directions. If I tell her to go get her shoes, put them on, and wait for me to tie them, she is likely to bring me her shoes instead of doing what I asked.

I have to be really careful about the way I phrase things when I talk to Isabel. If she doesn't want to do what I have asked, we really have a battle on our hands. I don't think I should give in after I ask her to do something.

❖ Standard
Follows simple oral directions.

What Is It?

Following directions isn't easy for young children. Doing so requires them to focus their attention, remember, and do what is asked. To help children learn this skill, teachers must encourage them to listen as well as to cooperate. You can help a child learn to follow directions by tuning in to her preferred learning style. A child who is auditory will need you to tell her what you want; a visual learner will do best when you show her; a kinesthetic learner will want you to let her try. To help a child learn to follow directions, you will also need to determine if she has heard what to do, if she knows how to do it, and if she is choosing not to comply.

Sometimes a child understands the directions and knows what to do but chooses not to do it. In part, this can be due to a child's need to develop independence. During the preschool years, children strive to do things for themselves, express themselves, and make their own decisions. Sometimes in their attempts to be independent, children resist following directions given by an adult. This resistance can escalate into a power struggle when an adult insists and a child continues to refuse. Teachers need to recognize the signs that a power struggle may be looming, learn ways to avoid it, and instead find ways to help a child cooperate. Adults working with young children must balance supporting children while they develop independence with encouraging cooperation.

Observe and Decide What to Teach

Watch a child who has difficulty following your directions or directions given by others. After you observe, consider the suggestions provided. Then develop a plan for teaching her to cooperate and follow directions. When you pinpoint what a child needs to learn, you can help her learn to follow simple oral directions.

> **Attention Grabber**
>
> One way to gain the attention of a group of children before giving directions is to play the game "If You Hear Me, Go Like This." Using a normal speaking volume, chant, "If you hear me, go like this," while rhythmically slapping your thighs. Then repeat, "If you hear me, go like this," this time rhythmically clapping. Repeat the chant, but switch to snapping your fingers or tapping your shoulders. Continue until all of the children copy your actions.

Does This Child Pay Attention to Directions?

Early childhood settings offer many distractions and temptations that compete for a child's attention. When you give a child directions, help her focus her attention before you begin. Use a signal to get her to look at you, say her name, clap a rhythm, or tap her on the shoulder. Move close to her and establish eye contact. Ask her to stop what she is doing. Reduce competing noise by turning off music or asking the group to be quiet before you proceed. Be sure to give this child time to think about what you have asked before expecting her to respond.

Does This Child Forget Your Directions?

Sometimes children have difficulty remembering things they hear. They tend to remember only the first or the last in a sequence of commands. Autumn, in the example that opens this chapter, was only able to remember the first in a string of directions made by her teacher. Help a child like Autumn be more successful by using the KISS principle: KISS stands for Keep It Short and Simple. Simplify directions. Provide only one step at a time. When a child can consistently complete one-step directions, add a second step. Aim to build up to three steps by the time she enters kindergarten.

Help a child remember directions by asking her to repeat them back to you. Or give three or four children in your group the directions and ask them to tell a friend. Each child tells a friend, who follow the directions, until all the children in the group have heard them. Repeating a direction helps to ensure that the child has heard it and helps her commit it to memory. Help her practice remembering what she hears and the order in which she heard it by asking her to retell a familiar story, such as *Goldilocks and the Three Bears*. Read a humorous story together about remembering directions, such as *Don't Forget the Bacon!* by Pat Hutchins or *Froggy Gets Dressed* by Jonathan London.

Does This Child Need Extra Help Doing What Is Being Asked of Her?

If children are unsure of themselves, they may not do as asked. They may also hesitate, watch others for clues about what to do, or walk away from a job that seems overwhelming. Be sure that children for whom English is their second language understand what is being asked of them. Use pictures, simplified language, and gestures to increase their understanding. Whether you are working with a child who is a native English speaker or a dual-language learner, if she is having difficulty, be sure to give directions that are clear and concise. Focus on telling her what to do rather than what not to do. Avoid vague instructions. Use understandable terms. For example, if you say, "Watch out!" you don't give a child much information about what to watch for. Instead, say something like "Your cup is tipping. Use two hands to hold it straight." Give your direction as a statement. Be careful not to ask a question or add "Okay?" to a direction that a child must follow. If you state it as a question, she may think she has a choice. For example, if you say, "Are you ready for cleanup?" the likely response is "No." What you really mean is "Please clean up now."

Be sure a child knows how to do what you request. Teach her the steps involved in cleaning the block area. For example, first you pick up a block, carry it to the shelf, find where it belongs, and place it there. Keep working until all the blocks are off the floor and any other toys are where they belong. It may be necessary to ask a child to do only one or two steps at first. Help her succeed by pasting a picture of the toy on the container in which it belongs. Place a second picture of the toy on the shelf where the container belongs. You can even post a photograph at the entrance to the center showing the area when it is clean, so the child knows how it should look.

Provide direction to match a child's learning style. For a child who is visual, demonstrate or provide picture cues of what needs to be done. Give verbal directions for a child who learns best by hearing things; a child who is kinesthetic needs to try out what must be done. If you give a verbal direction and she does not respond, wait for a moment to allow her to think about what you have said. Then restate the direction in a slightly different way to make sure she understands. If this is not enough to get her started, offer support at the level she needs. For example, you can offer hand-over-hand support, verbal directions with gestures, or verbal directions for every step. Compliment her attempts so she will feel encouraged to follow directions in the future. You can say, "I see you are putting all the square blocks where they go. You are really helping clean our room."

Practice following directions by playing games using songs like the "Hokey Pokey" or "Tooty Ta" from *Dr. Jean & Friends* by Dr. Jean Feldman. Provide the child with action cards to follow, such as a picture of someone turning around, closing her eyes, or jumping. Practice following directions with puppets. Have the child put a puppet on her hand. Tell the puppet to put a block in the box or hand you the crayon. Make cleaning up a game by asking a child to pick up only the blue blocks, then all the red ones; finishing cleaning up before the end of the song; or putting on mittens before cleaning up.

Is This Child Unable to Follow Two- or Three-Step Directions?

By the time children are entering kindergarten, most can follow simple three-part directions. As you build toward this goal, help this child practice following directions in games. Play games like Simon Says, Captain, May I? and Do What I Do. To play Do What I Do, the leader says, "Do what I do," then demonstrates two or three actions in a row for the others to imitate. For example, the leader might jump, clap, and then turn around before a child (or group) copies her. Create a treasure hunt for a child to follow. Give her directions like "Get the red block and put it in the closet." When she opens the closet door, she finds a sticker or other simple prize. Ask her to echo you as you clap various rhythms. Give her directions as part of play. In the housekeeping area, you can ask her to get a bowl, put some cereal in it, and give it to the baby doll. Give her extra practice in sequencing by asking her to use flannel board pieces to retell a simple story or to sequence simple pictures to tell a story.

Does This Child Choose Not to Follow Directions without Thinking?

Toddlers and some young preschool children automatically say no to all types of adult requests. For example, if you ask a young child if she wants milk, she may answer, "No," then become upset when you don't give her any. Understand that when a child says, "No," frequently, she may not mean it. Make requests more concrete by showing the milk container while asking her preference. Ask questions and give directions in a way that cannot be answered with a simple yes or no. Say, "How much milk do you want?"

Some children say, "No," in imitation of those around them. If a child is imitating things she hears, avoid modeling "No!" by substituting "Stop" when you must keep her from doing something. Arrange your play space so she can safely explore without hearing, "No, don't touch that." Find ways to say yes to her. You can say, "Yes, when the toys are cleaned up" or "Yes, you may, after you're done." When you must insist on a direction, briefly explain why. Say something like "I don't want you to run inside, because you might fall and hurt yourself."

One evening at an Early Childhood Family Education class, it was almost time for snack when a terrible noise came from the direction of the tables. Devon had overturned Jesse, chair and all. When the children's teacher investigated, Devon simply stated that he wanted that chair. (He always sat at that table, in that chair.) His teacher explained that someone else was sitting there. Then she pointed out the only other chair still available. Devon refused the other chair, stating, "But my mom said I could sit there." The teacher explained that if he did not sit down, he would miss snack. Then she turned her attention to the other children and ignored his protests. Devon stood throughout snack and did not join the group again until their next activity.

The next week, the teacher braced herself for another power struggle as snacktime approached. To her surprise, Devon walked straight to the spot he had so vehemently refused the week before and sat down.

Does This Child Refuse or Delay Doing as Asked Because She Is Involved in an Activity?

Children who are pulled away from an engrossing activity may delay a chore or a less desirable activity by arguing and complaining. Or they may passively agree to do what you have asked but continue to play or work on their project. Alert a child involved in an activity that she must soon stop or that it will soon be time to put her things away. Recognize that cleaning up may destroy an incomplete project. Save a block building by drawing or taking a picture of it. Or keep the pieces of a project in a bag so it can be completed at another time. If you are not asking a child to put things away but she is not paying attention, remove whatever is competing for her attention. Promise to return it when she has done what you have asked. Keep the daily routine and schedule predictable to cut down on arguments. Be consistent about cleanup and chores. Use picture schedules and job charts so she knows what to expect. Help her start her work on jobs she is asked to perform.

Does This Child Refuse When You Ask Her Directly?

Increase the likelihood that a child will cooperate by moving close to her before giving directions. State a direction once before helping her get started. Avoid getting upset and repeating yourself or losing your temper. Repeating yourself teaches her to tune you out until you have reached your limit. Losing your temper may give a child the impression she has power over your emotions. Take a few deep breaths to maintain your composure. If she doesn't begin to do as asked, offer her a choice: "Do you want to do it yourself, or shall I help you?" Sometimes a child will want help, and it is better that she has told you with words than shown you with inappropriate behavior. Offering a choice may spur independence. Let a child know that she can go on to the next activity after she has done what you have asked. Say, "When you finish hanging your coat, you can join the game" or "When you get your shoes on, I'll be able to tie them for you." Avoid power struggles in other situations by offering different types of choices. Ask, "Do you want to clean in the block or the housekeeping area?" Make sure you can live with either choice she makes.

Does This Child Continue to Argue Even after You've Set a Limit?

Some children have learned that if they argue long or effectively enough, they will get what they want. Some use arguing as a delay tactic. When you find yourself getting caught in an argument, end it. Say, "You're trying to get me to change my mind, and I am not going to. You need to stop asking now." Ignore further protests. Remove yourself from the situation by working with another child or moving to another part of the room.

If you responded to a child's request before thinking, you can change your mind. Let her know you have reconsidered. Say something like "I have thought about it a little more, and I've changed my mind." Give any other reasons you have.

A child may be arguing as a way to keep you involved with her. Be sure you have met her need for attention. Attend to her many times during the day when she is not arguing. Some children who push, push, push may be looking for boundaries. Set limits that are appropriate and reasonable for a child who is doing this, and stick to them. Reframe how you think about her behavior. For example, instead of telling yourself that she is arguing with you again, remember that she is learning to be more independent or is practicing being assertive. Be sure to recognize and comment positively on times when she does cooperate. Let her know how helpful this is.

Do Power Struggles with This Child Usually Turn into Tantrums?

Isabel, in the second example at the beginning of the chapter, refused to follow directions many times during the day. She, and others like her, loses emotional control during a power struggle, and her behavior dissolves into a temper tantrum. If this is the case for a child you are working with, choose your battles. Keep in mind that your goal is to gain a child's cooperation, not win a fight. Insist that things go your way only when it is really important. For example, it probably isn't a big deal if a child gets a drink just a few minutes before snack. However, you may need to insist that she stay within certain boundaries when you are on the playground. It

---

Techniques for Avoiding Power Struggles

Below are suggestions that may help to reduce power struggles:

◆ Develop a positive relationship

◆ Be firm, fair, and friendly

◆ Keep a sense of humor

◆ Give children opportunities to be powerful and to make decisions

◆ Offer choices

◆ Keep schedules and routines predictable

◆ Be consistent about expectations for cleanup and chores

◆ Move close to a child before giving directions

◆ State directions once, and then help a child get started

◆ Choose your battles; insist on your way only when it is really important—for example, safety

◆ Call an end to arguments

◆ Ignore protests; detach yourself from the argument

◆ Comment positively when a child is being cooperative and following directions

---

can be tempting to state the consequence for not following your directions. However, doing so often ends up adding to the struggle. Avoid threats that you cannot enforce. For example, don't threaten that she won't be able to go on a field trip if you can't leave her behind. Instead, try to find ways to phrase a direction that will elicit her help or entice her to do what she is asked.

Make sure you are not asking a child to do too much. Avoid overwhelming her with too many requests throughout the day. Try not to give a direction that is likely to result in a power struggle when you know she is tired or hungry. Reduce your expectations for the time being and see if doing so helps decrease power struggles. This child may be more willing to do as you have asked if she has plenty of opportunities to make decisions and control her own activities throughout each day. Allow her to be powerful by making her own decisions about what to do next, asking her to help rearrange the room, or lead a group game. Consider scheduling one of your free-play periods early in her day so she takes direction better the next time you ask. Be sure she has plenty of time to play; follow her lead by allowing her to direct the story line and what you do. Rebuild your relationship with her so she is interested in your approval and wants to please you. For information on how to respond to a tantrum that results from a power struggle, see chapter 8, "I'll Kick and Scream Until I Get My Way!" Temper Tantrums.

Work with the Parents

Parents may be understandably concerned and frustrated if their child is not following directions. Help them learn more about giving effective instructions and gaining cooperation by sharing the family information. Talk with them about techniques that work in your setting. Ask what they have found to be effective in their home.

If a child engages in power struggles, it may be tempting to think she has learned to argue because the parents give in to her at home. Perhaps you have witnessed the parent giving in to this child. Remember: some children try to control those around them from very early ages. You can understand how easy it is for a parent to become caught up in struggles when a child argues about almost everything. Avoid placing blame. Children who regularly engage in power struggles are challenging to teachers and parents alike. Sympathize with the parents while working with them to gain consistency between the home and early childhood setting. This can help reduce power struggles.

Develop a Plan for Action to help the child learn to follow directions the first time she is asked. If you remain concerned after completing your Plan for Action and giving the child time to learn the new skill, seek additional assistance.

When to Seek Assistance

If a child experiences challenges in any of the following areas when directions are given to her in her home language, seek assistance.

A child must be able to hear in order to follow directions. Ask yourself the following questions to determine if you should be concerned about a child's hearing:

- Does this child have a history of ear infections?
- Does this child respond to her name when she is not looking at you?
- Does this child follow simple requests like "Point to the ball" or "Run around the circle"?
- Does this child find or point to objects when they are named?
- Does this child respond to stories with appropriate laughter, smiles, or questions?
- Does this child make comments that are related to a conversation?
- Does this child seem to watch others in order to know what to do?

Seek a hearing screening for this child if you see a pattern that concerns you.

Other situations that may cause concern include

- A child who seems to be able to express herself but consistently is unable to follow directions
- A child who is unable to screen out distractions
- A child who has difficulty hearing and processing information unless in a one-on-one situation
(Greenspan 2001)

If you are seeing patterns of behavior that indicate a child is not hearing or that she is having trouble processing or remembering verbal directions, have her skills screened through her local school district, or seek an evaluation by a speech and language specialist.

If power struggles seem to occur frequently, look at your observation records. Determine how often they take place and how intense they are. Watch other children who are of the same age and temperament; compare your observations. You may find that the power struggles aren't as out of the ordinary as you thought. If something about them still pushes your buttons, try to determine what that is and problem solve what you can do to avoid them.

On the other hand, you may find that this child's upsets are more serious. Seek additional support if she shows a pattern of uncooperative behavior that escalates into angry outbursts, keeps her from being part of your activities, or interferes with her development (Keenan and Wakschlag 2002). Gain parental permission and have an early childhood consultant observe your interactions. This person may be able to give specific ways to implement these suggestions and others. Learning to work effectively with children who are uncooperative is an essential skill for early childhood teachers.

When refusing adult requests is the only behavior of concern, services are not readily available. However, if this is one among a number of upsetting or disruptive behaviors, such as difficulty controlling anger, negative attention getting, aggression, or severe tantrums, it may be appropriate to suggest that the parents seek parent education or family counseling.

A Plan for Action

To develop your Plan for Action, choose or modify one of the suggested goals to best match your situation. Add how well or how often you expect the skill or behavior to be demonstrated. Remember: you are looking for growth, not perfection. You want to move the child from where she is currently and to increase your expectations slightly. Next, determine three or four actions teachers and parents will take. Choose additional actions specific to the early childhood setting and the home. Record your choices on the planning form found in the appendix.

Sample goals for a child who does not follow simple oral directions:

- Looks at and pays attention to someone giving directions.
- Repeats one-, two-, or three-part directions (*Choose one.*)
- Works with an adult to complete one-, two-, or three-part directions (*Choose one.*)
- Completes one-, two-, or three-part directions with step-by-step verbal or visual cues (*Choose one.*)
- Completes one-, two-, or three-part directions independently (*Choose one.*)

- Follows one-, two-, or three-part directions with help (*Choose one.*)
- Stops an activity to follow directions
- Follows directions the first time she is asked
- Follows directions without arguing
- Follows directions without a tantrum

Sample actions parents and teachers can take:

- Use a signal to gain the child's attention
- Move close to this child and establish eye contact
- Ask this child to stop what she is doing
- Reduce competing noise
- Allow this child time to think before responding
- Play games that require her to follow directions
- Make cleaning up a game
- Use the KISS principle: Keep It Short and Simple
- Build up to three steps in a directive
- Ask this child to repeat directions
- Ask this child to retell a simple story
- Give directions that are clear, concise, and understandable
- Tell this child what to do rather than what not to do
- Use statements when you give directions
- Teach this child the steps involved in performing a task
- Give directions in a way that matches her learning style
- Restate a direction that isn't understood
- Offer the level of support the child needs
- Comment favorably when the child follows directions and cooperates
- Give this child direction as part of play
- Keep schedules and routines predictable
- Alert this child of changes in activities
- Find a way to save incomplete projects so this child can finish them at another time
- Use a picture schedule or job chart
- Make directions/questions concrete
- Break down tasks into manageable steps
- State directions once, and then move to help

- Remove yourself from further arguing
- Avoid losing your temper
- Make it clear that the current task needs to be done before this child starts her next activity
- Find ways to say yes to this child
- Choose your battles; insist only when doing so is really important
- Reduce your expectations for now
- Give opportunities for this child to feel powerful
- When saying no to this child, briefly explain your reasoning
- Call an end to arguments
- Ignore protests
- Avoid making threats

Sample actions teachers can take:

- Read books about sequencing lists or directions
- Create a treasure hunt for this child to follow
- Use puppets to practice following directions
- Provide picture cues to show where things belong
- Ask this child to echo you as you clap rhythms
- Schedule time for this child to be self-directed when she arrives
- Rebuild your relationship with this child
- Have a consultant observe your interactions; share pertinent information with the parents

Sample actions parents can take:

- Turn off the music or the television before giving your child a direction
- Pick out a cooking activity that requires you and your child to follow directions
- Make a picture checklist for daily routines
- Ask your child to repeat a short sequence of numbers
- Make decisions based on what is best for your child in the long run
- Make your child's sleep a priority
- Talk with a parent educator or counselor; share pertinent information with your child's teacher

Information on Following Directions

WHAT IS IT?

Following directions isn't easy for young children. Doing so requires them to focus their attention, remember, and do what is asked. To help your child learn this skill, you will need to determine if your child has heard what to do, knows how to do it, and is choosing not to cooperate. You can help your child learn to follow simple directions once you pinpoint what he or she needs.

Observe and Respond

Before you give directions, be sure your child is focused on you and paying attention. Call your child's name, touch your child's shoulder, or establish eye contact. Reduce competing noise by turning off music or the television before you proceed. Ask your child to stop and pay attention. Be sure to allow time for your child to think about your request.

Sometimes children have difficulty remembering things they hear. They may remember only the first or the last step of lengthy instructions. Keep directions short and simple. Simplify your directions by giving them one step at a time. When your child can consistently follow one-step directions, add a second step. Build up to three steps by the time your child enters kindergarten.

You can help your child remember directions by asking him or her to repeat them back to you. Repeating your directions helps to ensure that your child has heard and helps commit your instructions to memory. Asking your child to help retell a familiar story, such as *Goldilocks and the Three Bears*, can help your child practice remembering things he or she hears and the order of information. To help with daily routines, use a checklist; use a picture of pajamas as a reminder to put on pajamas and a picture of a toothbrush as a reminder to brush teeth.

Don't assume your child knows what is expected. Focus on saying what to do rather than on what not to do. Avoid vague instructions. "Watch out!" doesn't give much information. Say instead, "Your cup is tipping. Use two hands to hold it straight." Be careful not to ask a question or add "Okay?" to a direction. If you say, "Are you ready for cleanup?" the likely response is "No." What you really mean is "Please clean up now."

Be sure your child knows how to do what you are asking. Teach the steps involved in each task. For example, here is an effective two-part directive: "First, pick up all of the toys and put them in the toy basket. Then put all of the dirty clothes in the hamper." A photograph showing your child's room when it is clean provides a visual reminder of what cleanup looks like.

Give directions in the way that matches how your child learns best. A visual learner responds best to picture cues of what needs to be done; a verbal learner learns best by hearing things. Some children learn best by doing, so let them try. If you give a verbal direction and your child does not respond, wait to see if it takes awhile for the request to sink in. If he or she doesn't respond, restate the directive in a slightly different way to make sure your child understands. If this is not enough, help your child get started. Compliment your child for following directions. Say, "I see you are putting all the blocks in the bucket. Your room is really looking clean."

CONNECTING WITH SUPPORT

Sometimes you may find that you and your child argue about following directions. You have tried the approaches described here and believe your child knows how to follow the directions you have given but is choosing not to cooperate. If this is the case, ask your child's teacher for the handout "Information on Power Struggles."

You and your child's teacher may be concerned if your child is not following directions. Talk with the teacher about what works in the early childhood setting. Have your child's skills screened through your local school district if you are seeing patterns of behavior that suggest your child does not hear or is having trouble processing directions, remembering verbal directions, or can only follow directions with one-to-one help.

Information on Power Struggles

WHAT IS IT?

Sometimes children understand and can follow directions but resist in attempts to be independent. When this happens, children and adults can find themselves caught in power struggles that are difficult to end. You can learn to recognize the signs that a power struggle may be coming and how to avoid it, and help your child learn to cooperate.

Observe and Respond

When you and your child engage in power struggles, ask yourself two questions: First, does your child know how to follow directions? Second, how will you gain your child's cooperation? For ideas on how to give effective instructions, consult "Information on Following Directions." Suggestions on how to avoid arguments when you give your child directions follow.

Some young children say no when given a direction without even thinking about it. Perhaps your child frequently hears, "No." Help your child hear, "Yes," more often by finding ways to say yes. Say, "Yes, when the toys are cleaned up" or "Yes, after you're done cleaning."

Your child may argue when a job seems overwhelming. Be sure your expectations are realistic. Break a task into more manageable steps. Let your child know that other activities await after the task at hand has been completed. Say, "When you hang up your coat, we will be able to play a game."

Children who are accustomed to being pulled away from their chosen activities may delay chores by arguing. Or they may agree to do what you have asked but continue to play. If this is the case, tell your child that an activity is about to end. Avoid some arguments by being consistent about chores. Use a picture schedule or a job chart so your child knows what you expect. Recognize that from your child's perspective, cleaning up may destroy an incomplete project. Keep all the pieces of a project in a bag so your child can work on it another time.

If your child refuses to do as asked many times each day, make sure you are not asking for too much. Reduce your expectations, and see if this helps decrease power struggles. When you know your child is tired or hungry, try not to give directions. Cut down on how many extra activities your child is involved in. Make sure your child is getting enough sleep.

When you must give your child a direction, be sure your directions are effective. Avoid repeating yourself or losing your temper. Repeating yourself teaches your child to tune you out. Losing your temper gives the impression that your child has power over your emotions. Take a few deep breaths to maintain your composure.

Avoid power struggles by offering choices. Ask, "Do you want to do it yourself, or shall I help you?" or "Do you want to hold my hand or my jacket in this busy parking lot? You pick." Make sure you can live with the choice your child makes.

When you find yourself arguing with your child, base your decision on what is best for your child in the long run—not what is easier at the moment. End the argument. Say, "You're trying to get me to change my mind, and I am not going to." Ignore further protests. If you responded to your child's request before thinking, you can still change your mind. Let your child know you have reconsidered. Say something like "I have thought about it a little more, and I've changed my mind." Offer any other reasons you have.

Children may be more willing to do as adults ask when they are regularly offered opportunities to make their own decisions. Allow your child opportunities to be powerful by deciding what to do next. Provide plenty of time to play before asking your child to follow directions. Let your child direct the story line and what you do during play.

CONNECTING WITH SUPPORT

Work with your child's teacher so you both respond to power struggles in the same way. This will help your child learn that there are times when cooperation and agreement are necessary. Seek additional assistance if your child shows a pattern of uncooperative behavior that escalates into angry outbursts, prevents participation in activities, or interferes with learning. Find a parent education program or seek family counseling to learn more about how to help your child learn to follow directions and cooperate more readily.

15 "Read It Again!" Emergent Reading

FOR TEACHERS

Myles doesn't seem very interested in books. He prefers to play with the blocks or puzzles. I rarely see him choose the reading center. I worry he might not be ready for kindergarten.

❖ **Standard**
Shows interest in beginning to read.

What Is It?

The process of learning to read begins well before a child enters kindergarten or first grade and entails much more than learning the ABCs. Teachers can do a great deal to help children develop the strong vocabulary that forms the basis of understanding language, books, and stories. Children learn the important purposes reading serves when they see adults read for information and pleasure. When an adult and child read together, an emotional attachment can be built through snuggling and conversation. Teachers help children develop positive attitudes toward reading and important prereading skills by teaching children how to handle books, calling attention to print in the environment, and helping children begin to recognize simple words and letters. As they talk with teachers about stories, children learn the messages conveyed, relate them to their own experiences, and discover how reading can open new worlds they haven't yet explored.

Observe and Decide What to Teach

Ask yourself the following questions as you watch a child's developing interest in reading. The suggestions that follow will help you formulate a plan to further develop his emerging reading skills.

Does This Child Have a Limited Vocabulary?
Children usually need a language-rich environment in order to build an extensive vocabulary. Knowing a number of words and what they mean are keys to

Attention Grabbers and Interest Builders

Introduce books in a way that builds the excitement and curiosity of your group about what is to come. Once you've gained the children's interest in the story, keep it by involving them in telling the story. Below are some examples.

◆ Make a surprise box. Place toy animals or props that are found in a book inside a small box. Describe them one at a time and have the children guess what each one is. Lead into the book by saying, "All these animals are in the book we are going to read. Let's see if you can find them as I read the story."

◆ Read the book *Rosie's Walk* by Pat Hutchins. Find a toy chicken and place it somewhere in the room. Ask the children where Rosie is. Rosie might be under the table or on top of the easel. Another time, ask the children to follow Rosie around the chair, behind the shelf, and into the hallway.

◆ Spread out and have the children perform the same actions as the animals in Eric Carle's book *From Head to Toe*. When you read, "Can you do it?" the children respond, "I can do it."

◆ Use the doll bed from your housekeeping area and ten stuffed toy animals to tell the story *Ten in the Bed*. The next time, ask ten children to line up in front of the group. Tell the story again. Each time you say, "There were ten in the bed and the little one said, 'Roll over, roll over.' So one rolled over and one fell out," turn around the child on the end and send him back to his seat.

◆ Make an enormous mitten out of felt or find a parent who can knit one for you. Collect toy animals from *The Mitten* by Jan Brett. Tell the story using the props. When the bear sneezes, dump the mitten and scatter the animals around. Change the collection of animals but tell the same story. Let the children use the props to retell the story.

◆ Read and sing *Five Little Monkeys Sitting in a Tree* by Eileen Christelow. Find an alligator puppet or toy animal. Ask all of the children to stand up. When the alligator snaps, use the puppet to pretend to snap at the children. When you snap at a child, he sits down.

◆ Hide a large toy bear somewhere in the room. Gather the children for group time by moving to the smaller groups of children and saying, "We're going on a bear hunt, come on!" Look around the room until you spy the bear. Help the children settle down, and then read *We're Going on a Bear Hunt* by Michael Rosen.

◆ Draw pictures of the animals in *Brown Bear, Brown Bear, What Do You See?* by Bill Martin Jr. Place the pictures in a manila envelope and slowly pull out one picture at a time. Let the children guess the next animal while you tell the story.

understanding what one reads. For suggestions on helping a child build his vocabulary, see chapter 13, "It's My Turn to Talk!" Speaking.

Does This Child Lack an Interest in Books and Stories?

Children have varying experiences with book reading and storytelling when they enter early childhood settings. Some may not have had much exposure to books; others have been read to in one-to-one settings and others in group settings. Children show an interest in books by choosing to look at books independently, sitting with a small group to hear an adult read a story, asking to have their favorite book read, retelling parts of a story, and asking questions about a story.

Help a child develop an interest in books by reading books in different ways. Start by reading the book through without stopping. Return to interesting parts or to point out pictures later. During subsequent readings, stop to ask questions, or invite the children to make a prediction about what will happen next. When a story is well known, stop before a familiar phrase and ask the children to finish the sentence. Tell the story using props, puppets, flannel board pieces, or different characters. For example, when a child knows the predictable pattern of the story *Jump, Frog, Jump!* by Robert Kalan, change the animal and ask him to make up a similar story about "slither, snake, slither" or "buzz, bee, buzz." Use props to tell a story, or let a child hold a prop from the story. Each time a certain word is said, he can raise his prop in the air. Myles, in the chapter opening, really enjoys animals. He might be willing to listen to a story about animals. Choose a book such as *Little Gorilla* by Ruth Bornstein, in which a number of jungle animals come to a gorilla's birthday party. Ask the child to hold a stuffed animal that is a character in the book. Have him listen carefully, and when his animal is mentioned, he should hold it up for all to see. Or ask him to stand up when he hears a key word or phrase. He might stand up when he hears the phrase "chicka chicka boom boom" from the book of the same name by Bill Martin Jr. and John Archambault.

Collect a variety of books and place them in an independent reading center. Include predictable stories, wordless picture books, fiction, informational books, fairy tales, counting books, alphabet books, and nursery rhymes. Display them so children can easily make a choice. Join the reluctant reader where he is or invite him into the reading area. Reread favorite stories to help a child learn the sequence of events and the important features of the story. Add props, flannel pieces, and recordings of stories for a child to enjoy on his own.

Does This Child Understand Stories?

Not only should young children demonstrate an interest in stories, they also need to understand them and relate them to their own experiences. Typically, children demonstrate an understanding by asking and answering questions about a story, retelling it in their own words, or making predictions about what will happen next. If a child doesn't show these behaviors on his own, read a story through, and then ask him to tell how the characters were feeling at different points. Ask this child to draw his favorite part of the book. Make a class chart showing each child's favorite character. Ask open-ended questions to help this child relate a story to his own experiences. For example, ask, "Has anything like that ever happened to you?" Ask him to explain parts of the story. You might say, "What did it mean when they said . . . ?" Be careful not to ask so many questions that the child feels as if he's been quizzed rather than talked with.

Does This Child Handle Books Appropriately?

Children need to know many things about handling books, including how to hold them right side up and how to turn the pages carefully, and that print is read from left to right and front to back. Help a child learn these concepts by making them explicit when you read to him. Talk about the cover of the book. Look at the front and the back. Ask, "What is the same about them? What is different?" Point out the title and the name of the author and of the illustrator, if there is one. Make a comment like "Let's start at the front. It's the beginning of the story." When you read, say, "I start at the top of the page and read down." Run your finger under the words as you read to show that you read from left to right. When it's time to turn a page, invite him to turn it for you. If he is looking at the book with a recorded story and you hear the prompt, say, "Turn the page."

Aiden had been working at the writing center for a long time. He brought a booklet of pages to the teacher and said, "I'm writing a book. It's about a boy and his dinosaur. This is the dinosaur." The teacher said, "You could have a title for your book like other books. What do you want to call it?" He said, "Daddy Dinos. Can you write it for me?" The teacher said, "I'll write it on this paper, and then you can copy it onto the cover of your book." Aiden grabbed the sample and ran back to the writing center to copy what she had written. A few minutes later, he came back and said, "See my cover?" After commenting on his carefully copied title, the teacher suggested they look at the covers of other books to see what else was needed. Aiden and the teacher noticed that it needed a picture and the name of the author. Aiden went back to the writing center, this time to write his name and draw a picture. Once more, Aiden brought his book to the teacher and proudly showed her the cover. His teacher asked him to read his whole book to her. Unfortunately, she was briefly interrupted, so she said to Aiden, "Remember what page you're on so when I come back we can finish up." When she returned, Aiden finished his story and asked, "What else does it need to be a real book?" After looking at some more books together, Aiden decided the last detail he needed was to add page numbers. Back to the writing center he went. When the book was done, Aiden put it in his backpack and announced he was going to read it to his little brother when he got home.

Does This Child Lack an Awareness of the Smallest Sounds of Speech?

As they hear people talk to them, infants become increasingly aware of sounds. As children learn to imitate others, their babbling begins to sound more and more like the conventional sounds of the language spoken around them. Children need an awareness of sound so they can isolate the sounds of speech and connect them to letters they are learning. Being able to distinguish the smallest parts of speech helps children develop beginning reading skills and the skills they will need to sound out new words.

Children learn to distinguish these individual sounds of speech through rhyming and alliteration. Rhyming words are those that end the same, like *hat* and *cat*. Alliteration is a string of words that begin with the same letter or sound, like "the big, black bag."

Teachers help children learn to hear individual sounds of speech when they read nursery rhymes. Act out nursery rhymes like "Jack Be Nimble." Use a child's name and make a pretend candlestick to jump over. Let a child use flannel board pieces to tell "Hey Diddle, Diddle." Tell "Humpty Dumpty" by drawing a face on three hard-boiled eggs and one raw egg. Repeat the rhyme using one egg each time. Drop the raw egg into a pan to contain the mess when it falls off the wall.

Play rhyming games with a child's name by saying, "Get in line if your name rhymes with bed." Or say, "Someone is missing today. His name sounds like bike." Pretend you have forgotten a child's name and say, "Let me see, is your name Fillie? Tillie? Gillie? No, it's Willie."

Read books that use alliteration such as *Lilly's Purple Plastic Purse* by Kevin Henkes or *Sheep on a Ship* by Nancy E. Shaw. Try alliterative name games. Say, "Stand up if your name starts with the same sound as sing, sat, and silly." Call attention to the beginning of words by searching the room for things that start with the sound *b*, such as blocks, books, and beads. Or ask a child to say the first little bit of the words *table*, *turtle*, and *tank*.

Is This Child Unable to Recognize That Print Carries Meaning?

Many young children are unaware that there is print on a page. Through many readings with an adult, a child begins to differentiate the pictures from the print. He learns that print carries meaning when he watches adults read for many purposes. He learns about print by experimenting with reading and writing on his own.

If the child you are working with seems unaware of the print on a page, point to the words while you read a book. Read smoothly and with inflection while sweeping your finger under the words. Talk about the pictures on the page, and then say, "Now I'm going to read the words." If he holds a book so that the words are covered, point out the words and ask him to move his hands so you can see them. Find print throughout your environment. Look at food containers in a pretend grocery store and menus in your restaurant play area. Call attention to the names on lockers. Go on a word hunt throughout your school or neighborhood. Look for signs and read what they say.

A child may begin to recognize the letters in his name and the names of his friends, as well as some common words. Have magnet letters and boards so children can experiment with letter combinations and make words. Put letter stamps in your writing center and sponge letters in the art center. Use a sorter with lots of drawers (the kind you buy in a hardware store for nuts and bolts) to organize letter tiles. Children can use the tiles to make familiar names and words. Make books depicting common words for them to read. Write the words to a song or nursery rhyme on a chart and write each word on an index card. A reluctant reader can match the individual word to the word on the chart.

Work with the Parents

Talk with the child's parents about his emerging reading skills. Describe the things he is learning by seeing adults read for different reasons and what he learns from being read to. Talk with them about the importance of reading to their child each day. Emphasize the skills children learn when they cuddle with an adult to hear a story or read a book together. Talk about the skills you are working to develop when you read to their child. Describe their child's developmental level and what you intend to do to build additional prereading skills.

When to Seek Assistance

It is important for a child to hear the individual sounds of speech. If he seems to have trouble rhyming words, playing word games, or paying attention to the sounds of speech, have his hearing checked. If a child isn't speaking clearly, doesn't show an interest in book reading or nursery rhymes, or has difficulty understanding simple directions, have his skills screened for lags in development (Roth, Paul, and Pierotti 2006). Have the child's parents contact their local school district to schedule a developmental screening or consult with a speech and language pathologist for further information. Early intervention can help a child make significant progress in continuing to learn throughout the school years.

A Plan for Action

To develop your Plan for Action, choose or modify one of the suggested goals to best match your situation. Add how well or how often you expect the skill or behavior to be demonstrated. Remember: you are looking for growth, not perfection. You want to move the child from where he is currently and to increase your expectations slightly. Next, determine three or four actions teachers and parents will take. Choose additional actions specific to the early childhood setting and the home. Record your choices on the planning form found in the appendix.

Sample goals for a child when you are working on emerging reading skills:

- Shows an interest in books and stories by _____
- Demonstrates an understanding of stories by _____
- Handles books appropriately
- Makes _____ rhymes
- Isolates the first sound of _____ words
- Recognizes that print has meaning

Sample actions parents and teachers can take:

- Read books using different strategies
- Ask open-ended questions: ask the child to finish a sentence or make a prediction
- Engage the child in the story by asking him to hold up a prop or perform an action when he hears a key phrase

- Read a variety of books
- Reread favorite books
- Relate the story to the child's own experiences
- Talk about how to handle a book
- Sweep your finger under the words as you read
- Talk about the parts of a book
- Play rhyming and alliterating word games
- Read books with rhymes and alliteration
- Read the print in your environment
- Let the child experiment with sponge and magnetic letters and letter stamps

Sample actions teachers can take:

- Use puppets or flannel board pieces to tell stories
- Use attention grabbers and interest builders
- Make a class chart of favorite books or characters in a book
- Make books depicting common words
- Play a matching game with song charts

Sample actions parents can take:

- Read or tell stories to your child each day
- Check books out from your local library
- Take books with you and read them while you are waiting for appointments
- Go on a word hunt in your neighborhood
- Read road signs when you're in the car
- Let your child circle all the letters on a piece of junk mail that are the same as those in his name

Information on Emerging Reading

WHAT IS IT?

The process of learning to read begins well before a child enters kindergarten or first grade and entails much more than learning the ABCs. Parents do a great deal to help their children develop a strong vocabulary, learn how to handle books, recognize simple words and letters, and discover how reading can open new worlds they haven't yet explored.

Observe and Respond

Help your child develop an interest in books by reading or telling stories every day. Make reading part of your bedtime routine as well as other times of the day. As you read, ask your child to finish a sentence for you or make a prediction about what will happen next. Ask your child to hold a stuffed toy animal that matches a character from the story you are reading. Each time the animal is mentioned, your child can hold it in the air.

Visit your local library regularly. Check out a variety of books, including predictable stories, wordless picture books, fiction, informational books, fairy tales, counting books, alphabet books, and nursery rhymes. Reread favorite stories to help your child learn the sequence of events and the important features of the story. Encourage your child to retell parts of the story independently.

Talk about your child's favorite character and ask why that character is special. Ask open-ended questions that help your child relate the story to personal experiences. Ask, "Has anything like that ever happened to you?" If your child can't think of anything, provide a few hints. Say something like "Remember when Grandma was here and we made cookies?" Ask your child to explain parts of the story. Say, "What do you think it meant when they said they were uncertain what to do next?" Be careful not to ask so many questions that it feels more like a quiz than a conversation.

Help your child learn how to handle books by talking about how to turn the pages, the difference between the front and back, and how print is read from left to right. Point out the title as well as the names of the author and illustrator. Say, "Let's start at the front. It's the beginning of the story." Run your finger under the words to show that you read from left to right. Invite your child to turn the pages.

continued

Help your child learn to recognize print. Talk about the pictures on the page, and then say, "Now I'm going to read the words." If your child holds a book so that the words are covered up, point out the words and tell your child you need to see the words to read. Find print throughout your environment: look at food containers in the grocery store and menus in the restaurant. Look for signs when you are in the car, and read what they say.

Children need to be aware of sound so they can isolate the sounds of speech and connect them to the letters they are learning. Help your child hear sounds of speech by telling nursery rhymes and playing word games by saying, "My son Fillie? Tillie? No, Willie." Read books like *Lilly's Purple Plastic Purse* by Kevin Henkes or *Sheep on a Ship* by Nancy E. Shaw. Call attention to the start of words by searching for things in your house that start with the sound *b,* like blocks, books, and beds. Or ask your child to say the first little bit of the words *table, turtle,* and *tank.*

CONNECTING WITH SUPPORT

Work with your child's teacher to learn more about how children typically develop reading skills. Find out what you can do to support your child's efforts. If rhyming words, playing word games, or paying attention to sounds of speech seem difficult, have your child's hearing checked. If your child isn't speaking clearly, lacks an interest in book reading or nursery rhymes and has difficulty in understanding simple directions warrant a screening for lags in development. Contact your local school district or consult with a speech and language pathologist for further information. Early intervention can help your child make significant progress in continuing to learn throughout the school years.

"I Wrote My Name!" Emerging Writing

16

FOR TEACHERS

Vanessa likes to go to the writing center and write notes to her friends. When she shows me her writing, I see that she has made a number of marks and scribbles. Her lines aren't very controlled, and they lack fluidity.

❖ **Standard**

Shows interest in beginning to write.

What Is It?

Learning to write comes fairly naturally to many children as they explore writing materials, copy the adults they see writing, and then experiment with making lines and shapes of their own. When learning to write, children need strength and control of muscles in their hands and fingers. They need to be able to coordinate the use of their eyes and hands, hold writing tools, and learn to create vertical and horizontal lines, circles, and curves. Once they recognize that writing helps people communicate in many ways, they show an interest in combining basic strokes into conventional letters in their own efforts to communicate.

Children bring a wide variety of experiences with writing to your setting. Some may have had little exposure to writing tools and lack the opportunity to use them. Others may have had crayons and writing tools in their hands since they were toddlers. Their experiences will affect their emerging writing skills.

Children who are dual-language learners can print letters and words before they become orally proficient in their second language. They often use drawing to express themselves and their ideas. If they have learned to write in their home language, they do not need to learn to write again; they transfer the skill to their new language. Children can write in their home and their second language without becoming confused (Shagoury 2009).

Observe and Decide What to Teach

Ask the following questions as you observe a child who is learning to write. Your observations will give you ideas about activities that will help a child become interested in beginning writing.

Does This Child Use a Variety of Writing Tools?

Some children haven't had much opportunity to use writing tools. Allow a child who is new to using writing tools to explore by having plenty of tools available, such as an easel, writing center, and art materials. Don't limit writing activities to a table or desk. Place clipboards, paper, and writing tools in every area of the room. Allow this child to try writing in different positions. Tape large mural paper to a wall or fence, place long, narrow drawing paper on the floor, and vary the angle of the easel by spreading the legs different distances if possible. Vary the size of the paper and the surface the child uses to write on. Clip paper that has been cut into squares, circles, or triangles to the easel. Encourage this child to write on surfaces that are smooth, rough, bumpy, or patterned. Commercial textile boards are available; try cardboard, wax paper, aluminum foil, and sandpaper.

Find ways to include writing in this child's favorite activity. Move the easel out of doors, suggest she draw a picture of a building she has made in the block area, or work with her to make signs for labeling her buildings and towers. Add paper with the outline of a magnifying glass to the science area so she can draw her discoveries.

Get parents involved by offering traveling writing bags. Include items such as recycled paper, markers, stencils, paper punches, individual wipe-off boards and markers, and alphabet charts. Add things like coupons, stamps, washable ink, letter puzzles, and magnetic letters. Write a letter to parents that states you hope the materials will be well used. Encourage parents to add items to the bag like recycled printer paper, magazines, or junk mail. If a family uses up one of its supplies, ask that they let you know so you can replace it. Place the letter in a plastic page protector and slip it in the bag. Make a number of bags, and let this child as well as others take turns taking the bags home.

Stock Your Writing Center

Create a writing center in one area of your room. Include a variety of items that children can use to write or create:

- Recycled greeting cards
- Stencils
- Dot-to-dots (without numbers)
- Booklets made out of three or four pages of scratch paper stapled together
- Pencils
- Markers
- Crayons
- Staples
- Three-hole punch
- Stamps
- Envelopes
- Junk mail
- Old magazines (appropriate for children)
- Scissors
- Glue sticks
- Papers of different shapes and sizes
- Textiles for rubbings

Does This Child Hold a Writing Tool with an Unconventional Grasp?

Many children first grab a crayon or marker with an overhand grasp, making a fist around it. As they gain fine-motor skill, they develop the ability to bring their index finger and thumb together in a pincer grasp. When a child can pick up small objects in this way, she is likely to change to a more conventional grasp of a writing tool. If a child needs to learn to use a conventional grasp, be sure to give her lots of opportunities to strengthen the muscles in her hands by squeezing playdough, using tools like a small scissors or plastic screwdriver, and unscrewing the tops of different sizes of plastic jars to discover a surprise (a trinket or prize) inside.

Let Children See You Write

Let children see you write for a variety of reasons. As they watch you, they will begin to recognize that writing is a valuable way to communicate with others. When children understand the value of writing, they may be motivated to learn. Let children see you write:

◆ When you write what they say (for example, when a child dictates a note or story)

◆ When you tell someone something (for example, you write a note to the cook saying you will be five minutes late for lunch)

◆ When you need to remember something

◆ When you want to comfort someone

◆ When you take notes during group discussions

◆ When you make class graphs and charts

Help a child develop a pincer grasp by practicing other activities in which she brings her thumb and forefinger together. Lace sewing cards, string beads, place pegs in a board, or pinch clothespins and place them around the edge of a cardboard pizza round. Ask the child to tear strips of paper for an art project. Play a game in which this child pushes plastic chips through a slot in the plastic cover of a tin can. Make it a bigger challenge by giving her gloves to wear.

Make sure you have chubby crayons, large markers, and kindergarten pencils to use, because they may be easier to handle. Model the appropriate grasp for the child who is having difficulty. Describe the placement of your fingers when you pick up a writing tool. Try commercial pencil grips to assist this child.

Does This Child Make Only Marks and Scribbles?

In the beginning stages of learning to write, children make marks and scribbles and call it writing. Vanessa, in the story at the beginning of the chapter, often brought her teacher a row of poorly formed vertical lines and said, "That's my name." At this stage, a child may lack control of her strokes. As she becomes better coordinated, her lines become firmer and curves more fluid. Her increasing abilities may lead to greater confidence. Encourage a child who is making a variety of strokes to combine forms into letters.

At this stage, she might enjoy using personal-sized whiteboards and chalkboards. Encourage her to practice writing by placing a sign-up sheet near favorite activities like the computer. Show this child a picture of artwork signed by an artist. Encourage her to sign her artwork too.

Does This Child Produce Mock Writing?

When children engage in mock writing, they make lines, circles, curves, and loops and demonstrate a beginning awareness of writing (ITLC Online 2011). At this stage, children may make one or two recognizable letters along with vertical and horizontal lines. Sometimes when children use writing during dramatic play, they will quickly make a continuous line of hills and valleys as people do when they are using cursive writing.

A child at this stage needs you to provide things to look at when she practices writing letters. Place letter and number charts at eye level. Make personal-sized letter charts for this child to copy. Include writing materials in all dramatic play themes. For example, place order forms and menus to copy in the restaurant and note pads and pencils by the phone in the store or office. Use a pocket chart to make a classroom message center. Place a child's name on each pocket so each child can address messages to other children.

> *Ching Lan brings a colorful picture of an outdoor scene to her teacher. It is full of detail. The teacher describes the use of color and the way Ching Lan has included a little animal in the grass. Ching Lan points to several marks and symbols lining the bottom of the paper and says, "Yes, and that's Chinese writing."*

Does This Child Become Frustrated Trying to Write the Letters of Her Name?

A child who is trying to write her name or common words or to copy labels may be frustrated if she can't form the letters to her satisfaction. One reason for this is that children often find it difficult to hold the mental image of a word in their heads long enough to reproduce it. Help a child be more successful by providing verbal cues like "Start at the top; go down and around." In addition, provide models to copy or trace when she practices independently. Make name cards of her name and those of her friends. Make her a favorite word book by pasting pictures on an index card, writing a word under each picture, and placing the cards in a plastic photo album. Label common objects in the classroom. Ask parents who use a language other than English to write the label in their home language so one object can be labeled in English and the child's home language. Suggest that this child copy the labels of her favorite things at school or of all the blue things she can find. You can also play a game in which you give this child a picture of a labeled object for her to find, and then she can copy the object's name from the label onto paper. Or place a sticky note near certain objects and ask this child to copy the name of each object onto a new sticky note.

Give her meaningful opportunities to write too. Have her create a map of the room before parent night, make a greeting card for a sick friend, or copy a message to her parents. Place booklets with blank pages in the writing center. Encourage her to make a book. Have her add a title, signature, page numbers, pictures, and captions to her story.

Teprotha had been bent over his work at the writing table for some time. He finally looked up, brought his paper to the teacher, and asked, "What does this spell?" The teacher looked at the list of perfectly formed letters that spelled nothing. The teacher wasn't sure what to do, but she knew Teprotha's sense of humor, so she took a chance that she wouldn't hurt his feelings. She sounded out the sequence of letters the best she could. Teprotha laughed at the nonsensical word that she pronounced. He grabbed his paper and ran back to the writing center. A few minutes later, he brought back another string of perfectly formed random letters for her to read.

The teacher was pleased that this little game was so motivating to Teprotha. She knew that with another child, she would need a different approach. Perhaps with another child she could find groups of letters that suggested beginnings and endings to a word even if all the letters ran together.

Work with the Parents

Some parents want their child to learn to write by sitting and practicing letters. You and these parents may have the same goal for the child: to be ready for kindergarten. Work with parents to help them see all the opportunities their child has for developing writing skills within your classroom and at home. Save copies of their child's emergent writing and talk about the child's current stage of writing. Show the parents the next skill their child is likely to develop, and talk about how you are going to help her reach the next level. Give the parents the accompanying information, and use the Plan for Action to discuss the most useful steps.

When to Seek Assistance

Usually by the time a child is three years old, she can hold a writing tool in the typical position. Remember that skills may vary depending on the opportunity the child has had to practice using writing materials. If you are concerned, determine if the child can squeeze your hand firmly, and watch to see if she is strong enough to hold objects. Consider if she demonstrates fine-motor control by performing basic self-help skills like snapping her jacket or turning knobs. Observe a child who is struggling with fine-motor skills. If she is not making progress after three or four months of intentional instruction, encourage her parents to arrange for the developmental screening provided by their school district.

A Plan for Action

To develop your Plan for Action, choose or modify one of the suggested goals to best match your situation. Add how well or how often you expect the skill or behavior to be demonstrated. Remember: you are looking for growth, not perfection. You want to move the child from where she is currently and to increase your expectations slightly. Next, determine three or four actions teachers and parents will take. Choose additional actions specific to the early childhood setting and the home. Record your choices on the planning form found in the appendix.

Sample goals for a child when you are working on emerging writing skills:

+ Writes or draws with a variety of writing tools
+ Uses a conventional grasp to hold a writing tool
+ Makes marks and scribbles on paper
+ Makes vertical, horizontal, and curvy lines to convey meaning
+ Writes letters of his name or common words (*Choose one.*)
+ Copies labels

Sample actions parents and teachers can take:

+ Provide writing tools that are easy to handle
+ Allow the child to write in different positions
+ Vary the size, shape, and texture of paper to write on
+ Include writing in this child's favorite activity
+ Provide lots of opportunities for this child to strengthen the muscles in her hands
+ Help this child develop a pincer grasp
+ Model the appropriate grasp
+ Try commercial pencil grips
+ Find natural ways for this child to practice writing her name many times each day
+ Let this child see you write
+ Provide things for this child to copy
+ Include writing materials in pretend play
+ Offer meaningful opportunities to write

Sample actions teachers can take:

+ Include an easel, writing center, and art materials in your classroom
+ Place clipboards, paper, and writing tools in all areas
+ Circulate traveling writing bags
+ Offer personal-sized whiteboards and chalkboards
+ Make a classroom message center
+ Label common objects in more than one language
+ Encourage this child to write a book

Sample actions parents can take:

- Paint outside with water

- Draw letters in the sand with a stick or a small car

- Sit with your child and write

- Provide writing tools that will excite your child, such as hidden-color markers or a stick in mud

- Make a writing bag

- Collect, save, and reuse a number of things in your home for your child to write on

- Write notes to your child; ask her to write a note to you

- Write the grocery list together

- Make letters out of rolled ropes of playdough

- Encourage your child to make a greeting card or to write a letter

Information on Emerging Writing

WHAT IS IT?

Learning to write comes fairly naturally to many children: they explore writing materials, copy people they see writing, and then experiment with making lines and shapes of their own. When learning to write, children need strength in their hands and fingers; they need to hold writing tools; and they must learn to create vertical and horizontal lines, circles, and curves. Once they recognize that writing helps people communicate, they are motivated to write for a reason and are more likely to begin combining basic strokes into letters.

You may be anxious to have your child begin to write letters. Avoid the temptation to teach your preschool child to write through drill. Instead, look for ways to include writing in everyday activities.

Observe and Respond

Make sure you have plenty of writing and art materials available. Don't limit writing activities to a table or desk. Let your child put paper on the floor or a lap desk, or tape big pieces of paper to a fence. Vary the size and shape of the paper by cutting it into squares, circles, or triangles. Have your child write on cardboard, wax paper, aluminum foil, and sandpaper just for the fun of it.

Find ways to include writing in your child's favorite activity. Paint with water outside (it's especially fun to watch the water evaporate on a hot driveway or sidewalk); suggest that your child draw a bike or a favorite toy or draw letters in the sand with a stick or a small car. Make signs to label buildings and towers. Encourage your child to write when you are pretending to go to a restaurant. Give your child paper and pencil to write down an order or a prescription when you play doctor's office.

Make a special writing bag to use when you are waiting for an appointment. Include items like recycled printer paper, crayons, stencils, paper punches, markers, and alphabet charts. Add new items like coupons, stamps and washable ink, letter puzzles, and magnetic letters to keep it interesting.

Help your child develop the fine-motor control needed to hold a pencil or marker correctly by practicing activities that bring together index finger and thumb. Let your child lace sewing cards, string beads, place pegs in a board, pinch clothespins, or tear strips of paper for a pet's cage. Model the appropriate grasp for your child. Describe the placement of your fingers when you pick up a writing tool.

Many children learn the letters in their own names and the names of their families first. Once children learn these letters, they can easily transfer the strokes to other letters. Make name cards of your child's name and those of friends. Make a favorite word book by pasting pictures on index cards, writing a word under each picture, and placing the cards in a plastic photo album. Let your child practice copying favorite words.

Let your child see you write for a variety of reasons such as writing a thank-you note or making a list of things to do the next day. Then give your child meaningful opportunities to write. He or she can make a greeting card for a sick friend, write a letter to a grandparent, or sign a birthday card along with the rest of the family. Ask your child to write a grocery list or cross off the items on the list once you find them at the grocery store.

CONNECTING WITH SUPPORT

Work with your child's teacher to understand your child's developmental level in writing skills. Discuss the ways you can help your child reach the next level. If you are concerned about your child's skill development, pay attention to fine-motor skills like squeezing your hand firmly, holding objects tightly, snapping a jacket, or turning knobs. If your child is struggling with these skills, schedule an appointment for skills screening by your school district or health care provider.

Part 5

Cognitive Development

Cognitive development encompasses the thinking skills needed for everyday life. It includes mathematical and scientific thinking. Children learn how to count, count with one-to-one correspondence, and make comparisons. They learn to sort objects that are the same, classify things that belong together, and make simple patterns. They make comparisons and measure. Children are keen observers. They watch what is going on around them, ask questions, make guesses, test their thinking, and draw conclusions. They learn about the world through their senses and the use of simple tools like magnifying glasses and ramps. Through interactions with things and others, they learn to make sense of the world.

Children need early childhood programs that offer them opportunities to make hands-on discoveries—environments that are rich with materials they can count, group, and use in new ways. Children need to wonder out loud and have others wonder with them. Teachers can ask open-ended questions to spark their desire to know. A well-timed statement like "I wonder what will happen if . . ." can lead to experimentation and learning. Children need teachers who can help them link their prior experiences to current activities. For example, a teacher might say, "Last time, we used red and yellow paint. When you mixed them, they turned orange. I wonder what will happen if you mix the yellow and blue paint today," or "Is there another way you can group the toys?" Children need teachers who model counting, use graphs and charts, and help them recognize simple patterns.

Children thrive when they grow up in families in which they are included in daily activities that allow for learning. Sorting socks can be a lesson in matching.

Setting the table is a one-to-one correspondence activity. Cooking can be a time to learn about properties like wet and dry. Pretending to go to the store gives children a chance to count out pretend change for a purchase. When families talk about science concepts in their homes, children learn a vocabulary on which to build. They need their parents to talk to about what they see, hear, and smell. They benefit when the adults around them ask questions and make predictions. A parent can ask, "Do you think it will get runny when we add milk to the mix?"

Part 5, Cognitive Development, includes four standards. A discussion of each standard appears in the following chapters. As in all the domains, states may have more standards than those included in this book. The standards presented here, or similar standards, are commonly held by a number of states.

- ◆ Shows an interest in numbers, counting, and grouping objects, chapter 17

- ◆ Recognizes, duplicates, and extends simple patterns, chapter 18

- ◆ Uses observations to gather information, chapter 19

- ◆ Gathers information by asking questions and investigating the environment, chapter 20

Academics versus Play

A game my son played while he was growing up was to ask his friends who would win if there were a fight between Superman and Batman. Or who would win if there were a fight between Big Bird and Elmo? They would debate the pros and cons of each character and would eventually agree on a winner or agree to disagree on a particular contest. One day I asked, "What if the two superheroes teamed up?" The answer came, "That would be awesome!"

In some early childhood settings, parents and teachers find themselves in a similar debate, pitting academics against play. Some argue that children need to learn their letters and numbers, and others argue that they need to play and learn to get along with others. At times, it seems as if people engaged in the debate would like to see a clear winner. In truth, children need both academic and social-emotional skills (among others) learned through play.

Parents want to ensure their children have the skills they need to be fully prepared for kindergarten. Some believe that children need to know their ABCs and numbers so they can demonstrate school-readiness. Parents recall from their own educational experiences that the way to learn is to sit at a desk while the teacher provides information and you commit it to memory through paper-and-pencil tasks. They are most familiar with the instructional methods commonly used in first- through twelfth-grade classrooms. Unfortunately, many think this is the only way that teaching and learning can take place.

Those advocating for play know that children who are three, four, and five years old learn best through doing, with hands-on activities and meaningful, playful experiences. They envision a classroom in which children move about from one activity to another as their interests are piqued. They engage in book reading and acting out familiar stories. They write letters to one another and messages to their parents. They race cars down ramps and compare which one goes the farthest. They link pieces of a chain together until it stretches from one end of the classroom out the door. They stretch their imaginations and learn to get along with others while they pretend to climb into a boat to escape sharks in the water.

Instead of trying to determine if academics or play is the winner, what if they team up? An examination of the goals of academics and play show that they don't need to be at odds. It seems that the instructional methods envisioned for reaching goals are the bigger controversy. The goals of those who advocate for academics want children to learn how to "do school." Those who advocate for play want children to be ready for school, but they want to use instructional methods that meet the needs of young children. Children are prepared for school when they can pay attention to activities for short periods of time, follow simple directions, communicate with others, and show an interest in prereading and premathematics activities. They need to be able to do things like retell a favorite story, count to ten, and use writing tools to draw a picture. Academics don't have to be at the expense of play, and play doesn't have to exclude academics. Early childhood teachers can provide both.

To teach academic skills, early childhood teachers can use instructional practices that are appropriate for young children. When teachers have learning goals in mind, including academic skills, they can plan activities that teach children through everyday activities and play. Teachers can intentionally include writing materials in all areas of the room and guide children to use them for writing a message to a friend or a sales receipt for shoes at the pretend shoe store. Teachers teach measurement skills when they have string, rulers, measuring tapes, and yardsticks available and encourage children to see how long their paper chain is as it stretches across the room. They teach science skills when children race cars down a ramp and are then asked to guess which car will go the farthest and to hypothesize why. They teach social-emotional skills when they help children solve conflicts during play. Teachers encourage imagination and creativity when they support children's dramatic play themes.

Early childhood teachers are better able to demonstrate that they can do both academics and play when they articulate the learning they see taking place. One way to do this is to place a copy of the sales receipt created in the pretend shoe store on the family board and label it, explaining that this child used some letters in his name and other symbols as a step toward emerging writing. A teacher can show the learning taking place by creating a classroom scrapbook with pictures of children measuring their paper chain and a journal entry stating that children counted the number of steps it took to get from one end of the chain to the other. A teacher can ask a parent to join her in watching the children play, and then describe the observation, questioning, and investigation skills a child demonstrates when he races cars down the ramp.

Whatever method teachers use to document the skills practiced during play, the resulting evidence allows parents, children, and teachers to celebrate the learning taking place. Through their descriptions, teachers communicate to parents and others that children learn the skills to prepare for school by being involved in meaningful play activities. These efforts can help people see that when academics and play are teamed up, there are awesome results for young children.

"One, Two, Five, Six" Numbers

17

FOR TEACHERS

Although Darien can count to ten, when I ask him to count ten objects, he skips numbers or counts in the wrong order. If he counts to ten correctly, why can't he count objects correctly?

❖ **Standard**

Shows interest in numbers, counting, and grouping objects.

What Is It?

Children are learning about math and numbers from a very early age. They learn about numbers when they ask for *more* and get another strawberry. When they hold up their fingers to indicate their ages, they are learning about numbers. Even toddlers can often show their ages with their fingers and add one *more* block to a pile. To bridge this informal understanding of numbers to the more formal understandings used in school, children need the help of adults. Parents and teachers provide many experiences to help children gain this more formal understanding. As Darien's teacher accurately observed, Darien's ability to count numbers is a different skill from his ability to count objects. For Darien to go beyond rote counting and learn to count objects one by one, he needs planned activities targeting one-to-one correspondence.

English-language learners may have a language barrier that prevents them from demonstrating what they know. It is important to use as many visual cues as possible and to structure activities so children learning English can show you rather than tell you what they know. Try to learn to say the numbers one through ten in each child's home language.

Observe and Decide What to Teach

Ask the following questions while you watch how a child interacts with numbers. The suggestions that follow help the child gain a better understanding of numbers. Suggestions include both group and individual activities. A child benefits from a combination of the two methods. Use your observations and suggestions to work with the parents to design a plan that supports the child while he learns to show an interest in numbers, counting, and grouping objects.

Does This Child Lack an Interest in Numbers?

Most children like to play around with numbers and to learn to count. Occasionally a child may not show an interest. This child may avoid number activities during choice time, become restless while singing counting songs, or run away when you ask him to play math games. The reasons children show little interest in number activities vary. They may be more interested in other activities, or they may prefer to watch and observe before participating. Sometimes children may feel anxious or pressured to perform. For example, a child who watches before participating may need gentle encouragement to feel more comfortable. Another may need to participate in a variety of activities to build his confidence. Whatever the reasons the child isn't showing an interest, keeping the activities low-key, fun, and nonthreatening helps. Make sure you repeat the activities or vary them a little to give the child plenty of opportunities to succeed.

At first a child may be most interested in numbers that apply to him, such as his age or the number of days until a special event. Ask him to hold up his fingers to show you how old he is. If he is reluctant, hold up your fingers to show his age, and then count them together. Measure how tall he is, and show him the number on paper. Measure again in a couple of months, and show him how much he has grown. Ask the child to name or draw the people in his family. Then count them together.

Give this child opportunities to play with numbers. Create a store in your dramatic play area. Put a cash register on the table. Ask him to push the numbers to get the cash register to open. Put prices on play groceries, write prices on a list, and point them out when he pretends to shop. Put play money in the cash register, and point out the numbers on the money he uses. Help him count out pretend change for the shoppers.

Children become interested in numbers when they learn that they are useful and functional. When they see adults using numbers, they want to learn more about how numbers work. Talk about your work with numbers. For example, when you write down meal counts, speak the numbers out loud. Count the number of children in the line when you are coming in from outside, and declare, "We are all here." Consult the calendar when you talk about field trips coming up, and point to the date.

Is This Child Unable to Count to Ten?

Although counting to ten and counting ten objects are different skills, simple counting is an important beginning. It is a rote or memory skill, but it gives a child a way to move on to other math skills like counting objects. Because he knows the number words and the correct order, he has a foundation for the next steps.

If the child you are working with is a younger preschooler, he will start by counting up to four. An older preschooler can learn to count to ten and then twenty (Copley, Jones, and Dighe 2007). The English words *eleven, twelve, thirteen, fourteen*, and *fifteen* are particularly difficult for young children to remember because they don't follow a set pattern. Often a child will skip some of these numbers to get to twenty, because counting becomes easier after twenty since the numbers repeat a pattern he has learned before.

Help a child having difficulty learn to count by using normal, everyday routines. For example, count the number of chairs set out for a small-group activity. Ask this child to count the children with you as they sit down. Make a game of it by giving him a stop sign. He can put up the stop sign when the correct numbers of children are seated. Count the number of birds you see during a class walk or the number of houses on a block. If he is a younger preschooler, concentrate on smaller numbers until he is able to consistently count correctly.

Use games, songs, and books to reinforce counting. Games that require a child to count spaces in order to move help him not only with counting but also with one-to-one correspondence. Put out games such as Candy Land, Chutes and Ladders, and Hi! Ho! Cherry-O (Hasbro) during choice time and invite this child to play with you. Add math games to the themes you are studying. For example, make a game with drawings or pictures of the walk you took to see the community. Make a pathway with spaces that indicate what you saw along the way, such as a fire station, stores, and parks. Children can use a spinner or dice to determine how many spaces to go. Make a special effort to invite the child who is not counting to play. Change your inflection or voice when counting to create more fun and engagement. Play "Sit Down." To play, invite the children to stand in a circle. Tell the children they are to help you count. When you count the children up to a certain number, for example, three, the last counted child sits down. Once a child sits down, count to three again. You will end up counting to three over and over until only one child is left standing. Then use a different number. Sing songs featuring counting such as "Five Little Ducks" or "Five Little Monkeys" during large group. Use books, flannel boards, or props to help the children count while they sing. Read books such as *The Very Hungry Caterpillar* by Eric Carle. Ask children to count the food items the caterpillar chews through. Use a flannel board or story set to help this child count and to increase his interest. Leave the story set out for the child to practice independently.

Does This Child Count Objects One by One?

Counting objects one by one is called one-to-one correspondence. As children learn to count objects, they may make a number of mistakes. Often they keep counting even though they have reached and passed the correct number. Understanding that the last number counted is the number that indicates "how many" requires a sophisticated understanding of numbers. They may also start counting and then mix up the order. For example, when counting five objects, a child may point to each object and count, "One, two, five, six." Another common mistake children first make is to count an object twice. It takes them a lot of time and repetition to learn to count objects one by one.

To start, ask the child to match an object to an object. Start by placing one block on a table and ask the child to put another block on the table. When the child can consistently match one block to another block, increase to three and four blocks. Vary the activity by adding a magic bag. Ask this child to pull two or three objects out of a magic bag. Use objects he particularly likes, such as small cars or small toy animals. The next step is to ask the child to count the objects as you place them in front of him. Count them, and then state the total number: "One, two, three, four. You pulled four cars out of the bag."

When serving snack, ask this child to put a napkin by each place. Count them as he puts them in place. Help him place the cups and plates in the same manner. To vary this activity, put place mats in the house area and ask him to set the table for dinner. Help him count the plates, glasses, and silverware. Another variation is to place a number of plastic animals in a row. Ask this child to give each one something to eat (a cube). Have him place one cube in front of each animal. Count the animals; then count the cubes. Or ask this child to count as he places one penny on top of each spot on a playing card.

Survey your class and make a graph. Label three columns with variations of a theme. Theme ideas are endless. Three fun ones are favorite book, color, or flavor of ice cream. Put each child's name on a square of paper and have each child place his name in the column that indicates his favorite. Be sure that the list of names starts at the bottom of the chart and additional names are added above. This helps children read the data by determining which is the tallest, the shortest, and the in-between column. Count the names of the children in each column. Ask the child having difficulties to help you. Give him a pointer and guide him as he counts. After you are done counting with him, ask, "How many?" If the child isn't sure, count again more slowly to reach the correct number.

Is This Child Unable to Tell Which Has More or Less When Comparing Two Sets of Objects?

Children explore the concepts of more and less when they are very young. One of the first words spoken is *more*. Children quickly learn that when they say, "more," they get additional food, a second book read (or the same book read again!), or another loving hug. As they get older, they learn to transfer that concept to numbers. When young children first compare two sets of objects, they may think the longer or wider one has more. For example, when looking at two lines of objects, they think the longer line has more objects, even when the shorter line has more objects. They don't realize the objects are simply smaller or spaced farther apart from one another. As they gain skill in counting or matching objects one-to-one,

Books about Numbers

Read number books to help children begin to identify numbers.

Counting with Apollo by Caroline Gregoire

Five Green and Speckled Frogs by Constanza Basaluzzo

Five Little Monkeys Jumping on the Bed by Eileen Christelow

"More, More, More," Said the Baby by Vera B. Williams

One Duck Stuck by Phyllis Root

One Little Chicken: A Counting Book by David Elliott

Ten Little Fish by Audrey Wood

Ten Tiny Babies by Karen Katz

Ten in the Bed by Penny Dale

Ten in the Bed by David Ellwand

The Very Hungry Caterpillar by Eric Carle

What Comes in 2's, 3's, & 4's? by Suzanne Aker

they determine which grouping has more or fewer by counting. Children can soon recognize which has more or fewer just by looking at the grouping. Being able to identify more and fewer without counting is described below. The child who can't tell the difference between more and less or fewer will have a harder time learning to add or take away one.

A child who has difficulty recognizing quantities in groups needs a great deal of practice and repetition to help him grasp the concepts of more and less. Ask him which plate has more and which plate has fewer or less when you are serving snack. Line up two rows of cars to drive on a road built out of blocks; ask which line has more and which has fewer cars. When you are graphing favorites (see the last section), ask this child which columns have more and which columns have less or fewer once you have counted the items. By using the words *more* and *fewer*, you are helping him connect the words to the concepts.

When dismissing children from group time, ask each child to come up and draw *more* than two blocks from a bag or *fewer* than two blocks from the bag. Help a child who is having difficulty with the concepts of more and fewer count the blocks and decide if he has more or fewer.

Is This Child Unable to Recognize the Numerals 1 through 10?

When a child learns to count objects one by one, he is ready to learn to attach a number name called a numeral to a symbol. He probably will start with the lower numbers first and gradually add the later numbers. Or he may start with his age.

Provide a numeral-enriched environment. Put up numeral posters; provide numeral props, such as cash registers, numeral signs, telephones, calendars, and pocket planners in dramatic play areas. Post numerals by your writing center. Point out numerals when you are counting. If you observe a child who doesn't recognize numerals or isn't able to point to the numerals when you ask, keep encouraging him to participate during numeral activities.

Read books like *Five Little Monkeys Jumping on the Bed* by Eileen Christelow or *Ten in the Bed* by David Ellwand, and point out the numerals as you read. After the children are familiar with the story, give them numerals mounted on craft sticks to hold up when the numeral is spoken or sung. Make sure the child who is not recognizing numerals has one to hold up. As a variation, put five little monkeys on a flannel board with the numeral 5. When the monkeys fall off the bed one by one, take off one monkey at a time and put up the new numeral. The children associate the numeral with the number of monkeys left. The child who is not learning numerals easily can help you take the monkeys off or put up the numeral. Act out the story *Ten in the Bed* with toy animals while you sing the song. Put the toy animals and the book in your book area during choice time so children can act out the story with each other. Encourage the child who is not recognizing numerals to act out the story with a friend.

Make games this child can play in small groups. Make cards with the numerals and dots demonstrating the number. Show him a numeral and ask him to put out the same number of objects. For example, show him the numeral *3* and ask him to put out three objects. If he is hesitant, ask him to count the dots and then put out three objects.

Pair this child with a friend and ask them to do a numeral search in the room. First, ask them to find all the numerals they can in the room. Then, to make the game a little more challenging, give them a card with a numeral on it and ask them to find that numeral in the room. Have them match numeral to numeral at first. After they are able to match numeral to numeral, give them a picture of objects— for example, three objects—and ask them to find the corresponding numeral in the room.

Naomi was worried about a child in her class. Mikel was very active and had no interest in the number activities she was offering during choice time. Whenever he participated in number activities, he would roll around, wander off, or start pestering other children. Naomi thought that perhaps he wasn't ready for number activities because he needed better self-regulation skills. She watched him carefully over the next few days and recognized that he just loved to move all the time. When the class went outside the next day, she brought him over to the sidewalk and drew a hopscotch form with chalk. As she drew the numerals, she named them. When she showed him how to throw a small stone on a square and then jump, he became excited. He yelled to his friends to come and play. Soon they had a small group playing hopscotch every day.

Mikel was able to move and learn his numbers.

Is This Child Unable to Recognize Sets of Two, Three, and Four without Counting?

Young children develop the ability to recognize sets of two, three, and four without counting them. They build this ability through repeated exposure to groups of two, three, and four. When children learn this, they can add and subtract in their heads more easily.

Give a child who is not yet recognizing sets of numbers opportunities to practice. Put three blocks on a table, cover them with a scarf, and then ask the child to take off the scarf and tell you how many objects there are. If he can't recognize it quickly, ask him to count them. Vary the numbers of objects up to five.

Read the book *What Comes in 2's, 3's, & 4's?* by Suzanne Aker. This book groups shapes, colors, and everyday objects in sets of two, three, and four. Each page gives you ways to count the sets and talk about the pictures. See if this child can recognize the groupings without counting.

Make a lotto game board with nine squares. Paste pictures of objects in sets of two, three, and four in the squares. Make a second set of square matching cards. To play the game, hold up one card at a time and ask the child if he has a match. Point to the number of objects in the picture while the child finds the match. For a change, let him hold up squares for the lotto game.

Maya had just heard her program was requiring training on early math. She dreaded the training because she had always hated math and felt she didn't understand it. She did set out math activities in her classroom but didn't emphasize them. What if she couldn't even understand the training?

When she shared her feelings with other teachers in the center, they also expressed reservations and fears. When the trainer began with the observation that many teachers are afraid of math instruction, Maya knew she wasn't alone. Many teachers in the field of early childhood are uncomfortable with math.

During the training, she learned fun, easy, and engaging activities to teach math concepts and vocabulary. She found she was looking forward to trying them with the children. Her fellow teachers pledged to support each other as they experimented with learning new early math strategies.

When to Seek Assistance

The ages at which young children learn math concepts vary widely. However, younger preschool children are usually beginning to develop a sense of numbers one through four, and older preschoolers are able to understand both counting and one-to-one correspondence with numbers one through ten. If a child lags behind in these developmental steps, provide a variety of fun, engaging activities with numbers. Don't push but encourage participation. When the child experiences success, he will continue to seek out math activities. It is unlikely that a child would be eligible for additional services if the only area of concern is in early mathematics. However, if he is having difficulty in other cognitive areas as well, refer him for developmental screening through his school district.

Work with the Parents

As academic expectations have increased in elementary and secondary schools, many parents are more concerned than ever that their children be prepared for kindergarten. This includes exposure to literacy and math concepts. But just as teachers often feel ill-prepared to teach early math in their classrooms, so parents often feel overwhelmed when thinking about math at early ages. Help parents understand what their child is learning by sharing your strategies and goals, along with simple activities they can do at home. Give them the information for parents that follows. Help them recognize the ways they are already teaching math in their everyday interactions with their children. If a child isn't progressing in expected ways, develop the Plan of Action with the child's parents so you are working as a team.

A Plan for Action

To develop your Plan for Action, choose or modify one of the suggested goals to best match your situation. Add how well or how often you expect the skill or behavior to be demonstrated. Remember: you are looking for growth, not perfection. You want to move the child from where he is currently and to increase your expectations slightly. Next, determine three or four actions teachers and parents will take. Choose additional actions specific to the early childhood setting and home. Record your choices on the planning form found in the appendix.

Sample goals for a child who is learning about numbers:

- Shows an interest in numbers
- Counts to ten in the correct order
- Counts one to five or ten objects one by one (*Choose one.*)
- Tells which has more and which has less when comparing two sets of objects
- Recognizes and points to numerals *1* through *10*
- Recognizes sets of two to four objects without counting

Sample actions parents and teachers can take:

- Measure the child and show him how tall he is
- Set up a dramatic play area that involves numbers
- Count objects around the home and the classroom
- Ask this child to set the table for snack and set one napkin per chair
- Sing counting songs
- Read counting books
- Play hopscotch
- Ask this child to tell which line of objects has more and which has fewer
- Do a number search to find numerals in the home and the classroom

Sample actions teachers can take:

- Talk about how you use numbers
- Use flannel board figures or puppets to illustrate counting books and songs
- Ask the child to match three blocks to three blocks
- Make a graph of children's preferences; ask which column has more and which has fewer names
- Make lotto games with numerals and sets of objects to match
- Make pathway games; use a die to determine how many squares to move

Sample actions parents can take:

- Go for a walk with your child and count the objects you see
- Cook with your child; point out the numbers and measurements in the recipe
- Go for a ride and count the number of stop signs
- Shop for groceries with your child and point out the prices and numbers on boxes and cans

Information on Numbers

WHAT IS IT?

Children are learning about math and numbers from a very early age. They are learning about numbers when they ask for *more* and get another strawberry and when they hold up their fingers to indicate their ages. To bridge this informal understanding of numbers to the more formal understandings used in school, children need parents and teachers to provide many experiences with numbers.

Observe and Respond

Occasionally a child doesn't show an interest in numbers. If this is true of your child, use fun, nonthreatening counting activities like board games, measuring height, and singing counting songs to reinforce numeric concepts. When riding in the car, count the numbers of trucks or stop signs. When you are on a walk, count the number of stores, houses on your block, or cars on your street. Around your home, count the number of windows in a room, people in your family, or crackers on a plate. Don't pressure your child—more than likely, seeing you use numbers to cook or to consider the price of something will spark interest in how numbers are used.

Play store with your child. Collect empty cereal, oatmeal, and cracker boxes. Make play money together. Pretend to shop and then pay for the items. Ask your child how much you owe. Help your child count out the change. Cook with your child. Read aloud the numbers on measuring cups and tablespoons when you measure with them.

The ability to count from memory is an important step before learning to count objects. Young preschoolers can usually count up to four. An older preschooler can count to ten and then twenty (Copley, Jones, and Dighe 2007). The English words *eleven*, *twelve*, *thirteen*, *fourteen*, and *fifteen* are difficult for children to remember because they don't follow a recognizable pattern. Often a child will skip some of these numbers to get to twenty, since counting becomes easier after twenty because the numbers form a pattern he already knows (twenty-one, twenty-two, and so on).

Read books involving counting, such as *Five Little Monkeys Jumping on the Bed* by Eileen Christelow and *Five Green and Speckled Frogs* by Constanza Basaluzzo. Read *The Very Hungry Caterpillar* by Eric Carle and count the food items the caterpillar eats.

Counting out objects one by one is called one-to-one correspondence. As children are first learning to count objects one by one, they make a number of mistakes: they keep counting even though they have reached the correct number, mix up the order of numbers, or count an object twice.

Matching an object to an object can help your child learn one-by-one counting. Put out one block and ask your child to put out one block. Or ask your child to pull two objects out of a bag. Use objects your child likes, such as small cars or animals. When your child sets the table, see that one plate is put at each place. Have your child place one liner in each well in a muffin tin.

A child who has learned to count objects one by one is ready to learn to attach a number name to a symbol called a *numeral*. Point out numerals on the calendar, telephones, calculators, planning books, and rulers. When you are driving in the car, point out numerals on signs.

As children increase their math knowledge, they develop the ability to recognize sets of two, three, and four without counting them. Play a game with your child by placing three blocks on a table. Cover them with a towel and ask your child to remove it and tell you how many objects there are. A child who can't recognize the number quickly can count the items. Vary the numbers of objects up to five. Keep the game short and fun.

Most young preschoolers begin to develop a sense of the numbers one through four, while older preschoolers can understand both counting and one-to-one correspondence with the numbers one through ten. You may be surprised by how much math your child is already learning during everyday interactions.

CONNECTING WITH SUPPORT

If your child isn't showing interest or isn't progressing as expected, talk with your child's teacher. Ask her what she is observing and doing to help your child. Develop the Plan of Action with your child's teacher so you are working as a team. If your child's difficulty with math concepts seems linked to difficulties in other cognitive areas, seek a developmental screening through your school district.

"Red, Green, Red, Green" Patterns

FOR TEACHERS

I tried to get Samantha interested in patterns by putting out a matching game. All she had to do was match colored buttons to the patterns on the cards, but she didn't want anything to do with it. Now I don't know what to do. I guess she just doesn't like pattern activities.

❖ Standard

Recognizes, duplicates, and extends simple patterns.

What Is It?

Patterns are all around us. They can be found in checkers on a tablecloth, yellow dashes down the center of the highway, and the stripes of mowed grass on a baseball field. Actions such as *clap, clap, stomp, clap, clap, stomp, clap, clap, stomp* or colored blocks arranged *red, blue, red, blue, red, blue* are patterns. But adults and children don't always notice them. Patterns can be simple or complex. Once children start to see patterns, they enjoy finding new ones. They first begin to recognize patterns and then learn to copy them. Eventually they create their own patterns. Not only can adults help children recognize patterns, but they can also help them label and describe them verbally.

Patterns are not patterns unless they are repeated (Taylor-Cox 2003). Although this seems obvious, teachers need to remember this when they set up activities involving patterns. Repeat a pattern several times to ensure that children see how it evolves. Learning about patterns is an important component of early math. Seeing and making patterns helps children understand how things work together and encourages them to predict what comes next (Jain 2011).

Children typically pick out patterns involving bright colors more easily than patterns with shapes or numbers. Although patterns can be made using letters, it is best to avoid these with young children. Letter patterns may confuse children because they are concentrating on learning the names and sounds of letters (Copley, Jones, and Dighe 2007).

Observe and Decide What to Teach

Watch how each child interacts with patterns. The questions and the suggestions that follow can help you design a plan for a child who is learning about patterns. Many of the suggestions can be done with a group or an individual. Doing activities with the whole group benefits all of the children as well as motivates an individual child to recognize, duplicate, and extend simple patterns.

Is This Child Unable to Recognize or Identify Patterns?

Children enjoy learning about patterns but may need help recognizing them initially. Help them recognize that the daily schedule, the passage of day and night, and the Hokey Pokey all contain patterns. As you identify patterns, use the word *pattern* frequently so children become familiar with it. When a child cannot point to patterns in pictures, her clothing, or shapes you have placed on the flannel board, try the following suggestions to help her begin to identify them.

Clear a space from visual distractions so this child can concentrate on the patterns you make. Put colored cube blocks out. Blocks, or similar objects that differ in only one way, such as color, are a good choice when first introducing patterns. Sit with the child and build with her. Build a simple colored pattern, such as *blue, red, blue, red, blue, red*. Tell her, "Look, here's a pattern. See? *Blue, red, blue, red, blue, red*." Repeat with two other colors. If she seems to be catching on and is still interested, make a third pattern. Keep the pattern simple—only two or three items. End the activity before the child becomes restless or distracted.

Read the book *I See Patterns* by Susan Ring, which illustrates patterns that can be easily identified in colorful pictures of animals, insects, fences and posts, and rows in a field of corn. After reading the book, gather a small group of children and go on a search for patterns around your room. Make sure you have set out patterned materials especially for this activity so the children can succeed. Put patterned dishes in the house area, links arranged in a pattern on a tabletop, patterned fabric over a table, cutouts in a pattern on the flannel board, and books on patterns in the library area. Include the child you are concerned about in the small group. Point out the patterns while you walk with her. Ask her what patterns she sees. List the patterns on a sheet of paper and ask her to report back to the whole group. Gauge how eager this child is to share what she has learned about patterns. Encourage her to point to patterns or to describe them if she is willing.

During the month of March, Abby, a teacher in a four-year-old class, planned and offered a number of pattern activities. As she worked with the children, she noticed that Samantha and some of the other children, including a few of the dual-language learners in her class, were not progressing as she expected. They were having difficulty identifying patterns and even more trouble copying them. She wondered if these children might need more movement and less language in her lessons to better understand patterns. Abby decided to pull this small group together and focus on movement and demonstrations to teach them patterning. In her first lesson, she demonstrated a pattern sequence of clap, stomp, clap, stomp, clap, stomp. She asked the children to do the movements with her. After they performed the movement pattern, she repeated the word pattern. Then she tried another movement sequence and repeated the word pattern. Soon the children, including the dual-language learners, associated the movements with the word pattern. In her second lesson, she tried a pattern art project. She demonstrated how to glue ribbons, art feathers, and foam disks into a pattern. In a lesson later in the month, she paired one child learning English with an English-speaking friend and asked them to find patterns in the classroom. She found that the more she used movements and clear, minimal English, the more this group of children could comprehend.

Watch for a day when the child having difficulty learning patterns is wearing a shirt or pants with a pattern. At group time, ask the children wearing patterns to stand up. Have them point to or describe the patterns on their clothing—for example, red and green stripes. Talk with the child having trouble with patterning about what is on her shirt. For example, if she is wearing a blue-and-white-striped shirt, point to the stripes and say, "Look! Here is a pattern: *blue stripe, white stripe, blue stripe, white stripe, blue stripe.*" Then ask her to repeat your words or point to each stripe while you describe the pattern.

Present the daily schedule as a pattern. Help this child recognize that the class does the activities on the schedule in the same order every day. As you point to each item on your schedule chart, explain that washing hands comes first, then breakfast, then large group. The next day, describe the pattern in the schedule again. To make the pattern more obvious, put squares by the first two items—for example, a green square next to washing hands and a yellow square next to breakfast. Point out this same pattern daily (Copley, Jones, and Dighe 2007).

Is This Child Unable to Copy Patterns?

Once a child identifies patterns around her, she can begin to copy them. Most likely she will start with simple patterns involving just a couple of colored items or shapes and then move to more complex patterns.

Patterns can be made from a number of easily accessible items. Try making patterns from buttons, leaves, die-cut shapes, plastic animals, or flannel board pieces. You can make sound patterns using instruments, your hands, or your voice to make animal sounds. For example, divide the group in two. Assign one group to be ducks and say, "Quack." Assign the other group to be songbirds and say, "Tweet." Create a pattern by having the group say "Quack, tweet, tweet. Quack, tweet, tweet." Sing songs with repeated word patterns like those in "Old MacDonald": "Ee-I-Ee-I-O." Move to pattern songs like the one found at www.songsforteaching.com/math/beginning arithmeticconcepts/patterns.php.

Books about Patterns

Read pattern books to help children begin to identify patterns.

I See Patterns by Susan Ring

Pattern (Math Counts) by Henry Pluckrose

Pattern Bugs by Trudy Harris

Patterns Everywhere by Julie Dalton

Pattern Fish by Trudy Harris

Set blocks out in various patterns in the block area before children have choice time. When they enter the block area, sit with them. Point out a pattern and ask them to make one just like it. Use only five to seven blocks so they can use one-to-one correspondence to copy them. Use colored blocks at first—for example, yellow block, green block, red block—and repeat the pattern two to three times. Invite a child who is having difficulty copying patterns to do the activity with you. Encourage her to copy the pattern and let her know when she is right. Point out specifically how she copied the pattern. For example, tell her, "Look, you made a pattern. You put a yellow block, green block, and red block, and then you put a yellow block, green block, and red block."

Put out commercial or teacher-made pattern cards. Ask this child to place colored buttons in the same pattern she sees. Begin by asking her to put the buttons directly on top of the pattern on the card. Eventually have her make the pattern on the table next to the card. Start with the simplest patterns and gradually move to more complex ones. Include other children in the activity and talk about the patterns on the cards. Ask the children to describe the patterns to each other.

After this child becomes adept at identifying and copying patterns, take her on an outdoor pattern walk. Ask her to show you patterns she sees. She may notice patterns in apartment windows, doors, gates, or sidewalks, or patterns in nature, such as the brown and orange stripes on a caterpillar. Take pictures of the patterns to bring back to the classroom. Print the pictures and ask this child to pick out a pattern and draw it. Provide paper, markers, pencils, erasers, and crayons. If she is having difficulty choosing or drawing the pattern, sit with her and point out the pattern: "See? Here are three windows; underneath them are three more windows. Would you like to draw that?" Accept all drawings. Display the drawings next to the pictures you took with the camera. After a few weeks of studying patterns, take another pattern walk. Again take pictures and ask this child to draw patterns when she returns. Ask her to compare her first and second pictures. Discuss the differences in the pictures.

Is This Child Unable to Extend Simple Patterns?

Although extending simple patterns and copying patterns are very similar skills, extending patterns signifies that the child understands that patterns can be repeated almost limitlessly. If a child is having difficulty with this skill, she may just look at you when you ask her to extend or repeat the pattern, or she may avoid the activity. Making the activity nonthreatening and fun will help this child come to it in her own way.

Transition times when children are asked to line up or gather are opportunities to practice pattern activities. Once the children are together, start a simple pattern: each child holds up arms and hands or hangs them to the side. Demonstrate the pattern with four or five children. Ask the first child to hold her hands above her head, the second child to put her hands at her side, and then repeat this pattern two to three times. Give a verbal clue by describing the pattern: "Up, down, up, down, up, _____." Have the children fill in the blank. Ask the remaining children to repeat the pattern with their hands, and help as needed. Make sure the child who is having difficulty is placed near the end of the line so she can see the repeated pattern. Try another pattern like facing *forward, backward, forward, backward* or *sit, stand, sit, stand*. Make the pattern more complex by including a third position in the pattern, such as *sit, stand, kneel*. Use a movement pattern to get from one place to another, such as *slide, jump, jump, slide, jump, jump, slide, jump, jump* or *step, step, hop, step, step, hop*. Using body movements helps children understand patterns and how to extend them.

Create a pattern mural by putting a long piece of paper on the floor. Start a pattern that this child can repeat. For example, use a green marker to draw two straight lines and one circle; repeat this pattern a few times. Ask this child to extend the pattern. Demonstrate drawing two blue, two red, two blue, and two red straight lines. After she understands how to extend the simple pattern, make it a bit more challenging for this child by asking her to make the circle (in the two straight lines and one circle pattern) a different color, such as fluorescent pink. Now the pattern becomes two straight green lines and one pink circle.

Start several strings of beads with simple patterns, and ask this child to repeat the pattern. One pattern can be *red, green, yellow, red, green, yellow, red, green, yellow*. Introduce the activity and sit with her while she strings her first necklaces until she understands the idea. If she does not repeat the pattern, point out again how the pattern develops. Don't comment if she has made a mistake; instead, show her the right order. For example, if your pattern is *red, green, yellow* and this child has put in a blue bead, point out the pattern, ask her what the pattern is, and then ask if her pattern matches. If she says, "Yes," point to the blue bead and say, "I wonder if this blue bead matches." After you point this out, the child usually sees the broken pattern and corrects herself.

Is This Child Unable to Create Her Own Simple Patterns?

Once children can identify, copy, and extend patterns, they learn to create their own patterns. If a child is having difficulty creating her own patterns, determine if she understands and can do the steps described earlier in this chapter. She may not be able to create patterns until she understands how to extend patterns. Repeat previous pattern activities to help this child review earlier learning. Then ask her to create a pattern.

Invite this child to create her own patterns by lining up math counters (small plastic manipulatives, such as colored fruit or dinosaurs). When she is done, ask her to describe her pattern. If she is having trouble creating a pattern, limit the number of objects available. Have only two or three types of objects for her to use (such as bananas, apples, and pears). Introduce a weaving board (you can make one using an old picture frame; attach a number of strips of elastic across two parallel sides of the frame; and cut a variety of colors of ribbon the same length as the width of the frame). Ask the child to weave patterns using the ribbon. She may weave her ribbon over, under, over, and under the elastic. Or her pattern may be over, over, under, over, over, under. Ask this child to create a pattern at the easel using a long, narrow strip of paper and two or three rubber ink stamps. Or use long, narrow paper and dot art stamps.

Gather a small group of children together. Include the child who isn't creating patterns. Ask one child to create a pattern. Then ask the other children to copy or extend it. Take turns so all children have a turn creating their own patterns. Help the child having difficulty create a simple pattern. Being the leader and having others copy you can be extremely motivating to the children. The patterns can be made by drawing on paper with markers, connecting small plastic links, or using plastic disks like checkers.

Make pattern books using stickers. Put together booklets with blank pages. Have stickers available to place on the pages. Encourage this child to create patterns with the stickers. After she has finished, ask her to describe the pattern on each page and write down her words for a caption. Let children read one another's books.

Work with the Parents

Parents may not understand the importance of patterns in children's early math development. Help them better understand how recognizing and forming patterns helps children predict what comes next. Share information about their child's work with patterns. Help them think of pattern activities that can be done while the family is dressing, eating, or traveling in the car. Ask this child's parents what their child enjoys, and encourage them to find pattern activities related to her interests. Share the information for parents that follows and be sure to give them feedback about their child's progress in your setting.

When to Seek Assistance

A child's ability to understand and identify patterns partly depends on her experience and exposure to these concepts. Encourage a child having difficulty to continue to participate in pattern activities. Keep activities engaging, and give positive, specific feedback to this child when she has identified or accurately copied patterns. If you have been covering patterns in your setting and this child still cannot identify or copy them, particularly if she is four years old or older, look carefully at other measures of cognitive development. If you notice other cognitive difficulties, refer this child for developmental screening through her school district.

A Plan for Action

To develop your Plan for Action, choose or modify one of the suggested goals to best match your situation. Add how well or how often you expect the skill or behavior to be demonstrated. Remember: you are looking for growth, not perfection. You want to move the child from where she is currently and to increase your expectations slightly. Next, determine three or four actions teachers and parents will take. Choose additional actions specific to the early childhood setting and the home. Record your choices on the planning form found in the appendix.

Sample goals for a child who is learning about patterns:

- ◆ Recognizes patterns
- ◆ Copies patterns
- ◆ Extends patterns
- ◆ Creates own patterns

Sample actions parents and teachers can take:

- ◆ Point out patterns in the classroom or home
- ◆ Read pattern books
- ◆ Search for patterns around the classroom or the home
- ◆ Ask the child to copy a pattern with colored blocks
- ◆ Ask the child to draw patterns
- ◆ Ask this child to show you a pattern on her shirt or pants
- ◆ Ask this child to extend patterns with colored beads
- ◆ Ask the child to create a pattern for you to copy
- ◆ Make a pattern book with stickers

Sample actions teachers can make:

- ◆ Put out patterns (wallpaper, fabric, and dishes) for the child to discover
- ◆ Use pattern cards for the child to copy
- ◆ Take pictures of patterns on a walk and ask the child to draw them
- ◆ Lead pattern movement activities
- ◆ Make a pattern mural

Sample actions parents can take:

- ◆ Point out patterns you see
- ◆ Help your child recognize patterns in clothing, activities, and actions
- ◆ Take turns extending patterns with markers on a piece of paper

Information on Patterns

WHAT IS IT?

Patterns are all around us. They can be found in checkers on a tablecloth, yellow dashes down the center of the highway, and the stripes of mowed grass on a baseball field. Patterns can be simple or complex. Once children start to see patterns, they enjoy finding new ones. First they begin to recognize patterns, and then they learn to copy them. Eventually they create their own patterns. Not only can you help your child recognize patterns—you can also help him or her label and verbally describe them. Learning about patterns is an important component of early math. Seeing and making patterns helps children understand how things work together and helps them predict what comes next.

Observe and Respond

Help your child recognize that the daily schedule, the passage of day and night, and the "Hokey Pokey" contain patterns. Use the word *pattern* frequently so your child becomes familiar with it. Keep the patterns simple—at first, use only two or three items.

Read the book *I See Patterns* by Susan Ring, which illustrates patterns that can be easily identified in colorful pictures of animals, insects, fences and posts, and rows in a field of corn. Go on a pattern hunt around your house. Point out patterned dishes, wallpaper, and quilts. Keep a list of the patterns you observe. Ask your child to draw some of these patterns.

Point out patterns on your child's clothing. For example, if your child has a blue-and-white-striped shirt, point to the stripes and say, "Look! Here is a pattern: *blue stripe, white stripe, blue stripe, white stripe, blue stripe.*" Then ask your child to repeat your words or point to each stripe as you describe the pattern.

Children who can identify patterns can begin to copy them. Most likely your child will start with simple patterns involving just a couple of colored items or shapes and then move to more complex ones. Try making patterns

continued

from buttons, leaves, shapes, or plastic animals. Sing songs with word patterns that repeat, as in "Old MacDonald": "Ee-I-Ee-I-O."

Set colored cube blocks in a pattern or use markers on paper to create various patterns. Ask your child to make one just like it. Limit the pattern to only five to seven blocks so your child can use one-to-one correspondence to copy it. *Yellow, green, red, yellow, green, red* is a simple three-part pattern. When your child successfully identifies a pattern, point it out. For example, say, "Look! You made a pattern. You have a yellow block, green block, and red block, and then you have a yellow block, green block, and red block."

After your child can identify and copy patterns, take an outdoor pattern walk to look for patterns. Your child may notice patterns in apartment windows, rectangles in sidewalks, or patterns in nature, such as the brown and orange stripes on a caterpillar. Take pictures of the patterns. Print the pictures and ask your child to draw the pattern. If this proves difficult, sit down with your child and point out the pattern: "See, here are three windows; underneath them are three more windows."

Start a string of beads with a simple pattern and ask your child to repeat the pattern. Point out again how the pattern develops if your child doesn't see the pattern. Don't indicate mistakes; instead, show your child the right order. Then say, "I wonder if this blue bead matches." Your child is likely to see the broken pattern and self-correct.

Invite your child to create new patterns using rubber ink stamps. Or use long narrow paper and bingo daubers or stickers. Create patterns using small plastic links or plastic disks like checkers.

CONNECTING WITH SUPPORT

If you have been working on patterns for some time and your child is still having difficulty identifying or copying them, particularly if he or she is four years old or older, look carefully at other measures of cognitive development. If you notice other cognitive difficulties, have your child's skills screened through your school district.

19 ◆ "Come See This!" Observing

FOR TEACHERS

Owen was engrossed in the anthill he discovered. A number of ants were carrying crumbs of food, going in and out of a tiny pile of sand. When I asked him, "What do you see?" he did not respond.

❖ Standard
Uses observations to gather information.

What Is It?

When children see something they are curious about, they observe it, form questions, make guesses, "gather evidence, organize their ideas, and propose explanations" (Anderson, Martin, and Faszewski 2006, 32). This process is part of scientific thinking and forms the basis of scientific inquiry. Science is both the process and the content of inquiry. We all need to understand science so we can solve problems, make informed decisions, and join discussions about issues facing the world, such as pollution and climate change. Our society needs scientific thinkers to enter the fields of science, technology, engineering, and math.

Scientific learning takes place throughout early childhood settings. Children work on the concepts of gravity, symmetry, and balance when they build block structures. They learn about physical changes when they mix paint in the art area, and they learn about water flow and pressure when they experiment with water at the sensory table. Teachers can arrange designated spaces for scientific exploration. In these interest areas, teachers can offer science activities designed to expand children's natural inquisitiveness. Teachers can add tools for examining, measuring, and recording discoveries. Learning is extended when teachers walk children through the use of inquiry. Children deepen their understanding of their observations by talking with teachers about what they see, hear, touch, or experience.

Observe and Decide What to Teach

Keep the following questions in mind when working with a child who is learning to observe. Use the suggestions to build on his natural inquisitiveness and to help him learn to use his observations to gather information.

Does This Child Show Minimal Interest in Using His Senses to Explore Materials?

Children are active learners. They do more than look at an object; they engage all of their senses in order to learn about it. To learn about an object's physical properties, children look at it, taste it, give it a sniff, listen to hear if it makes a sound, and touch it. They manipulate it in order to see what it does, how it acts, and how it reacts.

Offer activities that help a child use his senses to explore taste during snack and mealtimes. Encourage this child to try a bite of new foods, but do not force him. Introduce a number of different vocabulary words that describe various tastes, such as *bitter*, *sweet*, *salty*, *spicy*, and *sour*. (But institute a "No tasting" safety rule during other science activities.)

Provide opportunities for a child to use his sense of sight by collecting a number of similar objects, such as large seeds, nuts, pinecones, stones, or leaves. Add magnifying lenses, measurement tools, and materials for him to record his observations. Gather a number of different types of leaves. Trace around the outside edges, sort them, and make prints of their veins by painting the backs and pressing them onto paper. Talk about what this child sees as he explores the leaves. Focus this child's attention on the items found within the confines of a section of grass roped off with string and craft stick stakes. Be aware of any allergies this child may have. If he is allergic to grasses, he may have to examine life found in the cracks of a sidewalk instead.

Give this child the opportunity to tune in to things he hears. Suspend three or four different-sized musical triangles. Let him strike each one to hear the differences in pitch. Or collect different-sized metal cans. (Be sure there aren't any sharp edges.) Let this child experiment with the sounds the cans make when they are tapped with different utensils, such as a pencil eraser, a metal spoon, or a drumstick. Draw or paint to different types of music, such as a lullaby, a waltz, or a march. Play a sound-matching game by filling two small containers with rice, two with beans, and two with sand. Mix up the containers. Ask this child to shake them and decide which ones sound the same. Ask, "What makes them the same? Which are the quietest? Which are the loudest?" Read the book *The Listening Walk* by Paul Showers. Then go on a walk with this child and listen for sounds. Take paper and a pencil to make a list of what you hear.

Explore different scents by placing a cotton ball in an empty salt shaker. Place a few drops of almond extract, orange juice, or lemon juice on the cotton ball. Let this child smell and describe what he smells. Add a scent to playdough by adding a few drops of peppermint or vanilla extract, or add a couple of drops of extract to tempera paint. Grow herbs, and let this child rub the leaves and sniff their aromas. Take a walk outdoors to smell lilacs in bloom or the fresh scent after a rain.

Use a sensory table to give this child a chance to feel different items. Fill it with water, sand, cotton balls, soil, or small pebbles. Make collages from textured fabrics, corrugated cardboard, yarn, and different types of ribbons. Go on searches for things that are rough, smooth, hard, or soft. In addition to experiencing how things feel, teach this child words to describe things, such as *jagged*, *smooth*, *rough*, *round*, *slimy*, and *bumpy*. Make a feely box by placing a long sock over an oatmeal container with the sole of the sock covering the container and the ribbing extending beyond the container to provide a sleeve for the child to stick his hand into. Place one textured item at a time in the box. Let this child reach in and guess what he feels only by touching it. If he is hesitant to touch various items, consider his threshold for sensory information; some children avoid textures that are uncomfortable to them (see information in part 6, Motor Development, on sensory threshold, pages 220–21).

Encourage Observation through Books

The following is a list of books that support observations. Ask open-ended questions to encourage children to make observations. Keep these and many like them in your collection of classroom favorites.

In the Tall, Tall Grass by Denise Fleming

Is It Rough? Is It Smooth? Is It Shiny? by Tana Hoban

The Listening Walk by Paul Showers

Mouse Paint by Ellen Stoll Walsh

My Five Senses by Aliki

The Snowy Day by Ezra Jack Keats

Take Another Look by Tana Hoban

What Is Round? by Rebecca Kai Dotlich

What Is Square? by Rebecca Kai Dotlich

Who Sank the Boat? by Pamela Allen

Is This Child Unlikely to Identify or Describe Objects by Their Physical Characteristics?

Children are often eager to learn about what they see. Once they become interested in an item, encourage them to describe its attributes, make observations, and draw conclusions. Usually children first identify and describe objects by a simple attribute or characteristic. They say it is red before they say it is red, round, and a ball.

Provide a child who isn't yet describing physical traits of objects with collections of objects to match and sort. Ask questions that correspond to his skill level. Start with an open-ended question: "What do you notice?" If you do not get a response, ask a closed question like "What color is the button?" If this child is still having difficulty, ask him to match the item to another item of the same color. Tell him that he has correctly matched two red buttons. At the beginning of the chapter, Owen's teacher noticed how engrossed he was in observing the anthill. She first asked Owen what he saw (an open-ended question). When he did not respond, she asked the closed questions "What are those? What are they doing?" Finally, she brought Owen a clipboard, paper, and marker, thinking he might be able to represent what he saw in this miniature world.

Display a collection of objects like rocks, leaves, or pinecones. Provide this child with a magnifying lens to look at the objects more closely. Taking a close-up look is highly motivating to young children and can help build enthusiasm in even the most reluctant young scientist. Most children can use a hand-held magnifying lens; offer a tabletop magnifier to children who have difficulty holding the lens, looking through it, and manipulating the object. Stand nearby and record what this child notices. Have a conversation about what he said. Reflect back to this child: "I heard you say the pinecones had prickles. What else did you notice about the pinecones? What did they remind you of?" Make a list of words that he uses as a record of this child's vocabulary.

Teach this child to document what he observes or experiences so he can remember and think about those things; ask him to dictate them to an adult so they can be written down. You can also ask him to record his observations in his own way. Encourage this child to represent what he sees using paper on a clipboard, a notebook and a marker, a whiteboard, playdough or other 3-D materials, a chart or graph, or a camera.

Is This Child Unable to Describe Changes He Observes?

Children are often amazed by changes they see. For example, a child will spontaneously describe how his view of the world is different when he is looking upside down. Teachers can help a child learn to describe changes by painting with water outside on a hot day to become familiar with evaporation, bringing snow into the classroom and watching it melt, or planting seeds and watching them grow. Measure the growth of grass seed or bean sprouts. Record the new growth you see in a science journal. Baking with children is another way to provide opportunities for discussing physical changes: the batter is baked and becomes muffins.

Talk with a child who doesn't describe change about how playdough changes shape when it is squeezed, rolled, or pounded. Draw his attention to the lines a rake makes when it is pulled through wet sand. Ask this child to describe what happens when he paints with more than one color or paints with a roller and then scrapes through it with a comb. Play a game in which you ask the children to close their eyes and then make a change, such as putting a chair on top of a table or taking off your glasses. Have them name what is different.

When to Seek Assistance

Examine your records to determine if this child is demonstrating a pattern of any of the following:

◆ Regularly wanders the room without becoming occupied in an activity

◆ Doesn't actively engage in exploration

◆ Is overly fascinated by something and you are unable to draw his attention away

◆ Tastes or puts nonedible items in his mouth after the age of three

◆ Is unable to describe one or more characteristic of an item by the age of four

If you recognize a pattern of any of these behaviors that lasts for more than a couple of weeks, talk to the parents about having this child's skills screened by the local school district.

Work with the Parents

Some parents may feel that preschool children are too young for science activities. Help them see that children are involved in science in their everyday activities. Encourage them to enhance their children's scientific discoveries by talking with them, joining them in their excitement, and asking questions that can lead to further discovery. Write newsletters highlighting simple science activities that can be done at home and by giving them the information presented for parents in this book. Post recordings of your classroom investigations to spark ideas of their own.

A Plan for Action

To develop your Plan for Action, choose or modify one of the suggested goals to best match your situation. Add how well or how often you expect the skill or behavior to be demonstrated. Remember: you are looking for growth, not perfection. You want to move the child from where he is currently and to increase your expectations slightly. Next, determine three or four actions teachers and parents will take. Choose additional actions specific to the early childhood setting and the home. Record your choices on the planning form found in the appendix.

Sample goals for a child who is not yet using observations to gather information:

- Uses his senses to explore materials
- Describes objects by one or two physical characteristics (*Choose one.*)
- Describes changes he observes

Sample actions parents and teachers can take:

- Offer new foods to taste
- Introduce vocabulary words to describe tastes, sights, sounds, smells, and textures
- Offer collections of similar objects
- Offer magnifying lenses and measurement tools
- Ask the child to draw what he sees in a section of grass or the cracks in a sidewalk
- Trace around the outside edges of items
- Sort items in a collection
- Experiment with musical instruments and household items that make sounds
- Read books that support observations, and describe what you see pictured in the book
- Go on sensory walks to focus on things you can see, hear, or smell
- Grow herbs and smell their aromas
- Go on a touch scavenger hunt
- Ask questions to prompt this child to describe objects
- Encourage him to record what he sees, hears, smells, tastes, or touches
- Plan activities that help this child describe changes he sees or experiences
- Play with playdough and talk about how it changes when you manipulate it

Sample actions teachers can take:

- Draw or paint to different types of music
- Make sound shakers and discover the sounds they make
- Explore different scents in smell containers
- Play with scented playdough or paint with scented tempera paint
- Fill a sensory table with various items
- Make texture collages
- Make a feely box and ask this child to guess what is inside
- Make impressions in wet sand
- Experiment with mixing colors

Sample actions parents can take:

- Talk about smells while you cook together
- Discuss how food changes while you cook together
- Fill a tub with water and let your child experiment with measuring cups
- Sort socks and describe how they are the same or different
- Note the signs that seasons are changing
- Talk about appropriate clothing for the weather

Information on Observing

WHAT IS IT?

Children engage in science when they explore their world. They work on the concepts of gravity, symmetry, and balance when they build block structures. They learn about physical changes while they mix sand or soil with water. They deepen their understanding by talking with people about what they see, hear, touch, or experience.

Observe and Respond

Many everyday experiences offer you and your child opportunities to explore science together. Children are active learners. They do more then look at an object; they engage all of their senses to learn about it. To explore an object's physical properties, your child will look at it, give it a sniff, listen to see if it makes a sound, touch it, and if it's something edible—taste it! Your child will manipulate an object to see what it does, how it acts, or how it reacts. Help your child learn to use the sense of taste by offering different foods to eat. Introduce words that describe various tastes, such as *bitter*, *sweet*, *salty*, *spicy*, and *sour*.

Provide opportunities for your child to use the sense of sight by collecting a number of similar objects, such as pinecones, rocks, or leaves. Give your child a magnifying lens, paper, and pencil to record observations. Rope off a section of grass with string and craft stick stakes, and ask your child to draw what he or she sees. Go on a fall walk together. Gather different types of leaves. Trace around their outside edges or sort them.

Give your child opportunities to tune in to sounds. Collect different-sized metal cans. (Be sure there aren't any sharp edges.) Let your child experiment with the sounds they make by tapping on them with different items, such as a pencil eraser, a metal spoon, and a wooden spoon. Go on a walk with your child and listen to the sounds. Make a list of all the things you hear.

Grow herbs and let your child rub the leaves and then sniff the aroma. When you cook together, talk about the different smells: vanilla, when it is added to cookie dough; orange, when you pour juice; lemon, when you make lemonade.

Fill a tub with water. Let your child splash, pour from various containers, or make bubbles by blowing through a straw. Go on

continued

a touch scavenger hunt; find something that is rough, smooth, hard, or soft. Help your child describe things that are jagged, smooth, rough, round, slimy, and bumpy. Children first learn to identify and describe objects by a single characteristic. They say something is red before they say it is red, round, and a ball. Provide your child with collections of objects that can be matched and sorted. If your child doesn't spontaneously describe physical characteristics of the items, ask, "What do you notice?" If you do not get a response, ask, "What color is it?" or "How does it feel?"

Children are often amazed by changes they see. Your child can experience changes by painting with water outside on a hot day—the water disappears. Bring snow in the house—it melts! Plant seeds—they grow! Talk with your child about how playdough changes shape when it is squeezed, rolled, or pounded. Take note of the signs that seasons are changing— for example, how dark it becomes on your way home from child care, if it is colder outside, or if grass is turning green. Talk about appropriate clothing for the season.

Cooking teaches children how substances change. Cook together and talk about how batter becomes runny when you add more milk and turns solid when you bake it. Let your child make juice by squeezing an orange.

CONNECTING WITH SUPPORT

If your child is not yet demonstrating an interest in science activities, look for science taking place around you. Share your enthusiasm for things you discover. Ask your child's teacher what else you can do to help your child learn to gather information through the senses. If your child regularly wanders around without becoming occupied in an activity other than television or electronics, is overly fascinated by something and cannot be drawn away, tastes or puts nonedible items in his or her mouth after the age of three, or is unable to describe one or more characteristic of an item by the age of four, consider having your child's skills screened by your local school district.

20 "I Want to Try It!" Investigating

FOR TEACHERS

Maddie usually comes up with her own explanations of the way things are. Her explanations aren't always right, but she is trying to understand things she sees.

❖ **Standard**
Gathers information by asking questions and investigating the environment.

What Is It?

Making sense of the world starts with a child's natural curiosity (see chapter 11, "Hey, What's This?" Curiosity and Questioning). To learn about an object or materials, children observe, wonder, and ask questions. Their drive to learn helps them focus on a question, make predictions, and set up an investigation. They use all of their senses and the tools available to collect and record data. Once they have gathered data, they analyze the evidence and make comparisons. They reflect on new information that challenges their current understandings and develop additional ideas and theories. As they communicate their theories to others, they deepen their understanding (Chalufour and Worth 2005). When adults around them encourage investigation, children engage in further study and revise their thinking until they arrive at plausible explanations.

Many early childhood teachers aren't comfortable teaching science. They may offer science activities for the children to explore but may not know how to take such activities to the next level to support children's investigations. If you are uncomfortable with science, try tinkering with materials before you put them out. Ask your own questions and engage in your own inquiry. Learning and practicing the process of inquiry is as important as the scientific concepts you explore. Consider partnering with a science expert in your community. This person may be able to provide you with an understanding of the underlying concepts of an activity and boost your confidence. You don't have to know every answer, but you can encourage children to ask questions, arrange an environment that encourages experimentation, help look for answers to their questions, and move beyond exploring to inquiry and understanding.

Observe and Decide What to Teach

It's important to offer many opportunities for children to ask questions and learn through hands-on investigations. Consider the following questions and suggestions as you help a child learn to ask questions and investigate the environment.

Does This Child Lack an Interest in Asking Questions and Seeking Answers?

Children ask questions and search for answers to their questions when they are in an environment that is physically and emotionally safe to explore. Create a setting in which all children feel free to ask questions. Accept all guesses and predictions. Ask open-ended questions so children needn't worry about making mistakes. Provide a model by asking questions and trying different approaches. For example, if you are trying to get a chain reaction from blocks stood on end (like dominos falling in a row), say, "I wonder how far apart my blocks need to be so when I knock one down, it will knock the rest over."

Pay particular attention to helping a child who is not yet asking questions. You want her to feel safe enough to take risks. Perhaps this child has questions but is not asking them out loud. Observe to see if she appears to have a question she is trying to answer. For example, does she place some objects on and take some objects off a balance scale? If so, she may be asking herself, "Do I put heavy objects on this side of the scale to make it balance?" Or does she restack a tower of blocks that have fallen, using a new approach? In this situation, her unspoken question may be "Which blocks do I need to put on the bottom so my tower won't fall?" Model asking questions for this child by guessing what she may be asking. When she does ask a question out loud, don't rush in to answer it for her. Instead, encourage her to discover the answer for herself by asking, "What have you tried? What else could you do?" or "How can you find out what you want to know?" Trying different approaches through various trials of an investigation teaches flexibility in thinking.

Does This Child Avoid Using Tools to Gather Information?

As children engage in their explorations and investigations, they gain further insights and can record their observations when they have access to a number of tools. Tools provide information, promote change, help measure, and assist in recording discoveries.

Problem Solving in Science

The processes involved in problem solving and scientific inquiry are similar. The language changes to reflect the situation.

Problem Solving	Scientific Inquiry
1. Identify a problem	1. Ask a question
2. Gather information	2. Observe and gather information
3. Generate solutions/ strategies	3. Make a prediction
4. Choose the best one or ones. Decide on a plan	4. Decide how to test your prediction
5. Implement your plan	5. Conduct your investigation
6. Evaluate how your plan is working	6. Analyze and evaluate your data
7. Revise your plan as needed	7. Develop additional ideas and theories and communicate these to others

If you notice a child who is not using tools for scientific discovery, use a tool together. Ask, "Have you seen anything like this before? Where? What is it used for? What does it do? How do you think you might use it?" (Chalufour and Worth 2003). Once a child becomes familiar with a number of tools, help her choose the best one for her investigation by asking, "What's the best tool to help you find out about this?" or "What's the best tool to help you record your work?"

Give this child a chance to take a closer look by offering a variety of magnifying tools, such as handheld, tabletop, or full-page magnifiers. Ask her, "What does the magnifier do? What did you notice when you used the magnifier? How do you make an item clear? Where can you see it best?" Once this child has had a chance to examine items up close, help her record what she has seen. Make an outline of a magnifying lens on a piece of paper and let her draw her discovery. Or give her a camera to take a picture of the item. Ask her to label the picture with her findings.

Help this child share her discoveries. Ask, "What did you do? What happened when _____? What did you notice? What will you try next time?" Record what she thinks her next step should be. Help her recall her thoughts so they can serve as the start of the next day's activities.

Open-ended Questions

Asking a few well-timed, well-phrased questions is critical to effective instruction. You can facilitate learning by asking open-ended questions that cause a child to think. (The opposite of an open-ended question is a closed question. These questions tend to be technical and require a memorized or single-word answer. Examples of closed questions include "What color is it?" "How many are there?") Examples of open-ended questions are

- What do you know about . . . ?
- What would happen if . . . ?
- What else can you try?
- What else can you do with . . . ?
- What did you notice?
- How do you know?
- What makes you think that?
- Why do you think that happened?

Some children may not be used to being asked questions. Others may be shy and uncomfortable about answering. If a child is shy, making your own comments or asking yourself a question may be a good place to start. Be sure to give all children time to think about a question you have asked before expecting them to respond or before asking another question. Accept their answers so they view themselves as successful.

Is This Child Unable to Make Comparisons between Objects That Have Been Collected or Observed?

Preschool children love to collect things. Their pockets bulge and their backpacks become heavy with treasures. These treasures, as well as teacher-collected items, provide opportunities for children to make comparisons. Collections may include rocks, leaves, pinecones, seeds, nuts, and shells. Display teachers' collections at children's eye level to spark their interest. Provide containers like buckets, plastic food containers, egg cartons, or ice cube trays for children to sort and classify their collections. If a child is not sorting items spontaneously, ask, "Do any of these go together?" or "Are there others like this one?" Accept the way a child groups things. Find out about her reasoning by asking, "What makes them the same?" Help her draw comparisons by asking, "What's different? What do you notice?"

Tools for Investigating and Recording

Preschool children can use many tools to conduct and record their investigations. Below is a list to help you think about tools children can use in your setting:

- Magnifying lenses
- Eyedroppers of various sizes
- Bulb basters
- Scoops
- Funnels
- Measuring cups
- Balance scale
- Stopwatch
- Computer
- Books on topics like plants, animals, birds, insects, machines, land, air, and water
- Thermometers
- Rulers, yardsticks, and tape measures
- Binoculars
- Rain gauge
- Sieves
- Flashlights or penlights
- Paper and pencil
- Camera

Help a child learn to make comparisons during different trials of an investigation. For example, you can arrange an investigation of gravity and motion by introducing ramps and inclines. Use varying lengths of wide boards, plastic rain gutters, or cove molding for ramps. Allow children to make inclines by placing one end of the ramp on a chair, table, or stack of blocks. Let this child try rolling different objects, such as balls, blocks, or cars, down a ramp. Add sandpaper or a bump to the inclines. As this child experiments with different angles, a variety of objects, and different obstacles, ask, "What do you notice?" Help her record her observations by charting which cars go farthest, or write her description of what takes place when a bump is added to the incline.

Teach her to organize and compare data by using charts and graphs. Make a life-sized graph by drawing a grid on an oil cloth. Lay it on the floor and ask her to place one item in each box. All items that are the same go in one row. When the items have been laid out, help this child step back and decide what the graph tells her. Help her conduct classroom surveys to discover what toys are the most popular, the favorite foods of the children, and their favorite books. Make a chart with three columns and a name card or photograph for each child. Have this child ask the others the survey question and then place their name or photo in the correct column. Be sure that the child starts her list at the bottom of the chart and adds other names to the top of each column. Help this child read the data by determining which is the tallest, the shortest, and the in-between column.

Does This Child Make Up Explanations about What She Observes?

As children attempt to understand what they see and experience, they devise preliminary explanations for their observations. Their theories go through a number of revisions when they investigate their explanations. Accept incomplete understandings and magical thinking. Ask open-ended questions and set materials out for children to test their predictions. As they experience more, children deepen their understanding and their ideas become more plausible and closer to current understandings (Chalufour and Worth 2005).

Maddie, the three-and-one-half-year-old in the story at the beginning of the chapter, told her teacher that it rains because a giant squeezes the water out of the clouds. Her teacher gathered a number of sponges and added them to the water table for Maddie to explore her explanation further. They also looked out the window on a rainy day at the clouds. Her teacher encouraged Maddie to describe what she saw. Then they read a book that describes clouds and what causes rain. Maddie used this information to modify her understanding of different types of clouds and what happens when it rains. Later that spring, Maddie called her teacher's attention to some dark, dense clouds and said, "I think those clouds are full of water."

Encourage this child to think about and describe the results of her experiments. For example, if she is interested in objects that sink and float, design activities that help her experiment. Offer boats of various sizes. Provide different materials to place in the boat, such as marbles, blocks, plastic animals, or metal washers. Ask, "What did you have to do to make the boat sink? Why do you think it sank?"

Work with the Parents

Some parents may think that teaching science is the school's responsibility. They may have had negative experiences with science or feel uncomfortable about their own level of scientific understanding. Help them see that children are engaged in scientific explorations all the time. Write newsletters with activity ideas that help them see science as part of everyday life. Encourage them to enjoy their child's awe as they experience new things. Help them learn to support their child's scientific exploration through questioning. Provide the written materials for parents that follows. Work with them to think of activity ideas that support the development of questioning and investigation skills.

When to Seek Assistance

Examine your records to determine if a child is demonstrating any of the following patterns:

- Regularly wanders around the room without becoming occupied in an activity
- Does not engage in scientific exploration after six months of gentle encouragement
- Is overly fascinated by something and cannot be drawn away from it
- Is overly fearful of most science materials after six months of introduction and modeling

If you recognize a pattern of any of the above behaviors lasting for more than a few months, talk to the child's parents about having her skills screened by the local school district.

A Plan for Action

To develop your Plan for Action, choose or modify one of the suggested goals to best match your situation. Add how well or how often you expect the skill or behavior to be demonstrated. Remember: you are looking for growth, not perfection. You want to move the child from where she is currently and to increase your expectations slightly. Next, determine three or four actions teachers and parents will take. Choose additional actions specific to the early childhood setting and the home. Record your choices on the planning form found in the appendix.

Sample goals for a child who does not gather information by asking questions or investigating the environment:

- Asks questions and seeks answers
- Uses tools to gather information
- Makes comparisons between objects that have been observed
- Makes reasonable explanations about what she observes

Sample actions parents and teachers can take:

- Create a physically and emotionally safe environment
- Accept questions, guesses, and predictions
- Guide this child through the process of inquiry
- Ask open-ended questions
- Give this child time to think about a question before expecting an answer
- Model asking questions
- Model trying different approaches
- State a question out loud that this child may be trying to answer
- Introduce this child to tools used for scientific discovery and recording
- Help this child choose the best tool for her investigation
- Offer this child a magnifying lens to take a closer look
- Help this child record what she sees
- Help this child talk about her discoveries
- Gather collections of similar objects
- Provide containers for sorting and classifying
- Accept the way the child groups things; find out how she reasons
- Accept incomplete understandings
- Provide additional opportunities to explore and deepen understandings

Sample actions teachers can take:

- Record what this child believes to be her next step; help her recall it when she starts her investigation again
- Help this child conduct surveys
- Teach the child to organize data
- Help this child decide what a graph or chart tells her

Sample actions parents can take:

- Encourage your child to answer her own questions
- Provide containers for your child's collections
- Encourage your child to sort her collections
- Encourage your child to draw comparisons
- Explore science in your community

Information on Investigating

WHAT IS IT?

Making sense of the world starts with children's natural curiosity. Their drive to learn helps them focus on a question, make predictions about what they might find out, and set up an investigation. Children use all of their senses and tools they have available to collect and record data. Once they have gathered data, they analyze the evidence and make comparisons. They reflect on new information that challenges their current understandings and develop additional ideas and theories. When adults around them encourage investigation, they revise their thinking until they arrive at plausible explanations.

The process of scientific inquiry involves a number of steps:

1. Ask a question
2. Observe and gather data
3. Make a prediction
4. Decide how to test your prediction
5. Conduct your investigation
6. Reflect on and analyze your data
7. Develop additional ideas and theories

Many everyday activities help children learn these important skills.

Observe and Respond

Children ask questions and search for answers when they feel free to risk making mistakes. You can help your child feel free to ask and answer questions by accepting even the wildest guesses. Provide a model for asking questions and trying different approaches. For example, if you are trying to place something on the top shelf but can't reach that far, say, "I wonder how I can get this up on the top shelf. Maybe I can reach it if I stand on my tiptoes, maybe I can ask Dad to put it up there, or maybe I can use the stool."

Does your child seem to have a question he or she is trying to answer? Does your child restack a tower of blocks that have fallen using a new approach? Model asking questions for your child by guessing what such questions might be. Say, "Which blocks do you need to put on the bottom so your tower won't fall?" Encourage your child to discover answers independently by asking, "What have you tried? What else could you do?"

Expand your child's thinking by asking open-ended questions. Open-ended questions include "What do you know about . . . ?" "What would happen if . . . ?" and "What else could you try?" Be sure to give your child time to think before expecting a response or before asking another question. Your child will feel successful if you accept his or her answers.

Provide tools your child can use to investigate. Offer measuring cups, a stopwatch, tape measures, funnels, sieves, flashlights, and a magnifying lens. Give your child a camera to take a photograph of the item; ask about your child's discoveries: "What did you do? What happened when _____? What will you try next time?"

Preschool children love to collect things. Collections may include rocks, leaves, pinecones, or shells. Provide containers like buckets, plastic food containers, egg cartons, or ice cube trays for sorting collections. If your child is not sorting items spontaneously, ask, "Do any of these go together?" or "Are there others like this one?" Help your child draw comparisons by asking, "What's different? What do you notice?"

Children make guesses as they attempt to understand what they see and experience. Their theories go through a number of revisions as they gain experience. Accept incomplete understandings and magical thinking (for example, the streetlight changes to green when I count to three). Your child's growing experiences will refine these theories and make them more plausible.

CONNECTING WITH SUPPORT

Ask your child's teacher what scientific explorations the children are doing in the early childhood setting. Find out what you can do at home. Look for opportunities to explore science in your community through classes for preschoolers and visits to a science museum and by getting outdoors. If after a few months of encouraging scientific investigations, your child remains fearful of science materials, does not engage in scientific exploration, or is overly fascinated by things that you cannot draw his or her attention away from, have your child's skills screened by your local school district.

Part 6

Motor Development

Children's bodies grow and develop physically throughout their early
years. As they explore how to move, they learn to sit, crawl, walk and hold a
spoon. This skill development is the basis for their understanding of space, coordination, and movement. As children move and are physically active, they build
strong muscles, healthy bones, and are more likely to maintain a healthy weight.
Good physical health and motor development allow a child to fully participate
in current and future activities and lead to self-confidence and pride in physical
accomplishments.

Through physical activity, children learn the fine- and large-motor skills
that make up this domain. They learn balance and strength, coordination of
large muscles, and build endurance. They learn eye-hand coordination and use
the small muscles in their fingers and hands. Early childhood teachers need to
understand that children need physical activity and nutritional food to develop
optimally. To promote the amount of physical activity that children require,
teachers should provide active indoor and outdoor play experiences. Indoors and
outdoors, children can be encouraged to engage in group games as well as to toss
a ball at a target on their own. Arrange an obstacle course to help children plan
how they will move through space, explore going fast or slow, and decide if they
will walk, run, or crawl.

Fine-motor skills are needed to become independent. Children use their fine-
motor skills to write a note to a friend, turn the pages of a book, button a shirt,
brush their teeth, and use a spoon to eat soup. To enhance fine-motor skills,
teachers should offer plenty of tools and materials for children to manipulate.

For example, they practice fine-motor skills when they use puzzles, art materials, writing tools, pegboards, blocks, and beads.

Children need their families to set schedules that allow them to exercise physically, rest when needed, and eat when hungry. Families can help children learn healthy habits by preparing healthy foods and engaging in physical activity. They can help children learn to use the small muscles in their hands and fingers when they encourage children to use utensils to feed themselves and offer them small toys to play with. Families should include children in everyday activities in which they can use their eyes and hands together.

As in all the domains, states may have more standards than those included in this book. Two standards used by many states are included in part 6, Motor Development. They are the following:

- Shows strength, balance, and coordination of large muscles, chapter 21
- Shows eye-hand coordination, strength, and control of small muscles, chapter 22

Joe and his mother were both scowling as they walked into the classroom. Natalia, Joe's teacher, could tell it had been one of those days. As Joe went to hang up his jacket and put his backpack away, his mom and Natalia stepped into the hall. His mom said, "Nothing went right this morning. It started with his socks. I'd put his socks on, and he'd rip them off. I'd put them on again, and he'd rip them off. He kept telling me it wasn't right. He started crying, and I asked if he could get it right. He tried, but he couldn't do it either. The best I could tell was he was trying to get the seam of the sock right across his toenails. We finally got it so he could tolerate it and started on his shoes. I must have tried to tie them six times. They were either too tight or too loose. As you can see, we gave up, and he's wearing his slippers. I'm sorry; we just got so frustrated."

Joe and his mom had mornings like this one pretty often. Something would be wrong while he got dressed: a tag was scratching him, his pants were too itchy, or his shoes and socks bothered him. Joe didn't like the feel of some things at school either. Sometimes he didn't want to go outside because he worried he'd get sand from the playground in his shoes. At other times, he didn't want to do an art project because he didn't want to get his hands messy.

Every child has a sensory threshold that is comfortable to him. It is part of a child's temperament or his inborn way of responding. Each child's threshold for sensory information is somewhere along a continuum. At one end of the line, a child responds minimally to his senses; at the other end, he has a high response. When you think of a child you are working with, ask how sensitive he is to things he sees, hears, feels, or smells. How aware is he of noise, textures, light, and temperature?

Most children fall somewhere in the middle of this sensual continuum. They may have a few sensitivities and avoid or seek out some things occasionally, but they take most sensory information in stride. Help children experience a variety of inputs by arranging an environment that is full of things to look at, touch, and smell but that is also calming and allows them to get away from sensations when they need to.

Joe reacted strongly to things he felt or touched. He avoided things whose textures were uncomfortable. At times, it was so difficult for him to cope with sensations that he would have tantrums, refuse to wear certain clothing, or throw the offending item across the room. Some days Joe wasn't as bothered by these sensations, and he could fully participate in activities. He seemed able to cope with taste and smell more easily than with other sensations. Other children may exhibit different sensitivities. For example, another child may plug his ears when the sound gets too loud or shade his eyes when the light is too bright.

Joe and other children with sensitivities may need a break from sensations. Look at and listen to what is going on in your environment. Reduce the number of items hanging from the ceiling or displayed on the wall. Play background music only occasionally. Try lighting some areas of the room with table lamps instead of overhead panels. Add rugs and fabric wall hangings to absorb sound. Be sure to include a place where children can get away from inputs to a quiet, restful space, such as a book corner.

Some children need more sensory stimulation. A child who needs more sensory information may seek sensations to get it. This child may lean on adults, lay sprawled out on the carpet, or hug others too tightly. Help a child like this take in information through his senses by encouraging sensory play, such as water and sand play or playdough. Try fine or coarse sand at different times to provide a change. Enhance art activities with a variety of sensations by adding a drop of peppermint extract to the paint or having different fabrics and ribbons available for a collage. Make a feely box and place different things inside like a cotton ball, a cube covered with sandpaper, or a yarn ball. Find ways for children to use their large muscles as often as possible. Have them practice holding up the wall by pushing against it or engaging in physical jobs like moving heavy objects or emptying the trash.

Some children fall at the extremes of the sensory continuum. These children react strongly or do not react at all to sights, smells, and textures that others take for granted. They experience difficulty organizing and processing the information they receive through their senses. Because they don't organize or process information in the same way as others do, they don't know how to respond to things around them in acceptable or appropriate ways.

If you are working with a child whose relationships, learning, or behavior are affected by his need for or avoidance of sensory stimulation, consult with the early intervention specialists or your local pediatric health care provider. Ask to talk with an occupational therapist or someone trained in theories of sensory integration. Describe some of the behaviors you are seeing and the intensity of the child's reaction. Ask if the parents see some of the same behaviors. Encourage the parents to seek an evaluation from a health care organization that specializes in sensory processing. If this child is experiencing a problem with sensory integration, early intervention can help him learn to cope.

 **"I Can Run, Hop, and Gallop!"**
Large-Motor Skills

FOR TEACHERS

Carlos doesn't show much interest in physical activity. When we're outside, he chooses to drive the trucks in the sand. He rarely goes on the climber, the swings, or down the slide.

❖ **Standard**

Shows strength, balance, and coordination of large muscles.

What Is It?

Young children are physically active in most things they do. Through their activity, they gain strength and coordination of the large muscles in their body. They also learn many of the skills that will be perfected and combined for later use in games, work, recreation, and sports.

Recent focus on academics and school readiness has led some programs to reduce the time and attention given to physical activity. This is exactly what they should not do, because studies show that physical activity helps with concentration and can enhance learning. Scientists have found that movement stimulates connections in the brain and that physical activity oxygenates and feeds the brain, producing a strong effect on children's ability to learn (Poole, Miller, and Church 2005). Physical activity also provides children with opportunities to release energy and relieve stress. They gain a sense of pride and accomplishment when they move fluidly and have the strength and stamina to participate in physical activities.

Both boys and girls need opportunities to explore movement and physical activities. Besides exploring, they need instruction in activities that help build muscles, enhance coordination, and build endurance. Providing these opportunities helps children develop necessary skills and habits for a healthy lifestyle.

Observe and Decide What to Teach

Ask the following questions as you watch a child move and participate in physical activities in your setting. The suggestions provided will help you formulate a plan to encourage strength, balance, and coordination of large muscles.

Does This Child Move through Space Using an Immature Form of Walking and Running?

By the time children are three years old, they should be able to walk and run with an even gait. They should alternate feet when climbing stairs and show increasing coordination when they perform complex activities like pumping their arms and legs on a swing (Sanders 2002). If a child you are working with has difficulty walking or running, provide lots of opportunities for him to move. Walk or run to music or to the beats of a drum. March to your next activity. Add movement to otherwise sedentary activities—for example, act out a favorite story rather than sit and listen to it. Act out favorites like *From Head to Toe* by Eric Carle, *The Carrot Seed* by Ruth Krauss, and *The Three Billy Goats Gruff* by Paul Galdone. Move to music by children's artists like Hap Palmer, Greg & Steve, and Raffi, as well as popular and classical music.

Is This Child Unable to Move through Space by Crawling, Jumping, Hopping, and Galloping?

Once children develop the basic skills of walking and running, they begin to develop additional locomotor skills, such as jumping, galloping, hopping, skipping, and leaping. At the same time, they are developing motor-planning skills: learning to coordinate their movements and their thinking so they can move from one point to another without bumping into other people or things. Help a child learn locomotor skills and motor planning by setting up obstacle courses. Encourage this child to move through the course in more than one way (on tiptoes, squatting like a duck, or slithering like a snake). Below are obstacle course ideas that are easy to assemble. Add your own ideas.

- Step or jump over (or slide under) hurdles like a yardstick held up by two chairs or large boxes
- Crawl or slither under a table or through a tunnel
- Run, pedal, or jump around traffic cones or plastic liter bottles
- Step or jump onto scattered carpet squares or into hula hoops
- Walk while balancing on a straight, squiggly, or zigzag line of tape or rope on the floor
- Climb up a three-step ladder; jump onto a mat or into a pile of cushions

Provide activities that allow this child to practice moving quickly and slowly, front to back, side to side, and up and down. Work on changing speed as well as direction. For example, he can work on changing speed and direction when you ask him to move like different animals, such as a bird, frog, horse, or snake. Hold up pictures of the animal so a child who is a dual language-learner can participate. Institute a no-crashes rule. Ask this child to move like a robot, a baby, or to sway in the wind like a tree. Practice games that require this child to stop and freeze. Call out an action to perform and then say, "Freeze." He should hold his position for three to four seconds before you call out the next action. You can say, "Wiggle, wiggle, wiggle, freeze. Jump, jump, jump, freeze." Provide verbal cues for this child while he learns new locomotor skills. As he is learning to skip, you can say, "Step, hop. Step, hop." Or for galloping, "Step together, step together."

Does This Child Lack an Interest in Using a Variety of Movement Equipment?

Children learn large-motor movements and control through interacting with things in their environment and repeatedly practicing. Often they find ways to practice without purchased or special pieces of equipment—for example, by balancing on a log, curb, or two-foot ledge. Early childhood settings are more likely to need equipment that allows children to practice large-motor activities. Basic equipment includes swings, slides, balance beams, pedal toys, romper stompers, climbing equipment, mats, balls, tumbling mats, plastic bats, beanbags, cones, hoops, movement CDs, and targets. If you don't have your own climbing equipment, visit neighborhood parks or community gyms regularly. By using a variety of equipment, children gain strength, coordination, and learn object control like throwing, catching, kicking, striking, and bouncing.

It isn't always possible or necessary to have enough equipment that each child has one to himself. But you will want to make sure that children are not required to wait for turns with most equipment. To give them plenty of opportunity to practice, divide children into small groups. Set up stations and rotate. Repeat activities; offer them throughout the year so young children get the practice they need.

If you are working with a child who is hesitant to use large-motor equipment, encourage him to take appropriate risks. He will need to try new and

---

Supervision and Safety

Supervision and safety must be priorities when children use large-motor equipment. The equipment should be kept free of hazards and in good working condition. Children need to be watched carefully to keep them out of harm's way. It can be tempting to take a break from a busy day when children are playing. But your careful supervision should protect a child from being hit as he walks in front of a swing or from sliding into another child who is sitting at the bottom of the slide. Here are some safety tips to follow:

◆ Check equipment regularly—make sure nuts and bolts are securely fastened

◆ Keep equipment in good working order

◆ Use equipment that is the right size for the child

◆ Pick up and dispose of garbage appropriately

◆ Use space that is large enough to allow movement and avoid collisions

◆ Teach children the appropriate use of equipment

◆ Establish a few important safety rules: one person at a time on the slide; go down the slide; and walk on the sidewalk, not in front of the swing

◆ Provide verbal direction or physical support when a child is close to performing a task on his own

◆ Stay alert and supervise closely

slightly challenging things to learn he can perform difficult tasks. He may be afraid to catch a ball, thinking it will hit him. Help him learn to take a risk by starting with soft balls, such as a Koosh ball or a beach ball, and standing close to him until he gains confidence. If other children are very active, a child who isn't very confident may need to play near or with an adult. Let this child self-select the level of challenge for which he is ready. Offer a variety of similar objects—for example, rubber balls, beach balls, Ping-Pong balls, tennis balls, and yarn balls. Find ways to ensure his success. You can offer him a large bat for ease in striking. Offer scarves for him to toss and catch—they float slowly and give him more time to grab for them. Find ways to encourage physical activity as part of dramatic play. For example, this child can pedal his tricycle to a pretend store to get gas or use large cardboard blocks to build a house.

Carlos started moving once his teacher found a large, pedal-toy dump truck. At first he didn't try to ride it. Instead, he pushed it around the track, hauling and dumping the rocks he and the other children collected. He loaded it with balls and threw them into a basket at cleanup time. He sat on it while others pushed him. Eventually he learned to pedal it when his teacher said, "Push hard with your foot. Now the other foot."

Does This Child Avoid Active Play Using Large-Motor Skills?

Young children aren't ready for long uninterrupted periods of strenuous activity. They need ten- to fifteen-minute periods of structured or guided physical activity that add up to at least sixty minutes each day. They also need

Ideas for Indoor Large-Motor Activities

There are many large-motor activities that can be included in your indoor space. Below is a list of suggestions. Add your own ideas.

- Use yarn or chalk to create a series of loops. Children walk in the loops or jump from opening to opening.

- Place boxes, baskets, or hoops on the floor, a chair, or a shelf to change the angle of the toss. The children can throw beanbags into the targets. Let them determine how far from the targets they want to stand.

- Keep beach balls in the air by having the children bounce them off their heads, elbows, knees, or hands.

- Suspend a beach ball from the ceiling. Children can use a rolled-up newspaper to bat at it.

- Clear a wide space. Children can pretend to go skating by placing each foot in a shoe box or box top and sliding around the room.

- Make a hopscotch pattern on the floor with tape or chalk. Let children use a checker or coin to mark the square to jump over.

- Tape two lines on the floor in a V shape. The tops of the V should be about eighteen inches apart. Bring them to a point on the other end. Children can jump from one side to the other, starting at the narrow end and increasing the distance with each jump.

- Create stick horses from yardsticks and set up chairs or cones to make a track. Invite children to straddle a stick horse and gallop around the track. To avoid crashes, establish a direction for all horse riders to follow.

- Set up chairs or cones to make a track. Children can stand inside old pillowcases and jump their way around the track. Time the children for added fun; have them try to improve on their own best time.

a minimum of sixty minutes of unstructured activity (Pica 2006) each day. They benefit from indoor and outdoor movement spaces. Create a large-motor learning center within your setting so children can practice large-motor skill development in a space for active play. It can be a corner of the room or a wide hallway. Ensure there is enough space so that children can move safely. If necessary, limit the number of children using the center at one time.

If a child is not participating in active large-motor activities, join the play yourself and invite him to join or to be your partner. Be sure to emphasize cooperation rather than competition so he feels a part of the group. Encourage him to try activities and make improvements rather than perfecting a skill within the first few tries. Entice him to become more active through highly motivating activities: chasing bubbles is a good one. Invite the child to join movement activities in which each child moves in his own way—for example, "Show me how you would move like a leopard." Follow a vigorous action with a more restful one: "Show me how you would move like an elephant."

Help a child who has been involved in strenuous activity transition to something more restful. Show him a rag doll. Talk about how it slumps over and its arms and legs are loose. Ask him to bend over at the waist and hang his head down. Have him stand up, wiggle his arms, and then let them fall to his side. Or teach him to hold out the fingers of one hand to represent the candles on a birthday cake. Have him slowly blow out one candle at a time.

Does This Child Lack Age-Appropriate Large-Motor Strength, Balance, and Coordination?

Children need to develop coordination and balance to move throughout their environment and to take part in routine activities like climbing stairs and riding a tricycle. They need strong muscles for everyday activities like carrying heavy objects. They need to be physically fit to prevent injury and to maintain healthy posture. Children benefit from instruction to learn more complex movement skills like throwing and catching. For example, when a child throws an object, he needs to be taught to step forward with the foot opposite his throwing arm. Give a child who needs practice instruction in how to perform a skill, followed by activities that allow him to try it on his own. Children can practice large-motor skills by playing Clean Up the Backyard. Divide the space in half with a row of chairs or a tape line on the floor. Place half of the children on each side of this fence. Explain to them that they are standing in their backyard. If it gets dirty, they are to throw the object over the fence into their neighbor's yard. Then throw a bunch of yarn balls to each group of children. The children throw them over the fence. Periodically ask the children to stop and count the balls on each side. See which side is dirtier. Start the fun again.

Give a child instruction in how to jump by saying, "Stand with both feet on the ground. Bend your knees; straighten your legs and push off the ground with your feet; land on both feet." Practice with carpet squares. Ask this child to jump around a square, jump in front of it, jump onto it, and jump from one square to another. Give instructions on how to kick a ball: "Keep your eye on the ball. Put your kicking foot behind it. Push it forward with the side of your foot." Then set up an indoor bowling alley where he can kick a foam ball to knock down plastic liter bottles. Teach him to hop on one foot by reminding him to bend his knee to hold up one foot and to use his arms for balance. Follow guided practice time with a self-directed game of hopscotch.

Work with the Parents

Parents may be concerned if they see their child struggle to perform motor tasks. They may also worry about an overweight child. And others may fondly remember their own involvement in sports or physical activities and want the same for their child. As you work with parents, emphasize the importance of establishing healthy habits. Keep in mind that some families may not have much space to allow their child to be active at home or have access to safe outdoor play space. The climate in which you live and how busy they are also influences parents' ability to help their child engage in physical activity. Talk with them about simple ways to encourage physical activity; highlight activities that can be done with materials found in the home. Talk about how a child can improve his abilities rather than compete with others. Encourage parents to look for and comment on improvement: "Last time, you threw four socks in the basket. This time you got six in." The suggestions for parents include some at-home activities. Work with parents to brainstorm others.

When to Seek Assistance

Seek assistance for a child who exhibits more than one of the following:

+ Muscles seem loose or floppy
+ Has trouble sitting up in a chair
+ Complains about going for long walks or standing in long lines
+ Lacks strength
+ Has poor balance
+ Lacks coordination

Encourage the child's parents to have his large-motor development screened by the local school district or an occupational therapist. Early intervention that includes guided exercise can improve this child's skills and help him live a healthy lifestyle.

A Plan for Action

To develop your Plan for Action, choose or modify one of the suggested goals to best match your situation. Add how well or how often you expect the skill or behavior to be demonstrated. Remember: you are looking for growth, not perfection. You want to move the child from where he is currently and to increase your expectations slightly. Next, determine three or four actions teachers and parents will take. Choose additional actions specific to the early childhood setting and the home. Record your choices on the planning form found in the appendix.

Childhood Obesity

Too many young children are overweight. This problem seems to be caused by inactive lifestyles and poor eating habits. Adults are responsible for providing healthy food for children to eat and encouraging children to move more.

Teachers and families can help by

◆ Serving healthy food choices

◆ Encouraging children to try new foods (new foods may need to be introduced a number of times before a child will try them)

◆ Serving vegetables and other healthy foods in a variety of ways, such as raw, with dip, or in soup

◆ Talking about "sometimes foods" (foods that are treats and can be eaten on occasion) and "always foods" (foods that are good for you and can be eaten at any meal or snack)

◆ Teaching appropriate serving sizes; a child's stomach is only the size of his fist, and that's all the volume it takes to fill it (Maimon 2008)

◆ Never forcing a child to clean his plate

◆ Never using food as a reward or motivator

◆ Offering a minimum of one hour of unstructured physical activity each day

◆ Integrating physical activity into daily activities—for example, taking the long way when you walk from one place to another; filling transitions with movement activities; taking movement breaks when children are sitting

◆ Modeling physical fitness and healthy eating

◆ Offering health and nutrition tips in family newsletters and on bulletin boards

◆ Consulting with a health care professional for advice on ensuring that your program is helping children establish healthy, lifelong habits (Maimon 2008)

Sample goals for a child who needs to work on developing strength, balance, and coordination of large muscles:

◆ Uses a mature form of walking and running

◆ Jumps, hops, or gallops (*Choose one.*)

◆ Moves from one point to another without bumping into things

◆ Uses a variety of play equipment

◆ Takes appropriate risks

- Engages in active play
- Shows strength, balance, or coordination (*Choose one.*)

Sample actions parents and teachers can take:

- Move to music or to the beat of a drum
- Practice moving quickly and slowly, front to back, side to side, and up and down
- Work on changing speed as well as direction
- Institute a no-crashes rule
- Practice games that require this child to stop and freeze
- Provide verbal cues for this child as he learns new skills
- Supervise closely
- Encourage this child to take appropriate risks
- Adapt activities to ensure this child's success
- Find ways to encourage physical activity as part of dramatic play
- Participate in physical play and invite the child to join you
- Emphasize cooperation rather than competition
- Encourage the child to try activities and make improvements
- Help this child transition from strenuous activities to more restful ones

Sample actions teachers can take:

- March to your next activity
- Find ways to add movement to sedentary activities
- Set up movement stations and rotate through them
- Set up obstacle courses; encourage the child to move through them in more than one way
- Offer a variety of the same large-motor equipment (for example, different types of balls)
- Let this child self-select his level of challenge
- Provide periods of ten to fifteen minutes of guided physical activity that add up to sixty minutes each day
- Provide a total of sixty minutes each day of unstructured physical activity time.
- Give instructions on how to perform a skill
- Create a large-motor learning center within your setting
- Provide movement activities in which this child can move in his own way

Sample actions parents can take:

- Use household materials to help your child be physically active
- Gather materials, such as beanbags, balls, plastic liter bottles, plastic bats, hoops, movement CDs, and baskets
- Turn off the television and the computer; have fun moving together
- Encourage ten- to fifteen-minute bursts of activity
- Visit neighborhood parks or playgrounds regularly
- Keep a log of the physical activities you do together

Information on Large-Motor Skills

WHAT IS IT?

Young children are physically active in most things they do. Through their activity, they gain strength and coordination of the large muscles in their body. They also learn many of the skills that will be perfected for later use in games, work, recreation, and sports. Physical activity helps children concentrate and enhances their learning. It helps them release pent-up energy and gain a sense of pride in being able to participate in physical activities. Boys and girls need opportunities to move and to develop the skills and habits needed for a healthy lifestyle.

By the time children are three years old, they should be able to walk and run with an even gait. They should alternate feet when climbing stairs and should show increasing coordination while performing more complex activities like pumping their arms and legs on a swing. Once they develop the basic skills of walking and running, they begin to develop additional skills like jumping, galloping, hopping, skipping, and leaping. They learn to coordinate their movements and their perception so they can go from one point to another without bumping into things.

Observe and Respond

You can do a lot to help your child learn these skills. Encourage different ways of moving, such as on tiptoes, squatting like a duck, or slithering like a snake. Play games that require your child to stop and freeze. Say, "Wiggle, wiggle, wiggle, freeze. Jump, jump, jump, freeze." While your child learns new skills, offer verbal cues. To teach your child to skip, say, "Step, hop. Step, hop." Gather materials to use like beanbags, balls, plastic bats, hula hoops, movement CDs, and baskets for targets. Find ways to visit neighborhood parks regularly.

If your child is hesitant to use large-motor equipment, be encouraging. Your child might be afraid to catch a ball and get hit by it. Start with soft balls and stand close to each other until your child gains confidence. Find ways to ensure your child's success. For example, use a large plastic bat to make it easier to hit the ball. Throw and catch scarves instead of

continued

a ball, because scarves float slowly, giving your child more time to grab them. Turn off the television and the computer and get moving. Here are a number of things you can do at home:

- Throw socks into boxes, baskets, or hoops; place the targets on the floor, chair, or shelf to change the angle of the toss

- Keep beach balls in the air by bouncing them off your head, elbow, knee, or hands

- Help clean floors by putting on old socks or standing on scraps of fabric and pretending to skate

- Chase bubbles

- Throw laundry, one piece at a time, into the washing machine

- Use plastic liter bottles and a soft ball to bowl

- Use an old pillowcase as a jumping bag, and set up chairs to hop around

Entice your child to become more active by being active yourself and inviting your child to join you. Be aware that young children aren't ready for long periods of strenuous activity. They need ten- to fifteen-minute bursts of activity rather than the thirty-minute vigorous workout that adults do. When you play together, be sure to emphasize cooperation rather than competition. Encourage your child to try activities and make improvements. Keep a log of the movement activities you do together.

CONNECTING WITH SUPPORT

Work with your child's teacher to learn more about how your child develops large-motor strength and coordination. Work together to think of simple ways to engage your child in physical activities. Have your child's skills screened by your local school district or an occupational therapist if your child exhibits more than one of the following.

- Muscles seem loose or floppy

- Complains about going for long walks or standing in long lines

- Has poor balance

- Lacks coordination

Early intervention that includes guided exercise can help your child live a healthy lifestyle and improve your child's skills.

22 "I Can Cut, Draw, and Bead!" Fine-Motor Skills

FOR TEACHERS

Arianna uses both her left and right hand to cut. One day she'll use the scissor in her right hand; the next she'll switch to her left. I thought by three and one half years old, she would know which hand to use.

❖ **Standard**
Shows eye-hand coordination, strength, and control.

What Is It?

As children grow and develop, they begin to refine the use of the small muscles in their hands and fingers. Fine-motor activities require children to coordinate what they see in order to tell their hands what to do. As they pick up and place sequins in a collage, build a tower with small blocks, lace beads on a string, or use an eyedropper to add colors to paint, they develop the ability to use their fingers and thumbs for precise motions. Some fine-motor tasks are challenging for many children, such as zipping their jacket or tying their shoes. With practice and patience, most children show great gains in fine-motor control when they engage in tabletop activities and use writing and painting tools.

Fine-motor skills learned in early childhood offer a base for those skills used in later school activities, such as writing, handling tools, or manipulating science materials. If a child struggles with fine-motor activities, she may realize she is not skilled or she is having difficulties. Thereafter, she may want to avoid the activities that would improve her skills. Teachers and parents who are alert to a child's needs and creative in their approach can do a great deal to help her improve in this area.

Observe and Decide What to Teach

Watch a child who is not engaging in or who seems challenged by fine-motor activities. Ask these questions and use these suggestions as you encourage eye-hand coordination, strength, and control.

Fine-Motor in Every Learning Center

Teachers can encourage children to practice fine-motor skills in every area of the room. Below are examples:

Art
- Use drawing tools
- Sign name on paper
- Make a collage by placing small pieces of crushed tissue on paper

Large Muscle
- Pick up beanbags
- Write down score
- Make a bull's-eye for a target

Science
- Place small objects on balance scale
- Use magnet wand to test for metals
- Hold magnifying glass

Blocks
- Make tower with small blocks
- Make signs for block buildings
- Drive small cars on roadways

Dramatic Play
- Write orders for customers at restaurant
- Undress and dress dolls
- Conduct a pretend checkup with doctor's tools

Writing Center
- Make greeting cards
- Use ink stamps
- Write notes to classmates

Library Area
- Turn pages of a book
- Place flannel pieces on a board
- Turn CD or cassette player on and off

Computer Center
- Sign up for a turn at the computer
- Use keyboard
- Use mouse

Math

+ Pick up and place objects as they are sorted

+ Point with finger while counting objects

+ Write numerals

Sensory Table

+ Pour water into funnels

+ Search for objects buried in sand with a spoon

+ Pull, stretch, and squeeze glurch

Self-Help

+ Button, snap, zip, and tie

+ Grasp and pull paper towel from dispenser

+ Turn faucet knobs on and off

Snack/Meals

+ Use utensils

+ Pour milk from small pitcher

+ Hold cup

Does This Child Avoid Tabletop Activities?

One way early childhood teachers give children the opportunity to practice fine-motor skills is to offer tabletop activities. These require children to grasp, hold, and place small objects in order to play with small toys. Examples of tabletop activities include snapping together toys, small building materials, and puzzles. Display tabletop materials attractively on low shelves so children can make their own choices and bring them to the table. Make it clear where materials belong by labeling their spots or pasting pictures so children can return the materials to the appropriate places. Rotate materials periodically to create renewed interest when a toy is offered again. Repeat activities so children can practice many times. Most children will find something that piques their interest.

If a child avoids tabletop activities, don't force her to participate. Instead, move tabletop toys to an area that interests her. For example, place small blocks in the same area as unit blocks; place bristle blocks in the sensory table, or add bolt construction toys to a service station in the dramatic play theme area. Offer fine-motor activities in other areas of the room too. This child might stir or flip pretend pancakes in the housekeeping area, dress and undress dolls, use craft punches at the writing center, or dig in the outdoor sand area. Set up an ice cream shop in the dramatic play area. Use colored cotton balls and ice cream scoops to make sundaes. Put water in the sensory table, add measuring cups to pour from and bulb basters to squeeze.

Encourage this child to play with playdough or clay. She'll gain strength and dexterity when she pounds, flattens, rolls, or squeezes it. Encourage her to participate by joining the play yourself. Offer suggestions, resources, and materials that embellish or expand on what she is doing. Model how to roll ropes, pinch a nest for the pretend bird's eggs she has made, cut the playdough with scissors, or push cookie cutters into it. Provide toothpicks, straws, or craft sticks so she can poke or connect parts together. Place objects in the playdough and ask her to dig them out.

A child having difficulty with fine-motor tasks may prefer to work at a different angle and on surfaces other than a table. Encourage her to put puzzles together while lying down, paint while standing at an easel, or play with small figurines while sitting cross-legged on the floor.

Does This Child Lack Control of Writing, Drawing, and Painting Tools?

As young children practice fine-motor skills, they become more proficient in the use and control of writing, drawing, and painting tools. By four and one-half years of age, most children who have had fine-motor practice are able to hold a pencil or marker with a mature grasp. With more practice, they learn to apply the right amount of pressure and to make fluid strokes to draw and print letters.

Many children first grab a crayon or marker with an overhand grasp, making a fist around it. As they gain fine-motor skills, they develop the ability to bring their index finger and thumb together. When a child can pick up small objects this way, she is likely to adopt a conventional grasp for writing tools. Help a child who is having difficulty practice many activities in which she brings her thumb and forefinger together. Ask her to snap toys together, place pegs in a board, make shapes using Wikki Stix (flexible waxy strings), or pinch clothespins to hang a wet painting. Offer large crayons, large markers, and kindergarten pencils, which may be easier to grasp. Model the appropriate grasp. Describe the placement of your fingers as you pick up a writing tool.

Usually it becomes clear if a child is more proficient using her right or left hand by age four. Arianna, in the example at the beginning of the chapter, is still developing a hand preference at three and a half years. Like Arianna, some children may continue to use either hand up to the age of seven. Hand preference is "controlled by complex neurological connections" (Puckett and Black 2007). Before a hand preference is established, offer tools at a child's midline. Let the child take it with either hand. Eventually she will begin to pick up tools with the hand that becomes stronger and more skilled. Be sure to have left-handed scissors available for a child who chooses to use her left hand.

Provide time for exploration of art and writing materials for the child who needs fine-motor practice. Offer a variety of writing and art materials. Supplies include crayons, markers, colored pencils, chalkboards, ink stamps, variety of papers, brushes, rollers, cotton swabs, and finger crayons (with big bulbs on top). A child who is learning to control writing materials may prefer to use markers because the color flows without much effort. Make numberless dot-to-dot pictures for this child by spacing dots about a quarter inch apart to create an outline of a simple shape. Ask this child to connect the dots. Make wide, dark outlines of this child's favorite animal or toy. Fasten tracing paper on top and ask her to trace over the original lines to create her own picture. If she is reluctant to draw or write, try highly motivating activities like fingerpainting, writing in a tray filled with sand, or drawing in wet sand.

Offer a wide variety of open-ended art activities. Emphasize process rather than product. Encourage this child to tear paper for a collage, make an abstract using one-inch colored art tape (show the child how to pull the tape and tear it off the dispenser on her own); or make a collage from ribbons, fabric, paper, and sequins. Encourage her to paint, using chubby paintbrushes, double-handled brushes, or paint rollers. Use eyedroppers to drop colors onto a coffee filter.

Does This Child Lack Eye-Hand Coordination?

As children practice, they gain skills and demonstrate greater eye-hand coordination. Continue to provide tasks that give them opportunities to improve the precision of their movements. Usually this means that the materials they manipulate become smaller and more complex. A child needing help in this area will need success with big objects first and then encouragement and support while she works to manipulate smaller, more challenging items. Offer activities that are really interesting—for example, tweezers to pick up and place collage materials and craft paper punches with different shapes. String necklaces made of colored tubes, straws, or cereal loops at snacktime. Sort playing cards or play cards games such as Go Fish, Old Maid, or Concentration. Play board games with small pieces, such as Candy Land or Hi! Ho! Cherry-O. Ask this child to stretch rubber bands across the knobs on a geoboard. Encourage her to use the keyboard as well as the mouse at the computer. Give her a child's tape measure to measure the length of a chain she has made or the height of her friends.

Be sure to offer foods other than finger foods and encourage this child to use a fork and spoon to feed herself. Let her use a toy hammer to pound golf tees into Styrofoam blocks or pumpkins. Help her learn to use scissors by offering child-safe scissors and paper that is stiff enough to cut. At first, invite her to snip or fringe the edge of the paper. Next, encourage her to cut the corners off her paper. Talk about her working hand, the one holding the scissors, and her helping hand, the one holding the paper. Make a two-inch-long, quarter-inch-thick line for her to cut straight across a paper. Then expand the length to about a six-inch straight line and decrease the width to about an eighth of an inch. Finally, she may be ready to cut on curved and angled lines. Provide the level of support she needs. For example, she may need you to cut with her, using scissors with four finger holes, spring scissors that open up after she has closed them, or verbal cues like "Open, close, open, close." Promote additional practice by offering craft scissors that create scalloped, jagged, or wavy edges. Take breaks before she becomes frustrated.

Encourage this child to participate in everyday activities that require fine-motor skills. Ask her to turn the pages while you read a book. Have her use a squeeze bottle to mist plants. Support her while she learns to button, snap, and zip when dressing herself. Say fingerplays and sing songs with accompanying hand motions. "The Itsy Bitsy Spider," "Five Little Monkeys Jumping on the Bed," "One, Two, Buckle My Shoe," and "Open, Shut Them" all require fine-motor practice.

When to Seek Assistance

Children develop fine-motor skills at their own pace and depending on the experience they have had with materials requiring this type of precision. A preschool child will benefit from a developmental screening by her school district or an occupational or physical therapist if she lacks strength in her hand muscles, hands tool from one hand to the other rather than crossing the midline of her body, uses her fingers to rake objects rather than using a pincer grasp to pick them up, or applies too much or too little pressure when using writing tools.

Work with the Parents

Talk with the parents of the child who is having difficulty with fine-motor skills. Describe the importance of fine-motor skills in everyday activities and the relationship they have to later school activities. Some parents may be tempted to do things for their child rather than offering her the time she needs to complete a task. This is understandable when parents are in a hurry, but it robs the child of the opportunity to practice her skills. Other parents continue to do things for their child longer than you might, perhaps for cultural reasons. If you see this happening, encourage the parent to work on fine-motor skills during play or when they are not hurried. Provide the parents with the written materials that follow. Work with them to think of activity ideas and toys at home that support the development of these important skills.

A Plan for Action

To develop your Plan for Action, choose or modify one of the suggested goals to best match your situation. Add how well or how often you expect the skill or behavior to be demonstrated. Remember: you are looking for growth, not perfection. You want to move the child from where she is currently and to increase your expectations slightly. Next, determine three or four actions teachers and parents will take. Choose additional actions specific to the early childhood setting and the home. Record your choices on the planning form found in the appendix.

Sample goals for a child who needs to work on eye-hand coordination, strength of small muscles in her hands, and fine-motor control:

- Participates in tabletop activities
- Demonstrates control of writing, drawing, and painting tools
- Demonstrates strength, eye-hand coordination, and fine-motor control (*Choose one.*)

Sample actions parents and teachers can take:

- Offer a variety of materials that promote fine-motor skills
- Rotate materials
- Repeat activities periodically
- Encourage this child to use big items before small ones
- Build this child's success and confidence

- Take breaks before this child becomes frustrated
- Encourage this child to play with playdough or clay
- Allow this child to work in various positions and on various surfaces
- Practice activities in which this child brings her thumb and forefinger together
- Offer large crayons, large markers, and kindergarten pencils
- Model the appropriate grasp of writing tools
- Describe the placement of your fingers when you pick up a writing tool
- Offer tools at a child's midline
- Offer a variety of writing and art materials
- Sort playing cards or play card games such as Go Fish, Old Maid, or Concentration
- Play board games with small pieces such as Candy Land or Hi! Ho! Cherry-O
- Encourage this child to use the keyboard as well as the mouse at the computer
- Encourage this child to use a fork and spoon
- Help this child learn to use scissors
- Ask this child to turn the pages while you read a book
- Have this child use a squeeze bottle to mist plants
- Support this child as she learns to button, snap, and zip when dressing herself
- Say fingerplays and sing songs with accompanying hand motions

Sample actions teachers can take:

- Offer tabletop activities that are displayed attractively on low shelves
- Offer fine-motor activities in many areas of the room
- Offer fine-motor activities as part of dramatic play themes
- Offer materials in a variety of sizes from which the child can choose
- Provide time for exploring art and writing materials
- Offer a wide variety of open-ended art activities
- Emphasize process rather than product in art activities
- Provide opportunities to use simple tools successfully

Sample actions parents can take:

- Ask your child to stir the ingredients while you cook
- Offer bathtub crayons to draw with in the bathtub
- Provide sidewalk chalk for drawing outside
- Give your child time to do as much for herself as possible

Information on Fine-Motor Skills

WHAT IS IT?

As children grow and develop, they refine the use of the small muscles in their fingers and thumbs to make precise motions. Fine-motor activities require children to coordinate what they see in order to tell their hands what to do. Most children show great gains in fine-motor control as they play with small objects and use writing and art tools. These skills provide the base for later school activities.

Observe and Respond

You can do a great deal to help your child develop skills in this area. Building or playing with materials that require your child to grasp, hold, and place small objects helps to develop fine-motor skills. Examples include snapping together toys, using small building materials, lacing beads, and doing puzzles. If your child avoids these kinds of activity, don't force participation. Instead, find ways to work fine-motor activities into your child's favorite pastimes. For example, provide clothes for dressing and undressing dolls, or containers and shovels for digging in the sand. Encourage your child to work in different positions: puzzles can be put together while lying on the floor, paper can be taped to a wall for drawing on, and small figurines can be played with while sitting cross-legged on the floor.

Encourage your child to play with playdough or clay to gain strength and dexterity by pounding, flattening, rolling, or squeezing. Model how to roll ropes, pinch a nest for pretend bird's eggs, or push cookie cutters into dough. Provide toothpicks or straws so your child can connect the parts.

If your child struggles with small items, encourage the use of big items first. This can help build success and the confidence needed to try something more challenging. For example, make domino tracks out of blocks before using actual dominoes. Or try pegboards and pegs with large knobs before trying the pegs for a Lite-Brite or other small peg toy. Take breaks before your child becomes frustrated.

By four and one-half years of age, most children who have used writing tools can hold a pencil or marker with a mature grasp. If your child finds holding writing tools challenging, offer large crayons and markers, which may be easier to grasp. Model the appropriate grasp. Describe the placement of your fingers as you pick up a writing tool.

Your child may prefer to use markers because the color flows without much effort. If your child is reluctant to draw or write, try highly motivating activities like playing with bathtub crayons, sidewalk chalk, or a Magna Doodle. With practice, your child will learn to apply the right amount of pressure, make fluid strokes, and draw and print letters.

Give your child practice in activities that bring the thumb and forefinger together. Provide lacing cards, clothespins to pinch together, and place on the edge of pizza rounds or ice cream buckets, string necklaces made of cereal loops for a snack, play card games such as Go Fish or Concentration, and play board games with small pieces like Hi! Ho! Cherry-O. Encourage your child to use the keyboard as well as the mouse at the computer.

It usually becomes clear if a child is more proficient with the right or left hand by age four. Some children, however, may continue to use either hand up to age seven. If your child is unsure which hand to use, offer tools midway between your child's left and right hand. Let your child take it with either hand. Eventually your child will pick up tools with the hand that becomes stronger and more skilled.

Encourage your child to use fine-motor skills in everyday activities: turning the pages while you read a book; squeezing the toothpaste onto the toothbrush; using a spoon to eat. Give your child plenty of time to learn to button, snap, and zip while getting dressed. If your child is struggling, you can start the zipper and let your child zip it the rest of the way.

CONNECTING WITH SUPPORT

Work with your child's teacher to brainstorm activities and toys you can use at home to support your child's fine-motor skills. If your preschool age child lacks strength in his or her hand muscles, moves tools from one hand to the other rather than crossing the midline of the body, uses fingers to rake objects, or applies too much or too little pressure when using writing tools, ask your school district or an occupational or physical therapist to screen your child's skills.

Appendix

Use the following list to easily locate the section of each chapter called A Plan for Action. Use the suggested goals and actions in each chapter as a reference when completing the Parent and Teacher Action form that follows.

Parent and Teacher Action Form

Date: _____

Our plan for _____
            (child's name)

GOAL

_____

_____

ACTIONS PARENTS AND TEACHERS WILL TAKE

1. _____

2. _____

3. _____

ACTIONS TEACHERS WILL TAKE

1. _____

2. _____

ACTIONS PARENTS WILL TAKE

1. _____

2. _____

As you put your plan into action, reflect on the following questions. Use your reflections to develop your next plan.

- ◆ Which idea(s) worked best? How do you know?

- ◆ Did things improve? When? What seemed to lead to improvement?

- ◆ Did you encounter setbacks? What seemed to cause them?

- ◆ What other idea(s) do you think might work?

We will check in to discuss progress or modify our plan on _____
(set a date six weeks to three months from now)

Signed

_____

(teacher)

_____

(parents)

References

Anderson, Karen L., Dean M. Martin, and Ellen E. Faszewski. 2006. "Unlocking the Power of Observation: Activities to Teach Early Learners the Fundamentals of an Important Inquiry Skill." *Science and Children* 44 (1): 32–35.

Bedrova, Elena, and Deborah J. Leong. 2007. *Tools of the Mind: The Vygotskian Approach to Early Childhood Education*. 2nd ed. Upper Saddle River, NJ: Pearson Education.

Bernstein, Henry. 2011. "Stuttering Four-Year-Old." FamilyEducation. Accessed April 21. http://life.familyeducation.com/cognitive-development/speech/40432.html.

Brodkin, Adelle M. 2003. "Between Teacher & Parent: 'She Cries When I Leave.'" *Early Childhood Today*. www2.scholastic.com/browse/article.jsp?id=3747137.

———. 2006. "Between Teacher & Parent: 'Why Can't I Play, Too?'" *Early Childhood Today*. www2.scholastic.com/browse/article.jsp?id=4009.

Chacko, Anil, Lauren Wakschlag, Carri Hill, Barbara Danis, and Kimberly Espy. 2009. "Viewing Preschool Disruptive Behavior Disorders and Attention-Deficit/Hyperactivity Disorder through a Developmental Lens: What We Know and What We Need to Know." Child and Adolescent Psychiatric Clinics of North America 18:627–43. doi: 10.1016/j.chc.2009.02.003.

Chalufour, Ingrid, and Karen Worth. 2003. *Discovering Nature with Young Children*. St. Paul, MN: Redleaf Press.

———. 2005. *Exploring Water with Young Children*. St. Paul, MN: Redleaf Press.

Child Development Institute. 2011. "Language Development in Children." Child Development Institute. Accessed April 21. www.childdevelopmentinfo.com/development/language_development.shtml.

Copley, Juanita V., Candy Jones, and Judith Dighe. 2007. *Mathematics: The Creative Curriculum Approach*. Washington, DC: Teaching Strategies.

Croft, Cindy, and Deborah Hewitt, eds. 2004. *Children and Challenging Behavior: Making Inclusion Work*. Eden Prairie, MN: Sparrow Media Group.

Decker, Barbara Smith. 2011. "How Children Learn to Speak and What to Do if You Suspect Problems." Parenthood.com. Accessed April 21. www.parenthood.com/article-topics/how_children_learn_to_speak_and_what_to_do_if_you_suspect_problems.html.

Early Childhood Services Team: Community Living Toronto. 2011. *Supported Inclusion—Tip Sheet: Turn Taking*. City of Toronto. Accessed April 22. http://connectability.ca/2010/07/24/supported-inclusion.

Feldman, Jean R. *Dr. Jean & Friends*. Melody House B001AZ2HJQ, compact disc.

Gallagher, Kathleen Cranley, and Kelley Mayer. 2008. "Enhancing Development and Learning through Teacher-Child Relationships." *Young Children* 63 (6): 80–87.

Gartrell, Dan, and Kathleen Sonsteng. 2008. "Promote Physical Activity—It's Proactive Guidance." *Beyond the Journal:* Young Children *on the Web.* www.naeyc.org/files/yc/file/200803/BTJ_Guidance.pdf.

Gower, Amy L., Lisa M. Hohmann, Terry C. Gleason, and Tracy R. Gleason. 2001. "The Relation among Temperament, Age, and Friendship in Preschool-Aged Children." Paper presented at the Biennial Meeting of the Society for Research in Child Development, Minneapolis, MN.

Greene, Alan. 1998. "Learning to Share." www.drgreene.com/qa/learning-share.

Greenspan, Stanley I. 2001. "Meeting Learning Challenges: Working with Children Who Have Language Difficulties." *Early Childhood Today.* www2.scholastic.com/browse/article.jsp?id=3745967.

Heidemann, Sandra, and Deborah Hewitt. 2010. *Play: The Pathway from Theory to Practice.* St. Paul, MN: Redleaf Press.

Hewitt, Deborah, and Sandra Heidemann. 1998. *The Optimistic Classroom: Creative Ways to Give Children Hope.* St. Paul, MN: Redleaf Press.

Honig, Alice Sterling, Susan A. Miller, and Ellen Booth Church. 2007. "Ages & Stages: Understanding Children's Anger." *Early Childhood Today.* www2.scholastic.com/browse/article.jsp?id=3748144.

ITLC (Interactive Technology Literacy Curriculum) Online. 2011. "Stages of Children's Writing." Western Illinois University. Access April 22. www.wiu.edu/itlc/ws/ws1/docs/Stages_of_%20ChildWrit.pdf.

Jain, Sugandha. 2011. "Fun Family Activities Teach Patterns." EduGuide. Accessed April 22. www.eduguide.org/library/viewarticle/1785.

Keenan, Kate, and Lauren S. Wakschlag. 2002. "Can a Valid Diagnosis of Disruptive Behavior Disorder Be Made in Preschool Children?" *American Journal of Psychiatry* 159:351–58.

Koralek, Derry G., Amy Laura Dombro, and Diane Trister Dodge. 2005. *Caring for Infants & Toddlers.* 2nd ed. Washington, DC: Teaching Strategies.

Kostelnik, Marjorie J., Laura C. Stein, Alice Phipps Whiren, and Anne K. Soderman. 1998. *Guiding Children's Social Development.* 3rd ed. Albany, NY: Delmar Publishers.

Kurcinka, Mary Sheedy. 2006. *Sleepless in America: Practical Strategies to Help Your Family Get the Sleep It Deserves.* New York: HarperCollins.

Kutner, Lawrence. 2011. "Insights for Parents: Helping a Child Learn to Share." Accessed April 22. www.drkutner.com/parenting/articles/share.html.

Levin, Diane E. 2003. "Beyond Banning War and Superhero Play: Meeting Children's Needs in Violent Times." *Young Children* 58 (3):60–64.

Maschinot, Beth. 2008. *The Changing Face of the United States: The Influence of Culture on Early Child Development.* Washington, DC: Zero to Three.

Maimon, Martin. 2008. "Michelangelo and the Prevention of Childhood Obesity." *Exchange* 181 (May–June): 76–78.

Maxwell, Kelly, Sharon Ritchie, Sue Bredekamp, and Tracy Zimmerman. 2009. "Using Developmental Science to Transform Children's Early School Experiences." *Issues in PreK–3rd Education* 4: 1–6.

NAEYC (National Association for the Education of Young Children). 1995. *Responding to Linguistic and Cultural Diversity: Recommendations for Effective Early Childhood Education.* Washington, DC: NAEYC.

National Scientific Council on the Developing Child. 2007. *The Science of Early Childhood Development: Closing the Gap Between What We Know and What We Do.* www.developingchild.net.

NIDCD (National Institute on Deafness and Other Communication Disorders). 2000. "Speech and Language: How Do I Know If My Child Is Reaching the Milestones?" National Institute on Deafness and Other Communications Disorders. www.nidcd.nih.gov/health/voice/speechandlanguage.asp#mychild.

Pica, Rae. 2006. "Physical Fitness and the Early Childhood Curriculum." *Young Children* 61 (3): 12–19.

Poole, Carla, Susan A. Miller, and Ellen Booth Church. 2003. "Ages & Stages: How Children Build Friendships." Early Childhood Today. www2.scholastic.com /browse/article.jsp?id=3747174.

———. 2005. "Ages & Stages: How Children Develop Motor Skills." *Early Childhood Today.* www2.scholastic.com/browse/article.jsp?id=3747784.

Puckett, Margaret B., and Janet K. Black with Joseph Moriarity. 2007. *Understanding Preschooler Development.* St. Paul, MN: Redleaf Press.

Rivkin, Mary S. 2010. "Natural Learning: Guide Your Child's Curiosity Outdoors and Open Up a Love of Science." Accessed January 20. www.scholastic.com /resources/article/natural-learning.

Roth, Froma P., Diane R. Paul, and Ann-Mari Pierotti. 2006. "Let's Talk: For People with Special Communication Needs." American Speech-Language-Hearing Association. www.asha.org/public/speech/emergent-literacy.htm.

Sanders, Stephen. 2002. *Active for Life: Developmentally Appropriate Movement Programs for Young Children.* Washington, DC: National Association for the Education of Young Children.

Shagoury, Ruth. 2009. "Language to Language: Nurturing Writing Development in Multilingual Classrooms." *Young Children* 64 (2): 52–57.

Spiegel, Alix. 2008. "Creative Play Makes for Kids in Control." National Public Radio. www.npr.org/templates/story/story.php?storyId=76838288.

Stephens, Karen. 2004. "Reaching Out to Parents with Technology." *Exchange* 157 (May–June): 14–18.

Tabors, Patton O. 1997. *One Child, Two Languages: A Guide for Preschool Educators of Children Learning English as a Second Language.* Baltimore, MD: Brookes Publishing.

Taylor-Cox, Jennifer. 2003. "Algebra in the Early Years? Yes!" *Young Children* 58 (1): 14–21.

Tomlin, Carolyn R. 2011. "Managing Aggressive Behavior in Young Children." *Earlychildhood News.* Accessed April 20. www.earlychildhoodnews .com/earlychildhood/article_view.aspx?ArticleID=594.